LANGUAGE AND SEXUALITY

How are sexuality and erotic desire expressed in language? Do gay men and lesbians have a language of their own? Does 'no' always mean no? Is sexual desire beyond words? This lively and accessible textbook looks at how we talk about sex and why we talk about it the way we do.

Drawing on a wide range of examples, from personal ads to phone sex, from sadomasochistic scenes to sexual assault trials, the book provides a clear introduction to the relationship between language and sexuality. Using a broad definition of 'sexuality', the book encompasses not only issues surrounding sexual orientation and identity – for instance whether gay men and lesbians use language differently from straight people – but also questions about the discursive construction of sexuality and the verbal expression of erotic desire.

Cameron and Kulick contextualize their findings within current research in linguistics, anthropology and psychology, and bring together relevant theoretical debates on sexuality, gender, identity, desire, meaning and power.

Topical and entertaining, this much-needed textbook will be welcomed by students and researchers in sociolinguistics, linguistic anthropology and gender/sexuality studies, as well as anyone interested in the relationship between language and sex.

DEBORAH CAMERON is Professor of Languages at the Institute of Education, University of London. She is the author of numerous books, including *Feminism and Linguistic Theory* (1992), *Verbal Hygiene* (1995) and *Good to Talk* (2000).

DON KULICK is Professor of Anthropology at New York University. His published works include *Language Shift and Cultural Reproduction* (1992), *Taboo* (1995, with Margaret Willson) and *Travesti* (1998). He is co-editor of the journals *Ethnos* and *GLQ*.

LANGUAGE AND SEXUALITY

DEBORAH CAMERON AND DON KULICK

CAMBRIDGE
UNIVERSITY PRESS

PUBLISHED BY THE PRESS SYNDICATE OF THE UNIVERSITY OF CAMBRIDGE
The Pitt Building, Trumpington Street, Cambridge CB2 1RP, United Kingdom

CAMBRIDGE UNIVERSITY PRESS
The Edinburgh Building, Cambridge, CB2 2RU, UK
40 West 20th Street, New York, NY 10011-4211, USA
477 Williamstown Road, Port Melbourne, VIC 3207, Australia
Ruiz de Alarcón 13, 28014 Madrid, Spain
Dock House, The Waterfront, Cape Town 8001, South Africa

http://www.cambridge.org

First published 2003
Reprinted 2004

Printed in the United Kingdom at the University Press, Cambridge

Typeface Adobe Garamond 11/12.5 pt   *System* LaTeX 2ε [TB]

A catalogue record for this book is available from the British Library

ISBN 0 521 80433 7 hardback
ISBN 0 521 00969 3 paperback

For
Meryl Altman
and
Jonas Tillberg

Contents

Preface

A few years ago, US President Bill Clinton denied that he had 'sexual relations' with White House intern Monica Lewinsky, even though he admitted that she had performed oral sex on him on a number of occasions. Intrigued by this apparently illogical denial, two researchers from the Kinsey Institute for Research on Sex, Gender and Reproduction took it upon themselves to re-examine the findings of a 1991 study in which they had asked 600 undergraduates to complete a questionnaire (Sanders and Reinisch 1999). The question was: 'would you say you "had sex" if the most intimate behavior you engaged in was...'. There followed a list of eleven intimate behaviours, and in each case respondents were asked if they would label the behaviour 'having sex'. The results showed that, like President Clinton, 60% of respondents did not consider oral-genital contact as 'having sex'; 20% did not even consider penile-anal intercourse as 'having sex'.[1]

The Kinsey re-study, and the Clinton–Lewinsky affair that prompted it, illustrate several important points about the relationship between language and sexuality. They show that our ideas about sex are bound up with the language we use to define and talk about it. They show that what is or isn't considered to be 'sex' is by no means a simple or straightforward matter: if 60% of younger Americans agreed with the President that fellatio was not 'sex', then 40% thought it *was* 'sex'. The Clinton–Lewinsky affair also dramatizes the way in which sex is political: it raised issues of gender, power, exploitation and agency that galvanized an entire nation for months on end. Finally, discussions and opinions about whether Bill Clinton and Monica Lewinsky had had 'sexual relations' demonstrate that contests about sexuality – about what is good or bad sex, what is normal, permissible, acceptable or 'real' sex – are inevitably conducted on linguistic terrain.

It is that terrain that we have set out to map in this book. In the chapters that follow, we consider how linguists and other social scientists might think about, research and analyse the complex and multifaceted relationship between language and sexuality. This is the first book-length treatment of this topic, and one of our major goals in writing it is to draw together a wide range of research to form a coherent field of inquiry.

We are able to write this book because, during the past few years, there has been a steady stream of publications – most of them edited collections – devoted to various dimensions of the relationship between language and sexuality (e.g. Leap 1995b; Livia and Hall 1997a; Harvey and Shalom 1997; Campbell-Kibler, Podesva, Roberts and Wong 2002). Edited collections have the great advantage of presenting readers with a snapshot of the variety of scholarly work being undertaken on a particular topic at a particular time. Their disadvantage is that they cannot easily accommodate more sustained reflection. However skilfully the pieces in a collection are selected, ordered and introduced by the editors, a volume made up of relatively short contributions by numerous contributors does not allow for the cumulative development of a single line of argument or point of view. In this book, by contrast, we do want to be reflective and to develop extended arguments around particular issues. In doing those things, we seek to complement rather than duplicate the contribution made by other researchers.

In the chapters that follow, we try to represent the range and diversity of research on language and sexuality for the benefit of readers who may not be familiar with it. However, we do not claim to provide an exhaustive survey. If we discuss some topics in preference to others, or at greater length than others, this is a choice reflecting our own intellectual and political commitments: we see ourselves as making an intervention in current debates rather than simply giving an overview of them. The details of our position will become clear in the chapters that follow. Here, though, we think it is useful to give interested readers some sense of our general aims and some indication of the book's overall direction.

First of all, we want to reflect on the theoretical assumptions underlying research on language and sexuality. This involves revisiting some funda-mental questions, perhaps the most fundamental of all being: 'what do we mean by "sexuality"?' In a great deal of recent writing about language and sexuality, including most of the collections cited above, 'sexuality' is used as a synonym for what is often called 'sexual orientation' and what we will call 'sexual identity', a social status based on the individual's self-definition as heterosexual, gay, lesbian, bisexual, etc. Sexual identity in this sense has come to occupy a pre-eminent position in language and sexuality studies. For instance, the collection *Queerly Phrased* (Livia and Hall 1997a) is al-most entirely devoted to two topics: one is the expressions used in various languages to label and categorize people on the basis of their sexual identity, and the other is the styles of speech and writing used by people enacting queer sexual identities. That these are legitimate and interesting research topics we do not dispute. Sexual identity is certainly an aspect of sexuality, and it is also one that lends itself to sociolinguistic investigation. What we do want to take issue with, though, is the tendency to regard the study of language and sexuality as coextensive with the study of language and sexual identity. We are committed to the view that sexuality means something broader. All kinds of erotic desires and practices fall within the scope of the term, and to the extent that those desires and practices depend on language for their conceptualization and expression, they should also fall within the scope of an inquiry into language and sexuality.

This is a rather abstract formulation of a point which is central to this book's purpose, so let us elaborate on what we mean. In fact, the argument here has two steps. First, we are suggesting that any inquiry into sexuality, whatever else it may take to be relevant, should have something to say about *sex*, i.e. *erotics*. We imagine that few scholars would dispute this point in principle, but in practice sex has become a somewhat neglected topic in recent linguistic research on sexuality (an exception is the papers collected in Harvey and Shalom 1997). The relative neglect of sex seems to us to be a consequence of the 'identity' focus many researchers have adopted, since the linguistic construction of self and others as straight, gay, lesbian, bisexual, etc., can be studied without direct reference to sex as such. Granted, sex is invoked indirectly: to enact a sexual identity through language is to invite certain inferences about your sexual life (for instance that you seek sexual satisfaction with partners of the same / the other gender). But neither the identity nor its linguistic assertion is confined to specifically sexual contexts. It is not only when he engages in or talks about sex that an out gay man, say, can claim a gay identity or be perceived as gay by others.

At the same time – this is the second step in our argument – when our hypothetical gay man participates in a specifically sexual situation, his identity as a gay man is not the only thing he is likely to be communicating. *Just as sex is not all that is relevant to the construction and communication of sexual identity, sexual identity is not all that is relevant to the construction and communication of sexual meanings.* No doubt sexual encounters, like all human encounters, do involve what sociolinguists call 'acts of identity'. But they also involve many other kinds of verbal acts: acts of love and affection, domination and submission, aggression and humiliation, lying and concealment. If we ask what part language plays in such explicitly sexualized transactions as, for instance, courtship rituals, sadomasochistic scenes, interactions between clients and prostitutes, incidents of sexual assault, the telling of 'dirty' jokes and the composition or reception of erotic narratives, it will be evident that constructing sexual identities is only one of the things people involved in these transactions do with words – and not always the most interesting thing.

Part of our project in this book, then, is to map out a field of language and sexuality broader in scope than the inquiry into language and sexual identity which is currently its most salient manifestation. It is also part of our project to try to show how this broadening of scope – to encompass, for instance, questions about the linguistic construction and expression of erotic desire – can be achieved in practice by researchers using an empirical approach to data collection and analysis. Where we propose that a certain phenomenon is worth investigating or that a certain theory is worth applying, we will support that claim with concrete illustrations from our own or other people's work.

The arguments we pursue here are political as well as theoretical. It is not a coincidence that so much recent work on language and sexuality has dwelt so insistently on questions of identity. The same trend is evident in the study of language and gender (witness such influential recent collections as Hall and Bucholtz 1995 – a volume whose subtitle is *Language and the Socially Constructed Self* – and Bucholtz, Liang and Sutton 1999, which bears the title *Reinventing Identities*). The focus on language and identity that is so marked among politically committed scholars today is one reflex of the turn to a particular form of 'identity politics' in the late 1980s and 1990s. By 'identity politics' we mean, roughly, a kind of politics where claims are grounded and validated with reference to the shared experience of those who identify as members of a particular group. The two major sexual political movements that developed during the late 1960s and 1970s – Women's Liberation and Gay Liberation – were both examples of identity politics in this sense. Participants in those movements spoke out about their own personal experiences, and engaged in processes of 'consciousness raising', self-discovery and self-affirmation – 'coming out' as gay or lesbian being a classic example of this personal/political journey.

We are not decrying this form of politics, for it has clearly been crucial to the gains made by women and sexual minorities since the late 1960s. But by the late 1980s, certain problems that had always been latent began to manifest themselves more overtly. The less radical and more individualistic climate of the Reagan/Thatcher era produced a more inward-looking orientation among radicals, and many became preoccupied with the 'personal growth' element of identity politics – the part that focuses on self-discovery and self-definition. Identity categories proliferated (as witness the now-common listing of sexual minority identities that goes, with slight variations, 'lesbian, gay, bisexual, transgendered, queer or questioning'), and attention focused on the ways in which radical movements themselves might have been guilty of excluding or marginalizing certain constituencies. Gay and lesbian organizations debated whether and how they could accommodate the claims of people who identified as bisexual or transgendered. Lesbian feminists argued about whether women who defined their lesbian identities in terms of butch-femme roles could legitimately lay claim to a radical sexual politics. Women's groups grappled with the issue of male-to-female transexuals who claimed access to women-only space on the grounds that they identified as women.

What emerged in the 1990s was a greater emphasis within radical movements on acknowledging differences and respecting the diversity of people's identities. Among social researchers affiliated to radical movements, there was a corresponding upsurge of interest in documenting this diversity of identities, both to foreground diversity in general and to make particular identities more visible. In the case of linguistic research, this took the form of investigating how identity was constructed, displayed or performed in the language used by particular groups, ranging from women police officers in Pittsburgh (McElhinny 1993) to African-American drag queens (Barrett 1995).

While the turn to identity has had some positive consequences for linguistic research on gender and sexuality (in particular, the focus on diversity has curbed the tendency to overgeneralize about 'women' and 'homosexuals'), there are a number of political criticisms that could be made of it. We have already mentioned one problem that arises when sexuality and sexual identity are conflated: it tends to evacuate the sex from sexuality. This is politically as well as theoretically unsatisfactory, for if post-1968 radical sexual politics have taught us anything, it is that sex, in all its forms, is unavoidably a political issue. But there are other problems with the identity approach, of which three are particularly relevant to the arguments made in this book.

Firstly, identity politics tends to lay emphasis on the 'authentic' expression of identity through the shared practices, symbols and rituals of a community (e.g. spending time in community spaces like bars, cafes and bookshops, wearing pink triangle badges and displaying rainbow flags, celebrating Gay Pride). The linguistic reflex of this is an impulse to claim for the community 'a language of our own' – a distinctive way of speaking and/or writing which serves as an authentic expression of group identity. Thus the history of the study of language and sexuality has been punctuated by attempts to delineate what has variously been called 'the language of homosexuality', 'gayspeak' and 'queerspeak'. Although the more simplistic forms of this quest have been challenged, the underlying idea continues to exert a powerful influence on the popular (and in many cases, the scholarly) imagination. We believe it has done more to obstruct than to advance our understanding of the relationship between language and sexuality, and we will pursue that point at greater length in chapter 4.

Secondly, the politics of identity has a tendency to accentuate the positive: of course radicals protest their subordinate status, but at the same time they celebrate their identities as a source of pride ('Black is Beautiful', 'Out and Proud'). In the case of sexual identity, activists also counter mainstream disapproval by openly affirming the joys of gay and lesbian sex. In linguistic studies of (minority) sexual identity, research has typically been conducted with people who share this positive outlook, in the sense that they are open about their sexual preferences and appear to be comfortable with them. Yet while admittedly it would be much harder for researchers to recruit subjects who do not acknowledge or accept their own queerness, it does need to be remembered that such people exist. There is still gay shame as well as gay pride; indeed, it is not only members of sexual minorities who may regard their own erotic desires with anything from ambivalence to horror. More generally, sex itself is not an unequivocally positive force.[2] While it can bring us intense physical pleasure and deep emotional satisfaction, it can equally be the site on which we suffer the most appalling cruelty and endure the most profound misery. Less extreme but more common negative experiences of sex include embarrassment, disappointment and boredom. Although we live in a culture which tends to view negative sexual experiences or feelings as problems which can and should be remedied by education or therapy (hence all the 'how-to' manuals and self-help books on the subject), most serious attempts to theorize the erotic (the traditions of psychoanalysis, for instance) suggest that things are more complicated. Feelings of shame, disgust, envy, aggression and hatred are treated by many theorists as an integral part of human sexuality, which implies that they would play some part in shaping erotic desire in even a more sexually egalitarian and enlightened society than ours. In this book we will take that suggestion seriously, focusing on the negative as well as the positive aspects of sex.

Finally, a criticism that has been made of contemporary identity politics is that it downplays something that should be at the heart of any kind of politics worth the name: power. It has been asked whether cultivating and celebrating authentic selves has become a substitute for collective action to change the material structures that reproduce social inequality. Not everyone would accept the presuppositions of this question. Some activists would insist that when sexual minorities make themselves visible through acts of identity, they are subverting mainstream norms and so challenging the existing power structures. Versions of this argument have been made by linguists analysing 'deviant' uses of language, such as the substitution of feminine- for masculine-gendered forms among transgendered speakers (e.g. Hall and O'Donovan 1996; Moriel 1998). Whatever we make of the argument about subversion, though, it is noticeable that recent studies focusing on the performance of sexual identities seldom address the linguistic mechanisms through which dominance and subordination are accomplished. In this book, we will follow Gayle Rubin (1984) in arguing that sex is 'a vector of oppression', and we will examine in particular the complex interactions of power, sex and gender.

Although we are critical of contemporary identity politics, we recognize that our own identities have a bearing on our scholarly work. If readers feel impelled to ask, 'who are these authors and from what kind of experiences do they come to the subject they are writing about?', we are not going to dismiss that curiosity as irrelevant or impertinent. It seems reasonable for us to make explicit, for instance, that neither of us identifies as heterosexual: that we are, respectively, a lesbian and a gay man. This is relevant information for our readers to have, since it would be strange if our views on sexuality had not been affected significantly by our status as members of sexual minorities. Our whole outlook on life is affected by that status – and also, no doubt, by other social characteristics we happen to have in common, such as being white, having received an elite academic education, and belonging to the generation that came of age in the late 1970s: a decade after Stonewall, a decade before Queer Nation.

Yet while this biographical information may help the reader to situate our ideas and arguments, it does not in and of itself explain why we think what we do. There are plenty of people who could say exactly the same things about themselves that we have just said about ourselves, but who would not by that token subscribe to the same opinions. Clearly, educated white non-heterosexuals in their forties are not a homogeneous group. Even as a group of two, we have our differences and disagreements. We were trained in different academic disciplines (linguistics and anthropology). We are of different genders, and this has led us to follow rather different paths politically (mainly feminist versus mainly gay/queer/transgender activism); there are political issues on which we hold sharply divergent views. This is not exactly the same book that either of us would have written had we been working alone rather than together. It is the product of a dialogue, and we offer it to our readers in the hope that they will feel moved to engage in further dialogue with us.

As well as acknowledging our debt to one another, we would like to thank those who have offered us assistance and support during our work on *Language and Sexuality.* We are particularly indebted to Meryl Altman, Keith Harvey, Keith Nightenhelser and Christopher Stroud for helpful suggestions and comments. Thanks also to the various audiences in Europe and North America to whom we have presented work in progress. The Bank of Sweden Tercentenary Foundation (grant no. 99–5061) provided financial support to Don Kulick which we gratefully acknowledge.

CHAPTER I

Making connections

This book sets out to explore a particular set of connections, between 'language' on one hand and 'sexuality' on the other. Each of these terms encompasses what is really a complex range of phenomena, and in addition each has connections to other terms which are related but not identical. Before we do anything else, therefore, it is important to try and get as clear as possible what it is that we will be discussing under the heading of 'language and sexuality'.

SEX, GENDER, SEXUALITY

In 1975 a groundbreaking collection of feminist scholarship on language was published under the title *Language and Sex* (Thorne and Henley 1975). Today, this title appears anachronistic: the field of inquiry that the volume helped to establish is known (in English) as 'language and *gender* studies'. The change reflects a general tendency, at least among social scientists and humanists, for scholars to distinguish *gender* (socially constructed) from *sex* (biological), and to prefer *gender* where the subject under discussion is the social behaviour and relations of men and women. In a somewhat similar way (and for somewhat similar reasons), *sex* in its 'other' sense of 'erotic desire/practice' has been progressively displaced for the purposes of theoretical discussion by *sexuality*. *Sexuality*, like *gender*, is intended to underline the idea that we are dealing with a cultural rather than purely natural phenomenon.

In this book we will follow most contemporary scholars in using *sex*, *gender* and *sexuality* to mean different, rather than interchangeable, things. Nevertheless, we think it is worth remembering that the English word *sex* has only recently yielded to alternative terms. There are good reasons to prefer the alternatives, but we should not underestimate the significance, nor the continuing relevance, of the connection that was made explicitly in the term *sex* with its dual meaning. That connection (between the phenomenon we now call 'gender' and the phenomenon we now call 'sexuality') is not coincidental, and it has not been destroyed by the preference for different words with somewhat different and seemingly more precise definitions. On the contrary, it can be argued that old assumptions about *sex* are often a sort of ghostly presence, haunting contemporary discussions which claim to have transcended them.

The entry for *sex* in the *Concise Oxford Dictionary* (hereafter *COD*; 1991 edition) begins like this:

1 either of the main divisions (male or female) into which living things are placed on the basis of their reproductive functions. **2** the fact of belonging to one of these. **3** males or females collectively. **4** sexual instincts, desires, etc. or their manifestation. **5** *colloq* sexual intercourse.

Clearly, the first three definitions in the entry are variations on the first main sense of *sex*, the one which has to do with male–female difference. The fourth and fifth definitions go with the alternative, 'erotic desire and practice' sense. Yet the fourth definition gives no indication that we have moved on to a different and distinct sense of the word. From the point of view of the proverbial visiting Martian (or the bored schoolchild looking up 'dirty words' in the dictionary) it is a singularly uninformative definition, since it does not give any criteria for describing 'instincts, desires, etc.' as 'sexual'. It is as though the meaning of the word *sexual* in this context were wholly obvious and transparent, even though the entry is for the more 'basic' lexical item – *sex* – from which *sexual* is derived. This only makes sense if we take it that, covertly, the last two definitions are parasitic on the other three. We are supposed to understand what makes an instinct or a desire 'sexual' through the previous references to 'males or females' and their respective 'reproductive functions'. The most obvious inference is that *sex* in its second sense prototypically refers to what males and females instinctively desire to do with one another in order to reproduce.

Since the late 1960s, radical thinkers have attempted to unpick, criticize and transcend the assumptions embedded in the *COD* entry for *sex*. Those who coined and then popularized the terms *gender* and *sexuality* were deliberately trying to get away from narrowly biological/reproductive definitions, and also to make a clear distinction between the two senses of *sex*. But this strategy has still not met with uniform acceptance, and the two 'new' terms, *gender* and *sexuality*, have complex histories in recent English usage.

As early as 1949, Simone de Beauvoir in *The Second Sex* had observed that 'one is not born, but rather becomes, a woman' (Beauvoir 1989[1949]: 267).

DEFINITIONS OF 'SEX'

In the wake of then US President Bill Clinton's public denial that he had 'had sex' with White House intern Monica Lewinsky because no penile-vaginal intercourse had ever occurred, two researchers at the Kinsey Institute for Research in Sex, Gender and Reproduction re-examined data that they had gathered in 1991 on the sexual lives of US college students. As part of that research, 599 undergraduate students had been asked to fill in a questionnaire that contained the following question:

Would you say you 'had sex' with someone if the most intimate behavior that you engaged in was . . . (mark yes or no for each behavior):
(a) a person had oral (mouth) contact with your breasts or nipples?
(b) you touched, fondled, or manually stimulated a person's genitals?
(c) you had oral (mouth) contact with a person's breasts or nipples?
(d) penile-vaginal intercourse (penis in vagina)?
(e) you touched, fondled, or manually stimulated a person's breasts or nipples?
(f) a person had oral (mouth) contact with your genitals?
(g) you had oral (mouth) contact with a person's genitals?
(h) deep kissing (French or tongue kissing)?
(i) penile-anal intercourse (penis in anus [rectum])?
(j) a person touched, fondled, or manually stimulated your breasts or nipples?
(k) a person touched, fondled, or manually stimulated your genitals?

The results indicated that 60% of the respondents would not say that they 'had sex' with someone if the most intimate behaviour engaged in was oral-genital contact. Undergraduates who had experienced oral-genital contact but had never engaged in penile-vaginal intercourse were even less likely to consider oral-genital sex as having 'had sex'. In addition, one in five respondents said that they did not count penile-anal intercourse as having 'had sex'.

Source: Sanders and Reinisch (1999)

To be a 'woman' as opposed to a 'female' takes more than just being born with the 'correct' reproductive organs. It is a cultural achievement which has to be learned, and exactly what has to be learned is different in different times and places. To give a couple of examples (they are trivial, but a great deal of everyday gendered behaviour is trivial): Western women have to learn not to sit with their legs apart and to button their coats the opposite way from their brothers. On the other hand, most no longer have to learn to ride side-saddle or lace a corset, which were once important gender-markers for Western women of a certain class. None of the 'accomplishments' just mentioned, past or present, can plausibly be considered an innate biological characteristic, but they are part of what it means, or meant, to be a woman in a certain society. This sociocultural 'being a woman' is what the term *gender* is supposed to denote, while *sex* is reserved for the biological phenomenon of dimorphism (the fact that humans come in two varieties for purposes of sexual reproduction). But the conflation of the two terms remains pervasive, and one consequence is that, among people who are neither political radicals nor academic theorists, the term *gender* is very frequently used as a sort of polite synonym for (biological) *sex*. One of us once heard a biologist on TV explain that there was 'no accurate DNA test for gender'. He wasn't making the obvious and redundant point that things like which way you button your coat cannot be read off from your chromosomes. He meant that even the most up-to-date genetic testing methods cannot determine an individual's *sex* with 100% accuracy. Ironically, one factor that may be influencing speakers to prefer *gender* over *sex* even in contexts where the topic is biology, and *sex* would therefore be perfectly appropriate, is that *sex* has the additional meaning of erotic desire or behaviour – a subject speakers in some contexts try hard to avoid on the grounds that it is indelicate or impolite.

What has happened to *sexuality* in many English speakers' usage is that the broad meaning it was intended to have – something like 'the socially constructed expression of erotic desire' – has been narrowed so that it refers primarily to that aspect of sexuality which is sometimes called *sexual orientation*. *Sexuality* has entered common usage as a shorthand term for being either 'homosexual' or 'heterosexual' – that is, it denotes a stable erotic preference for people of the same / the other *sex*, and the social identities which are based on having such a preference (e.g. 'lesbian', 'gay'). This usage does take us beyond the purely biological and reproductive ways of talking about sex that prevailed in the past. It recognizes a kind of sexuality (homosexuality) that is not directed to procreation, and makes a distinction (homo/hetero) that is not about reproductive organs (whether one is straight or gay/lesbian does not depend on one's anatomy). On the other hand, the 'sexual orientation' usage of *sexuality* could be said to reaffirm the connection between the 'men and women' sense of *sex* on one hand, and the 'erotic desire and practice' sense on the other, because it defines an individual's sexuality exclusively in terms of *which sex* their preferred sexual partners are.

It seems, then, that new theoretical terminology has not entirely dispelled confusion around sex, gender and sexuality. Partly, this may be because some speakers still cling to traditional beliefs (e.g. that the way women or men behave socially and sexually is a direct expression of innate biological characteristics). But it may also be partly because the phenomena denoted by the three terms – having a certain kind of body (sex), living as a certain kind of social being (gender), and having certain kinds of erotic desires (sexuality) – are not understood or experienced by most people in present-day social reality as distinct and separate. Rather, they are *interconnected*.

Let us illustrate the problems this raises using a case where the relationship between sexuality and gender is both particularly salient and particularly complicated: the case of a group of people in Brazil known throughout the country as *travestis* (Kulick 1998). The word 'travesti' derives from *trans-vestir*, or 'cross-dress'. But travestis do much more than cross-dress. Sometimes beginning at ages as young as eight or ten, males who self-identify as travestis begin growing their hair long, plucking their eyebrows, experimenting with cosmetics, and wearing, whenever they can, feminine or androgynous clothing such as tiny shorts exposing the bottom of their buttocks or T-shirts tied in a knot above their navel. It is not unusual for boys of this age to also begin engaging in sexual relations with their peers and older males, always in the role of the one who is anally penetrated. By the time these boys are in their early teens, many of them have already either left home, or been expelled from their homes, because their sexual and gender transgressions are usually not tolerated, especially by the boys' fathers. Once they leave home, the majority of travestis migrate to cities (if they do not already live in one), where they meet and form friendships with other travestis, and where they begin working as prostitutes. In the company of their travesti friends and colleagues, young travestis learn about oestrogen-based hormones, which are available for inexpensive over-the-counter purchase at any of the numerous pharmacies that line the streets in Brazilian cities. At this point, young travestis often begin ingesting large quantities of these hormones. By the time they reach their late teens, many travestis have also begun paying their travesti colleagues to inject numerous litres of industrial silicone into their bodies, in order to round out their knees, thighs, and calves, and to augment their breasts, hips, and, most importantly (this being Brazil), their buttocks.

In many respects a travesti's linguistic choices index feminine gender. Travestis all adopt female names and they call and refer to one another as *she* (*ela* in Portuguese – we adopt their own usage in discussing them here). At the same time, however, despite these linguistic practices, and despite the fact that travestis spend so much time and energy (and pain) acquiring female bodily forms, the overwhelming majority still have, and highly value, their male genitals. The logic behind this is that travestis do not define themselves as women; they define themselves, instead, as homosexuals – as males who feel 'like women' and who ardently desire 'men' (that is, masculine, non-homosexual males). Their sexual preference (for masculine, non-homosexual men) is central to their identity. It shapes the way they think about and structure both their affective relationships (it is men they fall in love with – not women and not other travestis) and their professional life (travestis say clearly that their work is often sexually pleasurable, and not just a way of making money). They think transexuals of the North American and northern European variety, who say they are 'women trapped in men's bodies', are the victims of a serious 'psychosis'. The overwhelming majority of travestis would not dream of having their genitals surgically altered because such an operation would preclude having the kind of sex they desire.

Question: is 'travesti' a gender or a sexuality? The answer is surely that it has some element of both; neither one on its own would be enough to understand the travesti's behaviour and her sense of her identity. The 'crossing' practices that cause us to label travestis 'transgendered' are not *just* about gender, but also and perhaps even more importantly about sexuality. It is futile to try to separate the two, for the identity of a travesti arises from the complex interplay between them.

Travestis may be a particularly complicated case, but gender and sexuality interact in more 'ordinary' cases too. Even where it does not involve bodily alteration or renaming oneself or cross-dressing, homosexuality is very commonly understood as *gender* deviance. Prejudice does not focus only on the supposedly 'unnatural' sexual practices of gay men and lesbians, but also on their alleged deficiencies as representatives of masculinity or femininity. Gay men are commonly thought to be effeminate (hence such insulting epithets as English *pansy*), while lesbians are assumed to be 'mannish' or 'butch'. Conversely, straight people who flout gender norms are routinely suspected of being homosexual. Feminists of all sexual orientations come under suspicion of being lesbians, not necessarily because they do anything to signal that they are sexually attracted to women, but simply because their behaviour is not conventionally feminine. Heterosexual male transvestites (like the British comedian Eddie Izzard, who often appears in women's clothes though his performance is not a drag act) have constantly to explain that they are not, in fact, gay.

The conflation of gender deviance and homosexuality comes about because heterosexuality is in fact an indispensable element in the dominant ideology of gender. This ideology holds that real men axiomatically desire women, and true women want men to desire them. Hence, if you are not heterosexual you cannot be a real man or a true woman; and if you are not a real man or a true woman then you cannot be heterosexual. What this means is that sexuality and gender have a 'special relationship', a particular kind of mutual dependence which no analysis of either can overlook.

For that reason, the study of sexuality (in relation to language or anything else) will inevitably need to make reference to, and may in some respects overlap with, the study of gender. That does not, however, mean that sexuality and gender are 'the same thing', or that the study of one is just an appendage to the study of the other. The title of this book suggests that we view 'language and sexuality' as a distinctive field of study. But in order to discover what makes it distinctive and what is distinctive about it, we will have to consider in some detail what the relationship between sexuality and gender might be, and how the linguistic 'coding' of one is similar to or different from that of the other.

Later on, we will review what twenty-five years of research into the relationship between language and gender has told us about the relationship between language and sexuality, and what it has neglected or left obscure. First, though, we need to clarify a few important points about what is encompassed by the term *sexuality* as we use it in this book.

SEXUALITY: SOME KEY POINTS

As we have already noted, probably the most common understanding of the term *sexuality* in contemporary English-speaking communities is as a shorthand term referring to same-sex (homosexual) versus other-sex (heterosexual) erotic preference, particularly where that becomes a basis for some ratified social identity such as 'gay man' or 'lesbian'. We might add that the preferences and identities most commonly under discussion when the word *sexuality* is used are precisely the 'minority' or 'deviant', that is non-heterosexual, ones. 'Heterosexual' or 'straight' is not regarded as a social identity in the same way (no one ever talks about 'the heterosexual/straight community', for instance, or asks a heterosexual: 'So when did you first realize you were attracted to people of a different gender?' When heterosexuality is used as a categorizing device it is usually in genres like personal ads, where finding a sexual partner of the preferred kind is the exclusive point at issue.) This is a predictable bias, also found in relation to the terms *gender* and *race*, which are not infrequently used as if only women had a gender and only non-white people a race. We have no wish to recycle this sort of unconsidered and untheorized (not to mention heterosexist[1]) common sense, and in later chapters we will return to questions about how sexuality may be understood theoretically. In the meantime, though, let us spell out some of the fundamental assumptions that inform our own use of the term *sexuality*.

Our first assumption is that all humans have sexuality – not just those whose preferences and practices are outside the (heterosexual/reproductive) norm, and not even just those who actually have sex (a word that can itself refer to many things, not only the kinds of genital contact it is most commonly understood to mean). This implies, also, that the study of sexuality cannot limit itself to questions of sexual orientation. Rather the study of sexuality should concern itself with desire in a broader sense; this would include not only whom one desires but also what one desires to do (whether or not with another person).

Everyone may have sexuality, but not everyone defines their identity around their sexuality. Our second assumption is that sexuality does not include only those preferences and practices that people explicitly identify as fundamental to their understanding of who they are. As we will see in later chapters, the very possibility of making statements like 'I am a heterosexual / a homosexual / a lesbian / gay / queer / bi . . .' (which is to say, explaining who one is in sexual terms) has not existed throughout history, and it still does not exist in all societies. Even in contemporary Western societies where there has been a proliferation of possible sexual identities, people vary a good deal in the importance they accord sexuality in their understanding of who they are and what group they belong to. For some, sexual identity has a very strong defining function; for others it comes second to other kinds of identity (e.g. some lesbians consider themselves 'women' or 'feminists' first and 'lesbians' second, whereas for others this ranking is reversed). Others again will say that they regard their sexuality as relatively unimportant to their identity. For instance, in an interview (*Guardian*, 18 March 2000) the movie actor Kathleen Turner, who is most famous for playing *femme fatale* characters, mused on what she represented as the ironic contrast between her public image and her own sense of self, saying that 'sexuality has never been the core of my personality'.

Thirdly, we assume that not only sexual *identities* (like 'lesbian', 'bisexual') but also *sexualities* (which we can gloss for the purposes of this discussion as 'ways of being sexual') are both historically and culturally variable. This assumption follows from our general commitment to the social constructionist view that human behaviour is never just a matter of nature or instinct. People do not just do things: they are constrained

THINKING ABOUT SEXUALITY

- Even identical genital acts mean very different things to different people.
- To some people, the nimbus of 'the sexual' seems scarcely to extend beyond the boundaries of discrete genital acts; to others it enfolds them loosely or floats virtually free of them.
- Sexuality makes up a large share of the self-perceived identity of some people, a small share of others'.
- Some people spend a lot of time thinking about sex, others little.
- Some people like to have a lot of sex, others little or none.
- Many people have their richest mental/emotional involvement with sexual acts they don't do, or even don't *want* to do.
- For some people, it is important that sex be embedded in contexts resonant with meaning, narrative, and connectedness with other aspects of their life; for other people, it is important that they not be; to others it doesn't occur that they might be.
- For some people, the preference for a certain sexual object, act, role, zone, or scenario is so immemorial and durable that it can only be experienced as innate; for others, it appears to come late or feel aleatory or discretionary.
- For some people, the possibility of bad sex is aversive enough that their lives are strongly marked by its avoidance; for others, it isn't.
- For some people sexuality provides a needed space of heightened discovery and cognitive hyperstimulation. For others, sexuality provides a needed space of routinized habituation and cognitive hiatus.
- Some people like spontaneous sexual scenes, others like highly scripted ones, others like spontaneous-sounding ones that are nonetheless totally predictable.
- Some people's sexual orientation is intensely marked by autoerotic pleasures and histories – sometimes more so than by any other aspect of alloerotic object choice. For others the autoerotic possibility seems secondary or fragile, if it exists at all.
- Some people, homo-, hetero-, and bisexual, experience their sexuality as deeply embedded in a matrix of gender meanings and gender differentials. Others of each sexuality do not.

Source: Eve Kosofsky Sedgwick, *The Epistemology of the Closet* (1990), 25–6

in what they can do or can imagine doing, and they imbue these doings or imaginings with meaning. This applies even – or perhaps especially – to the most 'basic' activities that humans must engage in to survive, like eating and, of course, sex. Clearly we do not only eat or have sex to survive and ensure the reproduction of our species: we use these activities for all kinds of other social purposes (for instance worshipping sacred beings, alleviating boredom, forging and maintaining intimacy, putting others under an obligation and displaying our power over them, giving ourselves and others pleasure). All kinds of meanings and elaborate rituals surround the supposedly 'natural' sexual impulse, and these are not the same meanings or rituals in every time and place.

One of the things a social constructionist view of sexuality should make us particularly cautious about is assuming that 'the same' sexual practice always has the same meaning, regardless of the culture and context in which it occurs and the way in which it is understood by those involved. For example, it is tempting for today's lesbian feminists to claim the married women who, 200 years ago, engaged in romantic and often physical 'passionate friendships' with their women friends as foresisters, lesbians who just did not realize, or could not risk acknowledging, that they were lesbians (see Smith-Rosenberg 1975). But these women almost certainly did not understand their sexuality in the way contemporary lesbians understand theirs: the ideas about sex they had at their disposal did not include the now-commonplace idea that every person has a fundamental 'sexual orientation' towards either their own gender or the other. Indeed, they may not have understood passionate friendships as 'sexual' at all. Our understanding of what is sexual, and what different ways of being sexual mean, is always dependent on the kind of discourse about sex that circulates in a given time and place – a point that is directly relevant to the issue of how sexuality can be connected to language.

LANGUAGE AND SEXUALITY

What does the collocation 'language and sexuality' most readily bring to mind? We suspect that for many readers it will be one or both of two things: the specialized language (slang or argot) used in sexual subcultures, and/or the issue of whether gay men and lesbians have an identifiable style of speaking, which distinguishes them from heterosexual men and women. Both these topics have been more extensively studied than most other candidates for inclusion under the heading of language and sexuality. Until recently the study of the terminology in use among homosexual men particularly was such a dominant theme that one collection of papers on language and sexuality announced itself as a radical departure with the title *Beyond the Lavender Lexicon* (Leap 1995b). Since then, a good deal of research interest has focused on the question of how gay men (and to a lesser extent lesbians) use patterns of discourse choices (rather than just words) to signal that they are gay. Another topic that has cropped up persistently is the phonetic characteristics of identifiably gay (typically, gay male) voices. We will review some of the research on these subjects later on. However, we do not think that on their own they should define the field of 'language and sexuality'.

It will already be clear from what we have said about our understanding of sexuality that we are not only interested in the voices, vocabularies or discourse styles of individuals who explicitly identify themselves as gay men or lesbians (or members of any other sexual subculture). That would be to fall into the trap of equating sexuality with *homosexuality* (or more broadly, minority sexualities), forgetting that sexuality is not the sole preserve of the subordinate group(s), and that there is more to it than whether one desires someone of the same or the other sex.

Questions about 'how gay men / lesbians speak' belong to what we would prefer to call the study of 'language and sexual identity'. It is a longstanding observation in sociolinguistics that language-using, whatever else it accomplishes, is an 'act of identity', a means whereby people convey to one another what kinds of people they are. Clearly, language-using can fulfil this function in relation to sexual identity as it can in relation to other kinds of identity (e.g. gender, class, ethnicity, regional provenance). It follows that the field of language and sexuality should consider questions of sexual identity. It does not follow, however, that the field is *reducible* to those questions. Furthermore, the study of sexual identity should in principle include normative heterosexuality[2] as well as the 'deviant' or marked cases. As we have already said, normative heterosexuality is seldom explicitly presented as an identity, whereas being gay or lesbian or bisexual is often presented in this way. But that does not necessarily mean that being straight has no impact on the way people use language. Later on we will present examples where it is clear that heterosexuality is an important influence on people's verbal self-presentation, shaping what they say, how they say it, and also what they do not say.

But sexuality is not only made relevant in language-use as a matter of the speaker's *identity*. When we attempt to define the scope of an inquiry into 'language and sexuality' our starting point is that sex, for humans, is not just the instinctive behaviour suggested by the dictionary definition we quoted earlier. It is cultural behaviour, meaningful behaviour, and as such it is always semiotically coded. In the domain of sex and sexuality as in other domains, there are culturally recognizable, conventionalized ways of doing things, and also of defining and representing what is being done. Language, arguably the most powerful definitional/representational medium available to humans, shapes our understanding of what we are doing (and of what we *should* be doing) when we do sex or sexuality. The language we have access to in a particular time and place for representing sex and sexuality exerts a significant influence on what we take to be possible, what we take to be 'normal' and what we take to be desirable.

It follows that the study of language and sexuality encompasses not only questions about how people enact sexuality and perform sexual identity in their talk, but also questions about how sexuality and sexual identity are represented linguistically in a variety of discourse genres. A list of potentially interesting genres might include: scientific and popular sexology, the 'Am I normal?' letters that appear on newspaper and magazine problem pages, pornographic narratives, romance fiction, personal ads and Valentine's day messages in newspapers, discussions on daytime talk shows, sex education materials designed for schoolchildren, medical literature about sexual 'dysfunction', legal texts defining sexual offences, radical political literature contesting mainstream representations, coming-out stories and other autobiographical genres. The two sets of questions, how sexuality is 'done' and how it is represented, are connected, because representations are a resource people draw on – arguably, indeed, are compelled to draw on – in constructing their own identities and ways of doing things. Who can truthfully say that nothing they know about sex and sexuality comes from any of the sources listed above? Conversely, representations draw, though often selectively, on people's lived experience and their ordinary talk about it.

Above, we referred in passing to the idea that sexuality shapes (and we would add, is shaped by) what is not said, or cannot be said, as well as what is actually put into words. The structuring significance of the not-said, of silence, is implicit in such oft-repeated formulas as 'the love that dare not speak its name' for male homosexuality, and in characterizations of women's sexuality as unspoken and somehow unspeakable: in Britain, the attempt to criminalize lesbian relations in the early twentieth century failed because the Lord Chancellor and other prominent citizens argued – in hushed whispers, one assumes – that to speak of lesbianism, even to forbid it, was to risk popularizing and spreading it among the 'untainted' female citizenry (Weeks 1985: 105).

Building on the theoretical work of Jacques Lacan, the editors of a book with the title *Language and Desire* (Harvey and Shalom 1997) suggest that sexual desire in general (not only those variants that are socially stigmatized) is an area of human experience that always exceeds the capacity of language to represent it. But if the importance of the not-said or the unsayable is a characteristic feature of discourse about sex and sexuality, that poses a problem for linguistic analysis. Techniques for systematically analysing spoken or written discourse are minutely attentive to the intricate patterning of what is 'there' in the text; but how do we begin to get at what is *not* there? In a later chapter we will consider some possible answers to this question, for we believe it is a question that any worthwhile study of language and sexuality must address.

HOW THIS BOOK IS ORGANIZED

Our investigation of language and sexuality begins with the way sexuality itself is represented in language (chapter 2). Language gives us categories with which to think about sexuality, and conventions for speaking and writing about it. We will look at how those categories and conventions have evolved over time, and how they reproduce ideological propositions about 'normal' and 'deviant' sexuality.

The next issue we address is the relationship of gender and sexuality. In chapter 3 we will focus critically on the common assumption that a speaker's identity as heterosexual is marked by the same linguistic strategies that mark her or his gender identity (and the corresponding assumption, also common, that homosexual identity is marked linguistically by using strategies more characteristic of the 'other' gender group). We will argue, using a number of examples from our own and other researchers' data, that this view is over-simplified. We will then move on in chapter 4 to consider a question that has been much debated in recent years: whether there is such a thing as 'gay language' or 'lesbian language' – in other words, a distinctive 'lect' or register which signifies the speaker's homosexual identity. In this chapter we will also discuss recent work on language that draws on queer theory, which has questioned the idea of an 'authentic' sexual identity – and consequently, of an 'authentic' language in which that identity is expressed.

As we have already noted, we believe that sexual identity should not be the exclusive focus of research on language and sexuality, and in chapter 5 we explore the broader question of language and desire. Here we return to the question we raised above about the significance of what is not said, or what cannot be said. We ask how the techniques of linguistic analysis can be used to illuminate the meaning of the unspoken, and whether linguistic researchers can make use of insights from psychoanalytic theory.

Finally, in chapter 6 we focus on language and sexuality as a new field of inquiry, summarizing the arguments we have made in this book and considering the most exciting future directions for theory, research and politics.

CHAPTER 2

Talking sex and thinking sex: the linguistic and discursive construction of sexuality

In the film *When Harry Met Sally* there is a famous scene in which the female protagonist Sally apparently has an orgasm as she sits fully clothed at a table in the middle of a busy diner. In fact, both the man she is with, Harry, and the audience watching the action on screen know that she is faking it, to demonstrate that you can't tell the difference between a competent performance of an orgasm and the real thing. Part of the joke is the surprise, amusement and embarrassment her performance causes other customers in the diner, who cannot be sure whether the orgasm is real or faked. Also part of the joke is the chagrin of the man for whose benefit the performance is being put on; for if this is not a real orgasm, perhaps the female orgasms he has been party to in more intimate circumstances were not real either.

This scene provides an illustration of what is meant by 'the discursive construction of sexuality'. The man who believes that you can always tell whether a woman's orgasm is genuine is holding on to one of our most cherished beliefs about sex: that the body does not lie. According to this view, the outward expression of orgasm comes directly from the inner physical processes and sensations of orgasm, and in the absence of the physical stimulus the outward expression cannot be convincing. The woman, however, sets out to show that you can communicate an orgasm without actually having one, by producing the signs that conventionally mean 'orgasm' (these include both nonlinguistic signs like gasping and moaning, and linguistic signs like uttering (in English) 'oh' and 'yes'). Sexual experience, like other human experience, is communicated and made meaningful by codes and conventions of signification. Indeed, without those codes we would not be able to identify particular experiences as 'sexual' in the first place. Codes of signification are not only relevant to the doing of sex (e.g. communicating orgasm) but also to the understanding of what it is that we are doing, which in turn exerts an influence on what we do. What we know or believe *about* sex is part of the baggage we bring *to* sex; and our knowledge does not come exclusively from firsthand experience: it is mediated by the discourse that circulates in our societies.

At this point it may be helpful to say something about the potentially confusing term 'discourse', which is used in rather different ways by the two main groups of scholars whose ideas we draw on in this chapter: linguists and critical theorists. For linguists, 'discourse' is 'language in use' – a discourse analyst differs from a syntactician or a formal semanticist in studying not the internal workings of some language system (e.g. 'English' or 'Arabic') but the way meaning is produced when a language is used in particular contexts for particular purposes. For critical theorists, on the other hand, 'discourses' are sets of propositions in circulation about a particular phenomenon, which constitute what people take to be the reality of that phenomenon. The critical theorist Michel Foucault (1972: 149) defined 'discourses' as 'practices that systematically form the objects of which they speak'. For example, the practice of administering certain kinds of tests to people, and then treating them for purposes of education and employment according to how they score on those tests, brings into existence such objects as 'IQ' and 'personality type', as well as categories of people defined on the basis of their IQ or personality, such as 'the gifted' or 'extroverts'.

Although the two definitions of 'discourse' are different, it is not difficult to make connections between them. On one hand, the critical theorist's 'discourses' clearly involve the linguist's 'discourse': the practices that form the objects of which they *speak* (or write) are to a significant extent language-dependent practices of definition, classification, explanation and justification. On the other hand, the instances of language-use studied by linguists under the heading of 'discourse' are socially situated, and must be interpreted in relation to 'discourses' in the critical theorist's sense. In this chapter we will not try to keep the two senses of 'discourse' separate and distinct, for we think of them as mutually implicated in the processes that interest us, namely the construction and contestation of the 'reality' of sex.

The dispute between Harry and Sally, for instance, is not just a self-contained speech event, but acquires much of its meaning from its relationship to discourses already in circulation about orgasms and the faking of orgasms. To interpret the scene, competent viewers must bring to bear certain presuppositions from that discourse, which need not be explicitly stated to be relevant. For instance:

• Orgasm represents the peak of sexual satisfaction for both women and men
• Orgasm is harder for women to achieve, but easier for them to fake
• Being able to bring a woman to orgasm is the sign of a skilled and considerate lover

These presuppositions (whether or not we take them to be true) are needed to understand why it has to be the female rather than the male character who fakes the orgasm in the diner, and why it is the man rather than the woman who wants to believe that orgasms cannot be convincingly faked. Since orgasm has come to be considered an indispensable element of good sex, and since the difficulties women may have in reaching orgasm during intercourse have been widely publicized, 'giving' a woman an orgasm has become a sort of test of a heterosexual man's sexual prowess. This constitutes a temptation for women to fake orgasms, in order to spare men's feelings (or perhaps to be rid of them faster). But from the men's perspective, the possibility that women are only pretending to have orgasms undermines their image of themselves as sexually skilled.

The presuppositions listed above are disputable, of course, and they would not be obvious, or even intelligible, in every time and place. For much of the twentieth century, the inability of some women to reach orgasm during heterosexual sex was not attributed to men's lack of skill and care, it was attributed to women's lack of sexual responsiveness, and, at the extreme, to the pathological condition of 'frigidity'. Men whose female partners did not have orgasms were not encouraged, as they often are today, to treat this as a challenge. Experts reassured laypeople that for many 'normal' women orgasm was not the most important goal of having sex, and the absence of orgasms was therefore nothing to worry about. Some held that not every orgasm was a good orgasm in any case: they asserted that there were two kinds of female orgasm, 'clitoral' and 'vaginal'. Only the latter represented true and mature sexual satisfaction.

Women's Liberation activists in the late 1960s and early 1970s set out to explode the presuppositions of then-current discourse on female orgasms. They seized on sexological findings suggesting that women are physiologically equipped for almost unlimited (clitoral) orgasmic pleasure. If many women were not realizing this potential, feminists saw the reasons as cultural, not physical. They pointed out that women are discouraged from exploring their own bodies and finding out what gives them pleasure; and also that the kind of sex that is held up as the norm and the ideal – sexual intercourse – is particularly poorly suited to ensure that women come. In her paper 'The myth of the vaginal orgasm' Anne Koedt argued that the idea of vaginal orgasm was not merely a product of widespread ignorance about female anatomy and physiology,[1] but a myth serving the interests of heterosexual men: it is they, rather than women, who find vaginal intercourse especially pleasurable. Koedt suggested that women 'must begin to demand that if certain sexual positions now defined as "standard" are not mutually conducive to orgasm, they no longer be defined as standard' (2000[1968]: 372).

What is illustrated by this discussion of changing ideas about female orgasm is that at any point in time, the ways people have of *discoursing on* sex shape

- their understanding of sex and how it should be (e.g. how important orgasm is in defining what counts as sex);
- their understanding of themselves as sexual beings (e.g. whether a woman's failure to achieve orgasm with a male partner is 'normal', a sign of 'frigidity' or the result of male incompetence); and
- their interpretation of sexual experience (e.g. whether a particular encounter constituted 'good sex', or whether a particular orgasm was 'vaginal' or merely 'clitoral' – not a question many people today would ask, because the discourse that supported that distinction is no longer current).

To say that sexuality is 'discursively constructed' is to say that sex does not have meaning outside the discourses we use to make sense of it, and the language in which those discourses are (re)circulated. Taken out of the context of other discourse, the orgasm-faking performance in *When Harry Met Sally* is just a party trick, like someone displaying their unusual ability to mimic the song of the humpback whale. Viewed in relation to other discourse, it becomes meaningful in other ways – for instance, as a comment on the sexual mores and gender relations of a particular time and place.

DEFINING SEXUALITIES: THE POWER OF THE WORD

It is a commonplace of contemporary discourse about sex that *talking about it* is intrinsically a good and liberating thing. There is a widespread belief that, until very recently, the subject was so veiled in shame and ignorance that it could hardly be broached in discourse at all, and that we are still in the process of breaking that silence. We are apt to congratulate ourselves on our openness to sex-talk, contrasting our modern, enlightened attitudes favourably with the prudishness of previous eras when such talk was taboo – censored in public discourse, and repressed even in private.

This account of recent history recognizes the significance of language and discourse in relation to sexuality, but from the perspective of most contemporary theorists it also misrepresents that relationship. It conceives of sexual desires, practices and identities as fixed realities which have always existed, just awaiting the sociocultural conditions that would permit them to be expressed openly in words. The alternative position, outlined in our earlier discussion of 'discourse' and adopted throughout this book, is that the 'reality' of sex does not pre-exist the language in which it is expressed; rather, language *produces* the categories through which we organize our sexual desires, identities and practices.

If it were true that we are only now emerging from millennia of silence on the subject of sex, the implication of what we have just said would be that, for most of human history, sex itself did not exist. (We would have to take literally the poet Philip Larkin's sardonic observation that 'Sexual intercourse began in nineteen sixty three / ... Between the end of the Chatterley ban / And the Beatles' first LP'.[2]) However, the notion that there was no discourse on sex before the late twentieth century will not withstand critical scrutiny. The most influential of all theorists of the discursive construction of sexuality, Michel Foucault, began his *History of Sexuality* (1981) by taking issue with the belief that discourse on sex is a product of modern ideologies of 'sexual liberation'. He pointed out that societies and institutions conventionally considered to represent extremes of sexual 'repression' may produce copious amounts of discourse about sex for exactly that reason. Thus Roman Catholics for centuries have been required to confess to the activities and the desires which their Church prohibits: far from maintaining silence about sex, the pious were obliged to put forbidden desires into words. It was also, of course, in discourse that religious and legal authorities defined what was forbidden and what legitimate sexual behaviour. In so doing they produced a set of categories defining what range of practices – both legitimate and proscribed – counted as 'sexual'.

The discursive categorization of practices as sexual, and the division of those practices into the 'permitted' and the 'forbidden', is clearly a very old phenomenon. One of Foucault's most influential observations, however, concerns the rather more recent historical emergence of categories of *people* defined by their sexual desires and practices, prime examples of such categories being 'homosexuals' and 'heterosexuals'. What prompted this development was the shift, in the late eighteenth and nineteenth centuries in the West, from treating the regulation of sex as the exclusive concern of religious and legal authorities to treating it as more properly the concern of medical and scientific authorities. The Church and the courts had based their regulatory practices on notions of what was 'sinful' or 'unlawful', and they had focused on actions rather than actors. Certain sexual acts were prohibited, but people who committed them were not thought of as a natural class or 'type': they were penalized for doing what they did, rather than for being what they were. Medicine and science, however, as bodies of knowledge whose aim was to uncover the laws governing the natural world, sought to regulate sex on the basis of a different distinction – not virtuous/sinful or lawful/unlawful but natural/unnatural or normal/abnormal. This shifted attention from the act to the actor, whose deviant behaviour was seen as manifesting his or her fundamentally abnormal nature. It gave rise to the novel idea that a person could be defined by their erotic desires – that those desires might constitute the core of their being and bestow on them a specific identity that linked them to others with similar desires.

The distinction we have just outlined, between treating sex as a form of behaviour and treating it as definitive of a person's identity, may seem arcane, but it can be clarified using a contemporary example: our understanding of the practice of paying a prostitute for sex. In English, there are terms in common use to describe those people (the great majority of them men) who pay prostitutes for sex, including 'customer', 'punter', 'john' and 'client'. However, words like 'client' allude to something a person does in a specific context (that is, exchanging money for sexual services), and it is not clear that the person's 'client' status has any relevance beyond that context. Is the same person still a client when he goes to work the next morning? Is he a client when he sits at home watching the news on a weekday evening, or when he reads his children a bedtime story? Do all clients have a similar nature, distinct from the nature of non-clients? Will researchers someday claim to have discovered a 'client gene'? Can we look at a six-year-old child and whisper, 'that boy's going to grow up to be a client'?

If these questions make little sense, it is because 'client' is not (at least at present) an *identity*. It remains a label for a specific relationship (of buyer to seller of sexual services), and only applies when the parties are actually engaged in a transaction. But if we substitute the word 'homosexual' for 'client' in the questions posed above, it becomes evident that we are dealing with a different kind of status – one that is considered to be both permanent and all-encompassing. A homosexual is not just a homosexual while having sex, but remains a homosexual in the office, watching TV or playing with the children. Some researchers have posited the existence of a homosexual gene, and many a concerned adult has looked at a six-year-old and seen a homosexual in the making.

Being a client and being a homosexual are both defined in some quarters as examples of sexual 'deviance'. Both carry a certain stigma, and each may attract legal penalties. The difference is, though, that in one case stigma and punishment are directed at a particular form of behaviour, while in the other they are directed at a category of persons whose sexual desires are held to constitute their identity. The latter approach is also the more recent, having emerged fully only in the nineteenth century. In a much-quoted passage from *The History of Sexuality*, Foucault explains how 'sodomy', a term that principally denoted anal intercourse but also included a wider range of forbidden sexual behaviours, was transformed into the identity category of 'homosexuality':

> The nineteenth century homosexual became a personage, a past, a case history and a childhood, in addition to being a type of life, a life form, a morphology, with an indiscreet anatomy and possibly a mysterious physiology. Nothing that went into his total composition was unaffected by his sexuality. It was everywhere present in him: at the root of all his actions because it was their insidious and indefinitely active principle: written immodestly on his face and body because it was a secret that always gave itself away. It was consubstantial with him, less as a habitual sin than as a singular nature. *The sodomite had been a temporary aberration: the homosexual was now a species.* (1981: 43, emphasis added)

The nineteenth-century homosexual was not alone as a new species to be diagnosed, studied, experimented upon and, ideally, cured. Typologies were produced, cataloguing the innumerable forms deviance could take; sexual 'perversions' proliferated. Homosexuals were joined by a carnivalesque ensemble that included onanists, frottists, nymphomaniacs, zoophiles and fetishists. Also temporarily included in this rogues' gallery were 'heterosexuals': the term, coined in 1869 (the same year as 'homosexual'), originally denoted a perversion – having sex with someone of the other gender for pleasure rather than in order to reproduce. The first 'heterosexuals' were thus men who had sex with pregnant women, or who engaged in oral sex rather than intercourse. Women too could suffer from heterosexuality, but this was less common; and if women enjoyed sex with men too much there were other names for them anyway, as we will see in more detail below.

In the late nineteenth and early twentieth centuries, heterosexuality lost its status as a perversion. This shift reflected the influence of arguments made by Freud and others to the effect that having sex for pleasure is not abnormal. It allowed the word 'heterosexual' to become what it has remained, an antonym of 'homosexual', denoting someone sexually attracted to persons of the opposite sex (see Katz 1995). With these contrasting terms in place, it became possible to think in the terms we consider natural and obvious today, assuming that every individual has a fundamental 'sexual orientation' towards either people of the same sex or else people of the other sex.[3] This assumption, in turn, makes possible the construction and public display of social identities that are based on sexual orientation, such as 'gay man' and 'lesbian'.

A DIFFERENT FRAMEWORK: ROMAN SEXUALITIES[4]

According to the classicist Holt N. Parker (1997), sexual categorization in ancient Rome was based on a fundamental distinction between sexual activity and passivity, with no special attention being paid to the homo/hetero distinction that is fundamental for modern Westerners. 'Active' sexuality in the Roman system meant using the penis to penetrate one of three bodily orifices, the vagina, the anus or the mouth. The person who was penetrated was 'passive'. The Romans had one or more Latin names for each position in the resulting classification, shown in the table below (adapted from Parker 1997: 49).

	vagina	**anus**	**mouth**
active (penetrator, male)	fututor	pedicator	irrumator
passive (penetratee, male)	cunnilinctor	cinaedus/pathico	fellator
passive (penetratee, female)	femina/puella	pathica	fellatrix

The active labels (*fututor, pedicator, irrumator,* meaning 'one who penetrates a vagina/anus/mouth') can only be applied to men, since only men have a penis with which to perform the act of penetration. Women are by definition passive: the labels for a vaginally penetrated woman, *femina* and *puella,* mean simply 'woman' and 'girl'. Male/female, then, is a crucial distinction in this system, but Parker argues that hetero/homo is not. Each of the three active terms denotes a preference for penetrating a particular orifice, and while *fututor* implies that the penetratee is female, since only women have vaginas, *pedicator* and *irrumator* do not specify the sex of the penetrated person. All the active positions were considered 'normal' male sexualities, regardless of whether the mouths and anuses men penetrated were male or female (or they didn't care which they were, which seems to have been a not uncommon attitude).

The passive positions may be occupied by either men or women, and the terms used to describe them are therefore gender differentiated. *Fellatrix,* for instance, is the grammatically feminine equivalent of *fellator* (both derived from *fellare,* 'to suck'). There is, however, an important difference between the masculine and feminine terms: a passive woman is normal, but a passive man is perverse. Both fellatio and cunnilingus were considered humiliating for men, because (however counter-intuitive we may find this) they were passive. Parker explains that 'for a man to give oral sex is for him to be passive with respect to his mouth [i.e. allow it to be penetrated], and the disgrace is the same whether he is servicing a man or a woman' (1997: 52).

It will be evident that (what we would call) lesbian sex is absent from this classification, though it was certainly known to the Romans. However, a system which defines sex as the penetration of an orifice by a penis cannot accommodate women having sex with women. The commonest terms for such women were *tribad* and *virago* (*vir* = 'man'), and the Romans thought of them as women who aped men, attempting to take active sexual roles for which they were not anatomically equipped.

Though some aspects of the Roman system may look familiar (e.g. the association of active/passive with masculine/feminine, which we return to below[5]), Parker argues that the ancient and modern systems simply do not correspond to one another – it is meaningless to ask about a Roman, 'was he a homosexual?', because homo/hetero preference was not what the categorization system was organized around. (Equally, it would be incomprehensible to inquire about a man today, is he an *irrumator*? Many men still do what the *irrumator* did, but there is no category or label for 'men who like to penetrate another's mouth'.)

One important motivation for categorizing people as 'homosexuals' (cf. other deviant groups such as 'criminals' or 'lunatics') was to subject the people so classified to various kinds of control, such as medical interventions purporting to 'cure' them. But when a classification of this kind becomes the basis for a shared social identity, that opens up the possibility that people who identify as members of the group will organize to resist their collective oppression. This is what has happened in the case of homosexuality. Movements for gay rights or gay liberation are based on an implicit acceptance of the categorization scheme (the division of people into two classes depending on their sexual orientation), but this is accompanied by an explicit rejection of the negative meanings that were originally attached to membership of the 'homosexual' class. Foucault calls this form of resistance a 'reverse discourse', because it appropriates the original gesture of classifying a group of 'deviants' ('yes, we are homosexuals') and turns it against the classifying authority ('and as a *bona fide* minority group, we now demand our rights').

One right which is often demanded when minority groups become politicized is the right to (re)name themselves – for instance, to substitute the community term 'gay' for the category label used by (often very unsympathetic) outside experts, 'homosexual'. Later we will return to the politics of naming and labelling; we draw attention to it here, however, to underscore the point that classification is a linguistic as well as a more broadly discursive practice: it simultaneously produces *and labels* categories, and the selection of labels is not unimportant in the process of defining what categories mean.

The kinds of expert discourse which have historically been most influential in shaping modern classifications of sexual desires, practices and identities are those of medicine, particularly psychiatry, and social scientific disciplines such as psychology and sexology. The work of early sexologists established many of the categories that are still in popular circulation today, such as 'sadism', 'masochism', 'fetishism', 'paedophilia'. 'Dysfunction' (e.g. impotence, premature ejaculation, frigidity) also provided grist to the classificatory mill. This urge to classify and label in the domain of sex has persisted: new categories still surface regularly, while older ones fall into disfavour and quietly disappear. Experts no longer have much to say about those once-familiar figures, the 'frigid woman' and her opposite, the 'nymphomaniac' – let alone the 'onanists' and 'frottists' who populated nineteenth-century texts. On the other hand we have recently made the acquaintance of the 'sex addict', an individual (of either sex, though represented more often as male than as female) who is pathologically dependent on the 'high' produced by sex, in the same way that other addicts are unable to function without alcohol or narcotics.

As these examples illustrate, the categories in existence at any given time are not just random and unmotivated, and change does not occur only because of advances in scientific knowledge. Dramatic changes in expert opinion often mirror what are clearly ideological shifts in the wider society, as opposed to startling new scientific discoveries. Thus masturbation, presented by medical experts in the late nineteenth century as a public health emergency threatening the wellbeing and possibly even the life of any child who engaged in it, is now treated by experts as a normal part of healthy sexual development. This turnaround was not prompted by a controlled trial in which the 'masturbation is bad for you' hypothesis was decisively disproved. Nor did any purely scientific investigation lead to the removal, in 1973, of homosexuality from the US *Diagnostic and Statistic Manual of Mental Disorders*. That followed political campaigning by gay and lesbian organizations, and reflected a climate of greater public support for gay rights. The fading away of 'nymphomania', similarly, is not unconnected to feminist critiques of the sexual double standard that category reproduced (women were pathologized for expressing desires which were seen as normal in men). The new category of 'sex addiction' fills a similar slot, pathologizing individuals who show an 'excessive' desire for sex, but it does not specify the gender of those individuals, and thus avoids the charge of sexism. The particular form this new pathology takes must be understood in a broader context. Discourse on addiction in general acquired extraordinary potency during the 1980s and 1990s, partly because of the public attention given to drug addiction as a major social problem (this was the time when the 'war on drugs' was declared) and partly because of the cultural salience of the 'recovery movement' whose prototype was Alcoholics Anonymous. The narrative of addiction and recovery, repeated constantly on television talk shows and in interviews with troubled celebrities, became – and indeed remains – an obvious discourse in which to talk about all kinds of behaviour viewed as self-destructive or antisocial, including sexual behaviour.

WHAT'S IN A NAME? THE POLITICS OF LABELLING

We said earlier that the classification of sexual desires, practices and identities does two things simultaneously: it produces categories and it labels them, gives them names. In the preceding section we concentrated on the significance of the first effect, the discursive production of sexual categories. We wanted to emphasize that this is not just a matter of hanging linguistic labels on a pre-existing chunk of reality which was always 'there' just waiting to be named. The production of the opposed categories 'homosexual' and 'heterosexual', for instance, reconfigures the reality which the labels purport to describe, bringing into view something – what we now refer to as 'sexual orientation' or 'sexual preference' – that had not been part of previous understandings of sexual behaviour. There was a great deal more to this reconfiguration than the invention of a couple of new vocabulary items. But since we use language to think with (individually as well as in conversation with others), any new way of thinking is likely to involve new ways of using language as well; and since the process of classification requires linguistic labelling, any novel classification of phenomena will tend to involve the coining of new words. All of which might prompt the question: how important are the words? Does it matter, not only whether we have a label for something, but also what that label is?

In order to answer that question, we need to consider what labels are used for and what arguments over labels are really about. Contests over what a particular group should be called (e.g. 'Black' versus 'African-American', 'the handicapped' versus 'people with disabilities', 'homosexual' versus 'gay') can easily appear – and are often presented by mainstream commentators – as pointless disputes about semantic trivia. Invariably someone will point out that 'reality' – material facts such as racial discrimination and violent homophobic attacks – cannot be changed merely by tinkering with names. But few if any of the activists who advocate renaming do so because they believe a change of label will magically eliminate material disadvantage. Rather they see renaming as a challenge to the *ideological* structures which make the subordinate status of the group appear natural, acceptable and inevitable.

This challenge is mainly directed outwards, to those sectors of mainstream society that actively oppress the group or tacitly condone their oppression. However, renaming may also have more 'inward-directed' objectives: in addition to challenging others' prejudices, one goal of proposing new identity labels is to satisfy the desire of group members themselves for names and self-descriptions they can readily identify with. Talking about, for instance, 'the gay community' or 'the Queer Nation' is one strategy for promoting group solidarity and cohesion, creating what the historian of nationalism Benedict Anderson (1983) calls an 'imagined community'. Anderson points out that even in a very small country, most people will not have direct contact with more than a tiny fraction of their compatriots: by contrast with, say, 'the village', 'the nation' is an abstraction, and identifying oneself with it requires some imaginative effort. Thus people's sense of themselves as members of particular nations has to be constructed through various symbolic representations of nationhood: stories about a country's origins and history; maps of its territory; discussions of the 'national character'; texts addressed by a country's leaders to the people (e.g. the US President's annual 'state of the Union' address); anthems; flags; and collective rituals commemorating key events (e.g. independence days). Labels and names may also be significant resources for the symbolic work of nation-building (think for instance of the way 'Rhodesia' became 'Zimbabwe' following the achievement of Black majority rule). This insight about nations can be extended to all kinds of groupings that go beyond members' immediate social networks – 'the African diaspora', 'the Roman Catholic Church', 'the Conservative Party' or indeed 'the gay community'. However, these larger groupings are not homogeneous, and when there are differences within the group as well as between it and other groups, labelling proposals that attempt to rally group members to a single, shared vision of what unites them may be contested internally as well as externally. Wherever the contests are located, though, they are essentially power struggles carried on at the symbolic level: they are both about who has the right or the power to label a particular group, and about whose ideological presuppositions will be foregrounded in that labelling.

As we pointed out above, the displacement of 'homosexual' by 'gay' is, among other things, a rejection of an expert, clinical label invented and used by people who typically do not belong to the relevant group, or necessarily support their struggle. 'Gay', by contrast, originated in the 1930s as an in-group term, part of a code which only insiders or sympathizers understood (Butters 1998). Although the two terms, 'homosexual' and 'gay', have the same referential meaning – they identify the same group of people – their meanings in actual usage are not identical. The selection of one or the other can signify the difference between conceptualizing homosexuality as deviance or sickness, and conceptualizing it in other and more positive ways: as an alternative personal and/or political choice, for instance, or simply as one 'natural' variant of human sexuality, less common than heterosexuality but not by that token deserving condemnation.[6] It can also be used by insiders to differentiate between those individuals who are 'out' and those who remain 'closeted' – the latter are 'homosexual' rather than 'gay' because 'gay' connotes a self-ascribed sexual identity, and closeted individuals deny their homosexuality.

In formal varieties of mainstream discourse there are signs that 'gay' has assumed the status of an unmarked and relatively neutral term, while 'homosexual' as a noun is now avoided in contexts where a non-pejorative term is wanted. The BBC, for example, uses 'gay' in news bulletins, particularly in contexts where the reference is to an individual (e.g. 'the first openly gay member of the House of Lords'). This suggests that 'gay' has come to be regarded as a conservative, middle-of-the-road choice, and that for many English-speakers it now occupies much the same semantic space that 'homosexual' did previously. For some of those speakers, of course, that semantic space is not neutral but markedly negative, and 'gay' can be used as an insult.[7] Nevertheless, it may be said that this particular symbolic struggle has resulted in victory for the in-group term: it has been accepted by important linguistic gatekeepers like the BBC, and consequently it is now the unmarked term in most 'respectable' public discourse. This should remind us how quickly things can change: as late as the early 1990s, anyone who used or advocated 'gay' in its 'homosexual' sense could expect to encounter vehement protests from people who argued that a deviant minority were stealing or ruining a word whose 'real' meaning the English-speaking community must preserve at all costs.

As we noted earlier, disputes about labelling may also take place within the group to which the labels apply. In the case we are concerned with here, one long-running dispute is about gender: many lesbians prefer the gender-specific term 'lesbian' to 'gay', which, they argue, obscures the presence of women by subsuming them under a label whose primary reference is to men. This argument was and is connected to a broader feminist critique of male dominance, from which gay men are not exempt (we discuss this issue further in chapters 3 and 4). Some lesbians question not just the gender inclusivity of the word 'gay', but more fundamentally the existence of a mixed 'gay community' in which women and men are united by culture and politics. Other lesbians feel they have more in common with gay men than with feminist women. This example illustrates another function of identity labels: adopting one label in preference to another is a way of signalling contrasting political stances.[8]

That point is also relevant when we consider the more recent emergence of the term 'queer'. 'Queer' exemplifies a labelling strategy that has been used by other subordinated groups too, that of 'reclaiming' a word whose primary use in the past has been to insult you. 'Black', at the time considered negative and insulting, was reclaimed within the Black Power movement; Women's Liberation activists in the 1970s reclaimed 'witch', 'bitch' and 'dyke'. A highly visible rap act in the 1990s named itself 'Niggas with Attitude', and there are radical groups of psychiatric patients which use the slogan 'Glad to be Mad'. The strategy is a confrontational one: it says, 'yes, we are exactly what you say – and what's more, we're proud of it'.

Queer activists had a similarly uncompromising message for their bigoted adversaries, trenchantly expressed in the slogan 'we're queer, we're here, get used to it'.

But in addition, 'queer' represented a bolder attempt to reshape the sexual-political landscape. It was not intended simply as a new label for the existing categories 'gay' and 'lesbian'; it was part of a whole discourse on sexuality whose aim was to produce a new category. That category was defined in a deliberately broad and loose way, to embrace all kinds of positions based on a rejection of orthodox, heteronormative assumptions. It would include, for instance, transvestites and other transgendered people – who might or might not identify as lesbian or gay, but who challenge heteronormativity in other ways. It would include people with 'deviant' desires regardless of their sexual orientation (e.g. sadomasochists and fetishists); it would even in principle include people who claim to have no sexual orientation, precisely because that claim challenges the logic of currently orthodox understandings of sexuality. 'Queer' was not conceived as a category of identity in the way that 'gay' was; what it signified was more a set of cultural-political positions, one of which, in fact, was being critical of the kind of identity politics represented by both the gay and the feminist movements during the late 1980s and 1990s. Queer activism was informed by queer theory (see chapter 3), an important strand in which was a sustained critique of the concept of 'identity', and the essentialist assumptions on which it depended.

We have made use of the past tense in some of the above remarks not because queer politics have ceased to exist, but because the *term* 'queer' has spread beyond the community that adopted it originally, and in the process it has acquired new uses and inflections of meaning. Today 'queer' is very often used as if it were equivalent to 'gay/lesbian', though with a hipper, more radical edge. One might say that 'queer' has moved into the space which 'gay' has vacated as it has replaced 'homosexual' in respectable mainstream discourse; one might also say that 'gay' was able to become 'respectable' for gatekeepers like the BBC partly because a new and more obviously 'extreme' word, 'queer', had entered the arena. Words do not change their meanings in isolation, but in dialectical relationships with other words. The near-equivalence of 'gay' and 'queer' in many contexts suggests that 'queer' has not succeeded in displacing the existing classification system and producing an alternative – or at least, it has not succeeded in doing this outside a small community of theorists and activists. But the present state of affairs is not the end of the story. Queer theory and activism have opened up a debate about identity and sexuality which is still ongoing, and the contested status of the label 'queer' (what it means, who it includes, whether it is preferable to other labels) needs to be understood as part of that broader debate. As the debate continues, the meaning(s) of 'queer' and its relationship to other labels will no doubt continue to shift.

In this section about names and labels, we have argued that although words matter – as witness the energy expended over the years on arguments about labels like 'gay', 'lesbian', 'queer', etc. – words in isolation are not the issue. It is in *discourse* – the use of language in specific contexts – that words acquire meaning. Whenever people argue about words, they are also arguing about the assumptions and values that have clustered around those words in the course of their history of being used. We cannot understand the significance of any word unless we attend closely to its relationship with other words, and to the discourse (indeed, the competing discourses) in which words are always embedded. And we must also bear in mind that discourse shifts and changes constantly, which is why arguments about words and their meanings (much to the irritation of the 'pointless semantic trivia' brigade) are never settled once and for all.

We have focused so far on a particular type or set of words – category or identity labels – because of their particular salience in both scientific and political discourse on sexuality. However, not all words are of this kind, and meaning does not reside only in vocabulary. In the following sections, we want to broaden the discussion by undertaking a more contextualized kind of analysis, examining specific instances of language in use, and paying attention to grammatical patterns as well as vocabulary. We begin by focusing on the role played by language and discourse in the construction of 'common sense' about women's and men's sexuality, and the way common-sense discourse functions to reproduce gender inequality.

'AND THEN HE KISSED ME': SEX, GENDER, SUBJECTIVITY AND AGENCY

The feminist Catharine MacKinnon once wrote: 'man fucks woman. Subject, verb, object' (1982: 541). This observation encapsulates a pervasive and persistent piece of common sense about gender and sexuality: that only men can be active sexual subjects, while the role of women is to be passive objects of male desire. This common sense has negative consequences for women: on one hand it restricts their freedom to behave as actively desiring subjects themselves, while on the other it can make them vulnerable to sexual exploitation and abuse by men who treat them as objects rather than equal human subjects. Put another way, women are frequently in the position of not being able to have the sex they want, while at the same time they may be forced to have sex that they do not want. Here we consider how language and discourse enter into this picture.

We will begin where Catharine MacKinnon does, with grammar. Elizabeth Manning (1997) analysed the grammar of verbs denoting sexual, romantic or intimate acts as these appeared in a corpus of 211 million words of (British and American) English. The verbs that particularly interested her refer to activities which are generally understood to be engaged in by two people on the basis of mutual desire (e.g. 'kiss', 'hug', 'caress', 'fondle'), and one mark of this is the fact that they can be used in 'reciprocal' constructions with plural subjects and no object (e.g. 'we kissed') and/or with 'each other' in the object slot (e.g. 'they caressed each other'). Verbs denoting sexual activity, such as 'fuck', 'screw', 'shag', 'make love', also permit these grammatical possibilities: one may say 'we fucked each other' or 'they made love'. However, Manning did not find such constructions to be as common in the corpus she analysed as the alternative pattern in which sex is represented as something done by one person to another. Furthermore, her analysis showed that for 'fuck', 'screw' and 'make love [to]', the commonest pattern in examples relating to heterosexual sex was for men to be in the subject slot and women in the object slot. Men are said to fuck / screw / make love to women far more often than the other way round. When women were the subject of the verb 'make love' it was more likely to be followed by the preposition 'with'; when men were the subject it was more likely to be followed by 'to'. The term 'shag' (an affectionate colloquialism for intercourse in British English) was more equally distributed in relation to the gender of the subject, though male subjects still slightly outnumbered female ones.

This pattern is not about grammar in the abstract, but about the way grammatical possibilities are actually deployed in discourse. In the English language as such, there is no grammatical rule that prevents speakers from representing sex as something women do to men, or something women and men do together; but in a large sample of discourse produced by users of English, the preferred representation of it was as something men do to women. The heading we have given to this section alludes to another notorious example. When the Beach Boys re-recorded a hit song originally performed by the all-female group The Crystals, 'And then he kissed me', they changed the lyric, as is usually done in these circumstances to preserve the heterosexual narrative of the original. They could in theory have done this by simply substituting 'she' for 'he', to yield 'And then she kissed me'; but in fact they changed it to 'And then I kissed her'. Speakers, writers and singers are not necessarily aware of any consistent logic underlying their decisions about the most 'natural' or 'appropriate' grammatical form for sentences like these. But in making the choices they do, whether consciously or not, they reproduce the underlying logic of men's agency and women's passivity, and recirculate it to the recipients of their discourse.

Even when a writer wishes to represent women actively pursuing their sexual desires in a positive way, this remains remarkably difficult to do. Consider, for instance, the following piece of discourse, from a feature in a British newspaper about a US girl group called The Donnas (*Guardian Weekend*, 28 July 2001: 35):

Mostly they sing about getting laid, about getting laid as often as possible, with as many people as possible, about whom they know as little as possible... It's classic slapper rock... rather than the rude-girl rap-sluttery of, say, Li'l Kim. 'I wouldn't say we were sluts though. That would be stupid. We all have boyfriends.' Ford [Maya Ford, one of The Donnas] seems affronted by the suggestion, which is a surprise coming from the woman who wrote, 'Gotta get out tonight / got an itch underneath my pants / I can smell your sex from here / so I think I'll take a chance'... In London... a DJ asked her about 40 Boys in 40 Nights [the title of the group's most recent hit song]. [The DJ said] 'That's a bit fruity, isn't it?' [Ford] paused for slightly longer than is radio-friendly. 'How about 40 Girls in 40 Nights? Is that fruity enough for you?' At the same time, she's keen to make clear that if they're not sluts, it's only because of the paucity of acceptable menfolk. 'I mean on our last tour me and the drummer were single, and we tried to make out with fans, and found, like, two really cute guys, but most of them aren't cute enough.'

The frame which the journalist has used for this feature is a 'good girl / bad girl' frame – The Donnas are contrasted with virginal teen idols like Britney Spears, and the thesis is that there are signs of what the writer calls a 'paradigm shift' in US youth culture whereby the 'good girls' have had their moment and 'bad girls' like The Donnas are the next big thing. The writer is overtly in favour of this paradigm shift, describing Britney and her ilk as 'a gruesome tranche of poppets singing about chastity'.

The first observation one might make about this is that it would not be so straightforward to draw the same 'good/bad' distinction for young men. More exactly, while one could talk about 'good boys' and 'bad boys', the contrast would not be framed in terms of an opposition between chastity/virginity and sexual activity. Sex is considered a normal and legitimate interest for all kinds of boys, though how they pursue it and with whom might differentiate them along good/bad lines. The Donnas' status as rebellious 'bad girls', however, is based entirely on the enthusiastic attitude they display towards sex in their song lyrics. The title '40 Boys in 40 Nights' occasions the description 'fruity' from a male British DJ (in British

English 'fruity' means 'risqué' rather than being an allusion to homosexuality, which is what the American Maya Ford appears to take it as). Since there is nothing novel or remarkable in men singing songs about how many women they've had sex with, the 'risqué' quality of '40 Boys in 40 Nights' must derive from the mere fact that it reverses the usual roles.

The second observation prompted by the extract of discourse reproduced above concerns the appearance in it of the terms 'slapper' and 'slut' (the latter appears three times). Both these terms come from the extensive lexicon of English words which may be used to refer to women as prostitutes ([Penelope] Stanley 1973). 'Slut' is defined in dictionaries as meaning a slatternly or dirty woman, one who does not keep house properly, and it can still be used in that sense, but in contemporary usage its more specifically sexual sense is usually to the fore: a 'slut' is a woman who sleeps around. 'Slapper' has achieved wide currency among British English speakers more recently, and refers to a promiscuous woman of vulgar appearance and behaviour. These terms, and related ones like 'tart' and 'slag', have no masculine equivalents.

In this piece of discourse the terms 'slapper' and more especially 'slut' function in a complicated way. When the writer describes The Donnas' music as 'classic slapper rock', in the context of the whole article this is evidently not intended as an insult; on the contrary, it displays approval of the 'bad girl' posture The Donnas have adopted. Maya Ford, on the other hand, seems to be caught between her allegiance to the group's rebellious public image and her awareness that 'slut' is a pejorative term, something she and the other Donnas would not want to be called in mundane reality. Ford 'seems affronted' by the suggestion that The Donnas might be sluts offstage as well as on, and rebuts the implied charge by saying 'We all have boyfriends.' Later on, when she asserts that they would be sluts if the available men were 'cute enough', she nevertheless makes clear that this would only be acceptable under certain circumstances, noting that when she and the drummer 'tried to make out with fans', they were not cheating on anyone, for at the time they were both 'single'. While making no bones about her desire for sex as such, Ford also stresses her allegiance to the more traditional ideals of romantic love and fidelity – the very ideals that separate the chaste woman from the whore. One problem she is trying to negotiate here is that terms which represent women as active sexual subjects also tend to represent them as prostitutes; and prostitutes as a class of women bear an enormous burden of historical contempt. Attempts have been made by some feminists to reclaim 'slut' (e.g. Califia 1983), but it is evident that the term still evokes ambivalent feelings, so that young women like Maya Ford cannot embrace it wholeheartedly.

Part of the difficulty of reclaiming terms like 'slut' for young heterosexual women is connected to the fact that the use of those terms is embedded in peer group practices with real and potentially devastating social consequences. In the 1980s, Sue Lees conducted research in British schools and found that the term 'slag' (which means much the same as 'slut') was a powerful weapon used by both boys and girls to police the behaviour of girls (Lees 1986). Girls lived in dread of being accused of being 'slags'; even if that accusation were totally groundless, it could lead to ostracism, both by the boys they might otherwise hope to form relationships with and by the girls who formed their primary peer group and support network. Therefore, girls consciously and systematically avoided forms of dress, speech and behaviour which they knew might call forth the epithet 'slag'. There was no corresponding epithet which could be used to police boys' behaviour, for unchastity or promiscuity does not devalue a boy's status in the way it does a girl's.

Debbie Epstein and Richard Johnson show in their more recent study *Schooling Sexualities* (1998) that not much has changed. Some young women do seem to enjoy the notoriety and the potentially glamorous 'outlaw' status that come from being known as sexually active, but the label 'slag' nevertheless retains significant power to shame, as is illustrated by this extract from a conversation involving Epstein, fifteen-year-old Tracy and Tracy's friend Sarah (Epstein and Johnson 1998: 120–1):

DE   cos you said people were looking at you like you were a slag. I wasn't quite sure what that meant.

T   oh it was like there were some rumours going round our area about me and this kid. And like, he spreaded it – someone spreaded it all around the Mid school, all around this school. People just looking at me, I couldn't hack it no more, and like I was

DE   you must have been really miserable.

T   oh no, not. I was really angry. I just wanted to take my anger out on anybody that come along really.

DE   sorry, what did you just say, Sarah?

S   no, I just said she was, she was upset and that.

T   I didn't come to school for about three days cos I couldn't face anybody.

Although Tracy initially describes a 'resistant' response to the criticism of her peers – anger – she admits, when challenged by her friend's statement that she was 'upset', that she absented herself from school because she 'couldn't face anybody'. It is significant, too, that in Tracy's story the rumour is presented by implication as untrue. 'Slag', like 'homosexual' or 'sex addict', is a term that produces the category it names, and while young women like Tracy can and do deny that they are members of that category, they strikingly do not challenge its ontological status – in other words, the presupposition that *some* women are 'slags'. Their insistence that they personally do not deserve the label only reinforces its power, and reproduces the assumptions about gender and sexual agency on which the label is predicated.

AGENCY, RESPONSIBILITY AND CONSENT

While women and girls are not supposed actively to pursue their own sexual desires, they are regularly held responsible for provoking men's desire. They are also supposed to help men to contain the 'male urges' that might otherwise be expressed in inappropriate or antisocial ways. One situation in which these contradictory demands regularly become an issue is where a man is charged with rape or sexual assault. In this situation it is common for the behaviour of the complainant to come under critical scrutiny, with a key question being whether she made sufficient effort to prevent or resist the alleged assault.

The critical discourse analyst Susan Ehrlich (1998, 2001) has made a detailed examination of the construction of agency and responsibility in the discourse of rape and sexual assault proceedings. Her data are taken from a court case and a quasi-judicial disciplinary hearing in a Canadian university, both relating to the same two incidents (separated in time by a matter of days) in which the defendant, a university student whom Ehrlich names 'Matt', went back to a woman student's room at her invitation, but then proceeded to engage in sexual acts which the women concerned said they did not consent to. As happens in most cases involving alleged sexual assault by a person the complainant knew, the defence offered by Matt was that the women had consented to sex. He did not deny that the alleged acts had taken place or that he had participated in them. What he denied was that the acts were unwanted and unconsented to by the women.

As Ehrlich points out, in rape and sexual assault cases which turn on the issue of consent, especially if no additional physical injury has been inflicted, the evidence presented is likely to consist entirely of discourse – the conflicting accounts offered by the complainant and the defendant. The jury or disciplinary panel is not privy to the disputed event itself, but must base their decisions on what the parties to the case say about it after the fact. Analysing the proceedings in this case, Ehrlich observed a difference between the way the same actions and events were represented by the complainants and prosecution lawyers on one hand, and by Matt and the lawyers defending him on the other. The women constructed sentences in which Matt was the agent and they the (unwilling) objects of his actions, such as: 'He took my shirt off and . . . he unclasped my bra . . . and he pulled my pants down'. Matt and his lawyers employed grammatical constructions that downplayed or elided his agency, such as plurals implying reciprocity and mutual engagement (e.g. 'we were fooling around', 'we started kissing') and passives which deleted the agent so that it was not clear whether Matt, the woman or both jointly should be held responsible for an action (e.g. Matt's lawyer asked, 'I take it that the sweater *was removed*?').

The grammatical strategy employed by Matt and his lawyers reverses the usual assumptions about gender and sexual agency. Matt, a member of the gender group which is usually cast as the 'active' partner in heterosexual sex, represented himself and was represented by his lawyers as having less than full agency, while the complainants, though members of the gender group which is usually cast in the 'passive' role, were persistently blamed for their passivity in not resisting Matt's unwanted advances more vigorously. Here it should be remembered that witnesses in judicial proceedings are not just free to tell their stories in any way they see fit, but constrained by questions asked by lawyers. In this case, a great deal of the questioning turned on why the women did not assert agency by resisting Matt with force. This was consequential for the outcome: Matt was not expelled from the university, and he was acquitted on one charge in court. The women's accounts attributing agency to Matt were not found convincing, because their own apparent failure to show adequate resistance was taken as supporting his claim that they consented to sex, or at least that he could reasonably have believed that they consented.

What lies behind the apparent contradiction here becomes clearer if we examine the discursive construction of 'consent'. Matt at one point in the proceedings elucidated his own definition of that term, explaining that if a woman 'didn't say "no", didn't say "stop", didn't say, uh uh uh jump up and say "no I want you to leave", I am assuming, OK? . . . that that is consent' (Ehrlich 1998: 155). 'Consent' on this definition is inferred from the absence of strong resistance. The women complainants, on the other hand, insisted in their own accounts that they gave Matt all the evidence a reasonable person could need that they did not wish to have sex with him, by being unresponsive physically and by making comments such as that they were tired and wanted to go to sleep. Matt in their view should have deduced the absence of consent from these clues, without their needing to use explicit commands like 'stop' or physically fight him off. (One explained that she was afraid to offer stronger resistance because she believed that if he became angry he would also become more aggressive and inflict serious harm on her.) The disciplinary panel seized on these conflicting accounts to interpret the incidents as cases of male/female misunderstanding. However, this is not an idiosyncratic or random kind of misunderstanding. It arises from a kind of discursive double-bind.

Sally McConnell-Ginet (1989) observes that whatever her individual intentions on a particular occasion, a woman cannot say 'no' to a man's proposal of sex and be confident she will be understood as meaning unequivocally to refuse. 'No' will often be interpreted as 'maybe', or 'keep trying'. This is not simply and straightforwardly because men do not understand what 'no' means in the English language. Rather it reflects societal assumptions about what is 'normal' (or normative) in this particular situation. The denial of sexual agency to women means that saying 'yes' to sex (or initiating it) is disapproved of. Nice girls should demur coyly in order to demonstrate that they are not sluts or nymphomaniacs, but this is a ritual, formulaic gesture and men should not be deterred – resistance is only to be expected from women, and women for their part are held to expect men to grind down their resistance.[9] But this understanding of heterosexual courtship rituals puts women in the position of the boy who cried 'wolf': when they do want 'no' to mean 'no' they cannot be sure it will be taken as they intend.

In response to feminist critiques of this state of affairs, an unusual discursive experiment was undertaken in the early 1990s at Antioch College, a small, educationally 'progressive' institution in Ohio, USA. The college introduced a campus-wide sexual consent policy (drafted by a group of students, faculty and administrators) in which consent was defined not as the absence of 'no', but as the presence of 'yes'. The policy's central feature was a requirement that an affirmative response must be elicited for every act performed during a sexual encounter. A spokesperson explained to the press, 'The request for consent must be specific for each act…If you want to take her blouse off, you have to ask. If you want to touch her breast, you have to ask. If you want to move your hand down to her genitals, you have to ask. If you want to put your finger inside her, you have to ask' (quoted Cameron 1994: 32). While the college did not install surveillance technology to police adherence to the code, it required new students to attend sessions explaining it, and stipulated that any subsequent complaints of harassment and assault would be adjudicated with reference to it – if the subject of a complaint had neglected to follow the code by obtaining their partner's consent, the complaint would be upheld.

This initiative occurred in the midst of public controversy about 'political correctness' on American campuses, and it soon attracted attention in the national and foreign media as an outstanding example of 'political correctness gone mad'. The tone of most coverage was incredulous, with incredulity focusing on two points in particular. One was the foolishness of the college authorities in imagining that the urgency of young people's sexual desires could be contained and regulated by *any* set of rules. The other was a more specific objection to the actual substance of Antioch's rules, and this objection is especially interesting in the context of a discussion of *language* and sexuality. What struck many critics as particularly absurd was the requirement that people must *speak* their desires. An idea that recurred was that talking about what you were doing or what you wanted to do must inevitably interfere with the business of actually doing it, destroying spontaneity and dissolving pleasure in a torrent of superfluous words. Good sex was implicitly represented as a passionate, wordless communion of bodies, a transcendent experience that cannot and indeed should not be verbalized.

However, interviews conducted with members of the campus community at Antioch (reported in Cameron 1994) suggested something rather different. The main aim of the consent policy had been rape prevention, and this was what administrators emphasized when they were asked what difference it had made. Yet when women students were asked the same question, a number spoke not of feeling safer, but of having better – more exciting, more varied and more pleasurable – sex. When asked how the policy had achieved that effect, they explained that it had impelled them to develop a language for representing their desires, both to themselves and to their sexual partners. They found themselves talking much more explicitly than they had previously been wont to do about specific sexual acts, and they claimed this enhanced the experience of sex. This view of what the code had accomplished for at least some members of the community[10] was at odds with the media representation of Antioch as a puritanical institution intent on suppressing young people's 'natural' sexuality; it was also somewhat different from the 'official' view of what the policy was about, as represented by the college authorities.

In the Antioch college spokesperson's explanation of the sexual consent policy that we reproduced above – 'If you want to take her blouse off, you have to ask...' – the conventional presuppositions are in place regarding gender, agency and consent: sex is figured as something men initiate and women either assent to or refuse. This is somewhat misleading about the actual workings of the Antioch policy, for although its main official goal was rape prevention, it was written to apply to both genders, and to same-sex as well as cross-sex encounters. Despite choosing the most common or conventional scenario (man coercing woman) to illustrate the principle of affirmative consent for the benefit of the press, the framers of the policy did not rule out the possibility that men, too, might wish to say 'no' to a sexual invitation.[11] This is an unusual move, for in conventional understandings of heterosex it is unimaginable that any man would ever pass up the opportunity to have sex. Refusing a woman's advance carries the risk that a man will be seen as somehow sexually inadequate – in particular, it may cast doubt on his credentials as a heterosexual and raise the suspicion that he is in fact gay.

So it is interesting that there is one circumstance in which male sexual refusal is construed sympathetically: when the unwelcome proposition comes not from a woman to a man, but from a gay man to a man who is or claims to be heterosexual. This suggests that there are conflicting discourses governing men's acceptance or refusal of a sexual invitation: if one assumption is that 'real men are always ready to have sex', another is that 'real men act in ways that affirm their heterosexuality, and do not act in ways that may compromise their heterosexuality'. Thus if the invitation comes from a woman, acceptance is the unmarked choice because refusal could imply non-heterosexuality; if the invitation comes from a man the reverse is true – refusal is the unmarked choice because acceptance implies non-heterosexuality. Not only is it seen as acceptable masculine behaviour to refuse sex if the invitation comes from another man, it is sometimes seen as reasonable for men to respond to such an invitation with physical violence. This is what lies behind the legal defence of 'homosexual panic', employed in cases where a straight man has responded to a (real, imagined or invented) advance from a gay man by assaulting or even killing him.

'Homosexual panic' was a psychiatric condition first proposed in 1920. In its original formulation, it did not refer to a fear prompted by advances from other men. Instead, 'homosexual panic' referred to cases where men who had been in intensively same-sex environments became aware of homosexual desires that they felt unable to control, and unable to act on. The original formulation of the disorder was based on the diagnosis of a small number of soldiers and sailors in a US government mental hospital after the First World War (Kempf 1920). These men were not violent – they were, on the contrary, passive. The disorder was characterized by periods of introspective brooding, self-punishment, suicidal assaults, withdrawal and helplessness.

Later, some experts extended the idea of 'homosexual panic' to explain acts of violence, suggesting that perpetrators had 'panicked' when a homosexual advance threatened to shatter their fragile heterosexual identity. In recent court cases where 'homosexual panic' has been offered as a defence, however, the argument has *not* been that the defendant overreacted because of his own sexual insecurities. Instead, his violent actions have been explained as an understandable and defensible response to an unwanted homosexual advance. To a heterosexual man, such an advance is said to constitute a kind of assault, and acts of violence committed in the resulting state of panic must therefore be regarded as justifiable self-defence.[12]

It might seem that there is a parallel between women resisting male heterosexual advances and straight men resisting homosexual advances, but on closer inspection there are important differences between the two cases. These may be linked to the point made above, that, for heterosexual men, refusing a proposition of homosexual sex is the unmarked choice – indeed the proposition itself is culturally construed as a provocation. When men make unwanted advances to women, the same assumptions are not in force. Thus women who complain of rape or sexual assault are frequently questioned about what they did to provoke or confuse the assailant, and it is considered important to establish whether they produced any explicit verbal refusal. (In Susan Ehrlich's study, Matt's credibility was strengthened and the complainants' weakened by evidence that they did not say 'no' or 'stop'.) In 'homosexual panic' cases, by contrast, courts do not seem to dwell on the issue of whether a defendant tried to deter the unwanted advance verbally before escalating to physical violence. Women are apparently considered responsible for saying 'no' to unwanted sex, but heterosexual men do not have the same responsibility. Their antipathy to propositions from other men is taken for granted. Furthermore, heterosexual men, unlike women, are not supposed to be in the position of refusing (or consenting to) someone else's sexual proposition anyway: they are supposed to be the ones who make propositions to others. In this sense, positioning a straight man as the object of another man's desire is a double provocation, impugning both his heterosexuality and his right to be the active initiator of sex. Whereas in many contexts, saying 'no' is a mark of the speaker's dominant status, in sexual contexts it is associated with a 'submissive' or 'feminine' role (this is a point we discuss further in chapter 5).

This is not the only peculiarity of 'no' when used in sexual situations. In many such situations, there appears to be a strong cultural presumption that 'no' does not straightforwardly or definitively indicate refusal: it is possible to construe it rather as a ritualized move in a game, used to signify a formulaic resistance whose function is, precisely, to be overcome. The sexual double standard we have already discussed is one relevant factor in this construction of 'no' (i.e. if everyone knows nice girls don't say 'yes' to sex, 'no' will not always be taken as an unambiguous refusal). Also relevant, however, is the cultural tendency to eroticize power differences,[13] so that initial resistance followed by eventual submission may be experienced as enhancing sexual pleasure. That tendency is acknowledged and discussed most explicitly among members of one particular sexual subculture, sadomasochists, who get pleasure from the ritual enactment of relations of dominance and submission. Because their erotic practices make explicit what is usually left implicit, it is instructive to look at how sadomasochists use the word 'no' and what they have to say about its use.

In consensual sadomasochistic (SM) scenes, where participants enact fantasies that may involve humiliation and pain, it is common to decide in advance on a 'safe word', a word whose utterance by one party will immediately cause the other to desist from whatever s/he is doing. However, one word that cannot function as a safe word is 'no' (another is 'stop'). Although its ordinary-language semantics might seem to make it the obvious choice, using 'no' as a safe word would rule out using it to indicate purely formulaic resistance. In SM scenes, which require one party's submission to the will of the other, the formulaic resistance function of 'no' is particularly important. If the submissive partner offers no token of resistance, the dominant partner cannot experience the pleasure of imposing his or her will on a powerless other, while conversely the submissive partner cannot experience the pleasure of being overcome by a more powerful other. Writers on SM often recommend choosing a safe word which will stand out in context as incongruous and therefore unambiguous (for reasons best known to practitioners themselves, the word 'pickle' seems a popular choice), or using a verbal 'traffic light' system where 'yellow' means 'be careful' and 'red' means 'stop right now'.

SM scenes are a clear case of sexual encounters in which 'no' conventionally does not mean 'no'. Other cases may be less clear cut, but since the eroticizing of power differences is not confined to SM, the potential exists in most sexual situations for 'no' to be interpreted as something other than an unambiguous refusal.

This might make us critical of the advice often given to women and children to protect themselves from sexual assault by making their refusals not only explicit but also as direct as possible – the 'just say no' approach. As well as glossing over the ambiguous status of 'no' in sexual contexts, advice of the 'just say no' type is difficult to follow for other reasons, as the

WHAT 'NO' MEANS IN SM: EXTRACTS FROM ADVICE
LITERATURE FOR SADOMASOCHISTS

Example dialogue from *The New Bottoming Book* (Easton and Hardy
2001: 39):

> Top: 'Seems to me you deserve a good spanking with this hairbrush,
> my little slut.' Bottom (in role as obedient slave): 'If it pleases you, sir
> or madam' – or Bottom (in role as reluctant victim): 'No! Please! Not
> the hairbrush!'

Advice on choosing a safe word, from *Consensual Sadomasochism: How to
Talk About it and Do it Safely* (Henkin and Holiday 1996: 89):

> Words other than No, Stop, or Slow Down are usually designated [as
> safe words] because SM is a *consensual* eroticism in the realm of *erotic
> theatre*. If a bottom could just say 'Stop' to end a [sexual] scene, the
> illusion that the Top has total control might be threatened. Besides,
> many bottoms enjoy the fantasy of nonconsensuality and scream 'No,
> no, please stop!' – or words to that effect – when the scene is going
> very well; they would be upset, confused, and even angry if a Top
> actually did stop in response to their outbursts.

Note: the terms 'top' and 'bottom' are used in SM subcultures to denote,
respectively, the dominant and the submissive partner in a sexual scene.

conversation analysts Celia Kitzinger and Hannah Frith (1999) have pointed
out. In a critical discussion of rape prevention advice, these researchers
present evidence from focus group discussions with a total of fifty-eight
young heterosexual women which suggests that successful sexual refusals
are very rarely performed in real life by saying 'no'. Kitzinger and Frith
argue that there is a very good reason for this: saying 'no' is not normal
conversational behaviour, whether in relation to sex or anything else.

In the terminology of conversation analysis, refusal is a 'dispreferred'
move in response to an invitation or proposition, contrasting with the
'preferred' move, acceptance. What this means is not that people have a
preference, in the non-technical sense of the word, for accepting invitations. Instead, it means that accepting an invitation is interactionally more
straightforward than refusing it. Acceptances can be bald and direct, but
refusals have to be more elaborate. Studies of naturally occurring invitations
have found that acceptances are typically produced immediately, directly
and briefly (e.g. A: 'how about a drink after work?' B: 'OK'). Refusals,

by contrast, are longer turns marked by hesitation, hedging, apologies, excuses and explanations (thus B might refuse A's invitation to have a drink by saying, 'uh, well, sorry, I'd love to but I've got people coming for dinner').

Kitzinger and Frith's data indicate that this pattern is also operative in sexual situations. Since it is not generally possible for social scientists to record naturally occurring sexual encounters, the researchers approached the question of how refusals are performed in real life by asking focus groups to talk about what they said when they were invited to have sex but did not want to. Participants were virtually unanimous that it was impossible to respond with an unelaborated 'no': only two said they would feel comfortable doing so. In general, 'no' was thought to be unnecessarily confrontational; some women added that they would feel foolish saying it. The approach they favoured instead involved the strategies mentioned above – hesitating, hedging ('well'), 'palliating' (e.g. 'I'm flattered / you're a really nice guy, but...') and providing face-saving explanations such as 'I'm really knackered [exhausted].'

The conventions for performing dispreferred conversational moves are not gender-specific: a large body of research on ordinary conversation in English has shown that they are used routinely by both women and men. Sexual refusals are not exceptional in this regard. Kitzinger and Frith's informants spoke about strategies they had *successfully* used to avoid having sex, and, in their experience, men had no difficulty interpreting such strategies as refusals. The point, then, is that it cannot reasonably be claimed, as Matt claimed in the case examined by Susan Ehrlich, that anything other than 'no' or 'stop' is unintelligible as a refusal. (What the women told Matt – that they wanted to go to sleep – actually emerged in Kitzinger and Frith's study as one of the commonest effective refusal strategies.) It is disingenuous for men like Matt to plead ignorance of commonplace conversational strategies – strategies that actually occur more frequently than the direct 'no' they insist they would have understood.

In fact, advice to women that revolves around 'saying no' is misguided in two ways. Kitzinger and Frith show that the utterance of 'no' is not a *necessary* condition for refusal. But our earlier discussion showed that it is not a *sufficient* condition either, since there is often potential for 'no' to function (or be strategically 'misunderstood') as a token of purely formulaic resistance. In real communication there are no 'magic words' that will always have the same meaning no matter where, when, how or by whom they are uttered. It follows that words in themselves are neither the cause of sexual communication problems nor the solution to those problems. The real problem lies in the contradictory discourses on sexuality, gender and power which are part of our culture's background knowledge about sex, and which are therefore brought to bear on interactions about sex. It is those underlying discourses, rather than specific verbal formulas, that should be the focus of efforts to change the sexual status quo.

CONCLUSION

As we have tried to show in this chapter, the notion that sexuality and sexual behaviour are expressions of natural impulses which cannot be constrained by rules, and that sex is or should be beyond language, could hardly be more misleading. Sexuality and sexual behaviour are always and everywhere constrained (and at the same time, importantly, enabled) by the rules and conventions, the categories and definitions, the conflicting stories and the competing arguments, that circulate in discourse. Since discourse about sex is not static and homogeneous, the rules, categories and definitions through which we organize our understanding of sex are not always and everywhere identical. They are, however, political. Many of the examples we have mentioned in this chapter – the discrediting of 'vaginal orgasm', the invention of 'sex addiction', the rise of 'gay' and later of 'queer', the redefinition of 'consent', the complex and contested meaning of 'no' – testify to ongoing power struggles over who may define and categorize sex, and from what point of view. Those struggles are conducted in discourse, and through language; it is clear, however, that their effects are felt not only in our discourse, but also in other aspects of our lives as social and sexual beings.

CHAPTER 3

What has gender got to do with sex? Language, heterosexuality and heteronormativity

In her essay 'Compulsory heterosexuality and lesbian existence' (1980), Adrienne Rich pointed out that heterosexuality and lesbianism are not just 'different but equal' choices women can make; one of them – heterosexuality – is 'compulsory', the other – lesbianism – forbidden. 'Normal' development for women is equated with movement through a set of life stages defined largely in terms of heterosexuality (dating, one or more serious 'steady' relationships, marriage or cohabitation, having and bringing up children). This trajectory is not simply left to happen 'naturally', even though it is always portrayed as a natural phenomenon. Rather it is aggressively promoted in every part of the culture. The other side of that coin is the persecution of women who refuse compulsory heterosexuality, especially if they show a positive preference for sexual and emotional relationships with other women. 'Lesbian existence', Rich notes, is a precarious and risky business; and she documents the point with many historical and contemporary examples of women being oppressed because they chose other women, rather than men, as their lovers and most cherished companions.

HETEROSEXUALITY AS A PATRIARCHAL INSTITUTION: THE RADICAL FEMINIST ANALYSIS

The idea of heterosexuality as a norm rather than simply one option among others is still part of feminist thinking, and is also current among queer theorists and activists.[1] But in the Women's Liberation Movement of the 1970s and early 1980s, that idea was connected to a particular set of arguments about the relationship of sexuality to gender. According to those arguments, compulsory heterosexuality is not just bad because it denies individual women, and indeed individual men, the freedom to define and express their own sexual preferences. Rather, heterosexuality is a political institution, and the 'compulsory' status of heterosexuality has a key political function in maintaining the gender hierarchy that subordinates women to men. Lesbians are threatening, not simply because of their erotic practices, but more fundamentally because they do not submit to the male dominance that is supposed to be all women's lot. As the radical feminist Charlotte Bunch expressed this idea in a 1972 paper called 'Lesbians in revolt' (Bunch 2000[1972]: 332–3):

Male society defines lesbianism as a sexual act, which reflects men's limited view of women: they think of us only in terms of sex. They also say lesbians are not real women, so a real woman is one who gets fucked by men. We say that a lesbian is a woman whose sense of self and energies, including sexual energies, center around women – she is woman-identified...Woman-identified lesbianism is, then, more than a sexual preference; it is a political choice. It is political because relationships between men and women are essentially political: they involve power and dominance. Since the lesbian actively rejects that relationship and chooses women, she defies the established political system.

Bunch's term 'woman-identified lesbianism' implies that there may be other kinds of lesbianism. This is not the place to detour into the history of feminist political arguments – which were prolonged and sometimes acrimonious – about who counted as a lesbian and on what criteria (did you have to have sexual relationships with women or was it enough to declare yourself 'woman-identified'? Were lesbians 'in sexual practice only' 'real' lesbians?) We cite the work of radical feminists like Charlotte Bunch and Adrienne Rich in order to illustrate the point that for these women and many others who were active feminists, the analysis of sexuality as a social/political phenomenon was not separate from the analysis of gender as a social/political phenomenon. The power structures at issue were taken to be the same ones in both cases, and in essence these were gendered power structures.

The 'established political system' which the lesbian 'defies' is the system of male supremacy, which depends on the normative or compulsory status of heterosexuality. It is within heterosexual relationships (prototypically, within marriage) that men's power over women has been most directly affirmed by the law as well as by custom and practice. It is not so long since husbands in Western bourgeois societies legally owned their wives' property and earnings, and could chastise their wives physically and rape them with impunity. Even after legal reform, many old assumptions about men's rights in marriage have persisted (domestic violence is still prevalent, and it remains difficult to get legal redress in cases of marital rape).

Feminists also pointed to the economic inequality that is institutionalized in heterosexual relationships – historically men have been paid more than women on the grounds that they are responsible for the financial support of their households, while women are expected to contribute most of the unpaid domestic labour (this pattern has persisted even in the age of the dual-income family). And Women's Liberation activists like Charlotte Bunch were critical of the *emotional* dependence on men which heterosexuality entailed for women. A woman who has primary sexual and emotional relationships with men has an interest in being the kind of woman men want to have those relationships with, and in male supremacist society, feminists argued, that essentially means a subordinate woman. As Martha Shelley noted (2000[1970]: 305) '[men] don't like women who aren't dependent on them – who aren't sitting at home waiting for the phone to ring, waiting for "him" to come home, women who don't feel totally crushed by the thought that some man doesn't love them any more, women who aren't terrified at the idea that a man might leave them'.

The radical feminist analysis reverses the common-sense assumption that heterosexuality arises from the natural attraction between pre-existing 'opposites', men and women. The alternative analysis is that heterosexuality as a political institution *requires* men and women to be 'opposites', and that is why they are socialized to be as they are – different in very particular ways. From this point of view, a lesbian is as much a gender deviant as she is a sexual deviant: since she is outside the heterosexual system, she can reject the oppressive forms of femininity it requires. The French feminist Monique Wittig takes the same thought a step further with her notoriously bold claim '[l]esbians are not women' (1992: 32).[2] 'Woman' for Wittig is not a biological category, but a social and political status which only exists within a sociopolitical system based on compulsory heterosexuality; just as the racist term 'nigger' does not denote a biological category, but a social and political status within a system that grounds and naturalizes white superiority.

A similar sort of analysis can also be applied to gay men, even though this was not a central concern of most radical feminist analysis. Indeed, given the tendency to analyse sexual oppression in terms of gender, it is not surprising that many feminist writers saw gay men first and foremost as men, and hence as beneficiaries and supporters of patriarchal institutions and values. Significantly, one much-discussed piece of evidence for this view (which we will return to in the next chapter) centred on language: the parodic use of female names and of stereotypical 'Woman's Language' by gay men. However, while gay men may indeed benefit from the privileges that a male-dominated society confers upon men (privileges that differ, of course, along lines of class and race, and that also are affected by the degree to which individual men choose to make sexuality a political issue), the open rejection of conventional masculinity, which is defined as heterosexual, is not without penalties. Like lesbians, gay men can be seen as traitors to their gender; even though in the case of men what is being refused is the powerful social position, not the subordinate one. In both cases, though, the rejection of compulsory heterosexuality constitutes a challenge to its status as natural, necessary and desirable. And one consequence of that rejection is harassment and persecution.

We have presented these radical feminist ideas at some length because they are relevant to the history of the field of inquiry this book deals with, language and sexuality. As we noted in our introductory chapter, the study of language and sexuality has been closely bound up with the study of language and gender. More exactly, while some lines of investigation (e.g. research on the special vocabularies associated with sexual subcultures) developed separately, questions about the broader linguistic correlates of sexual identity have tended to be seen as falling within the scope of language and gender studies. Since that field, which emerged in the early 1970s, drew its theoretical apparatus from feminism, it is not surprising that its treatment of sexuality or sexual identity reflected the analyses which were current among feminists at the time.

LANGUAGE, GENDER AND COMPULSORY HETEROSEXUALITY

In fact, early work on language and gender had rather little to say about sexuality, at least explicitly, and this omission has been noted critically by more recent scholars. In their editors' introduction to the collection *Queerly Phrased*, Anna Livia and Kira Hall (1997b) suggest that early feminist work is flawed by its apparent assumption that 'women' means 'heterosexual women', and its failure to consider lesbians. But while the body of linguistic research they are talking about can indeed be criticized for neglecting questions about diversity among women – it rarely attended to class and racial or ethnic differences either – the specific criticism made by Livia and Hall overlooks an important point. What was assumed by feminists in the era of the Women's Liberation Movement was not that all women were heterosexual (after all, this was a time when issues of sexuality were hotly debated, with many feminists publicly rejecting heterosexuality). Rather feminists claimed that *femininity* – the gender-ideal against which women's behaviour was judged by society at large – was inextricably linked to the *institution* of heterosexuality.

Some feminist researchers investigated the linguistic dynamics of heterosexual relationships directly. Pamela Fishman (1983) described the interactional work (in an earlier version of her paper she dubbed it 'interactional shitwork') done by women in conversation with their male partners, basing her account on data from a sample of heterosexual couples. She found that the women in her sample asked large numbers of questions whose function was to facilitate men's contributions to conversation. Since men did not return the favour, the result was a pattern whereby women offered men the floor and supported them in holding it, while receiving little or no encouragement to talk on subjects of interest to themselves. Fishman likened women's responsibility for the work of keeping conversations going to their responsibility for doing the housework. One implication of that analogy is that the unequal division of linguistic labour, like that of domestic labour, is part of the heterosexual contract.

Other feminists were interested in the kinds of language that symbolically signal femininity. Probably the best known of all the early feminist works on language and gender, Robin Lakoff's book *Language and Woman's Place* (1975), proposed the idea of a distinctive feminine register which Lakoff called 'women's language' (WL). The characteristics of WL as Lakoff described them included superpolite forms and the avoidance of strong expletives ('fudge' rather than 'damn' or 'shit'), rising intonation on declarative sentences, question tags added to propositions whose validity the speaker does not need to check (e.g. 'it's a beautiful day, isn't it?'), and 'trivial' vocabulary items such as 'lovely', 'divine' and elaborate colour terms (e.g. 'mauve' rather than just 'purple'). What the items on this list have in common is that they tend to reduce the force of utterances which include them, making the speaker sound less certain, less confident and less authoritative or powerful than she would otherwise. The implication is that one marks femininity linguistically by symbolically minimizing one's power. Lakoff opposed this way of speaking not to 'men's language' but to 'neutral language'. She did not suggest that all women used WL all the time – for instance, she said they might well avoid WL in professional or academic contexts – but she did suggest that the existence of this socially meaningful register faced women speakers with a dilemma. They could use neutral language and be judged unfeminine, 'less than a woman', or use WL and risk being judged less than a fully competent human being.

CHARACTERISTICS OF LAKOFF'S 'WOMEN'S LANGU

1. Women often seem to hit phonetic points less precisely than me. lisped 's's, obscured vowels.
2. Women's intonational contours display more variety than men's.
3. Women use diminutives and euphemisms more than men . . .
4. Women make more use of expressive forms (adjectives and not nouns or verbs and, in that category, those expressing emotional rather than intellectual evaluation) than men: *lovely, divine.*
5. Women use forms that convey impreciseness: *so, such.*
6. Women use hedges of all kinds ['Well . . .'; 'I don't really know, but maybe . . .'] more than men.
7. Women use intonation patterns that resemble questions, indicating uncertainty or need for approval.
8. Women's voices are breathier than men's.
9. Women are more indirect and polite than men.
10. Women won't commit themselves to an opinion.
11. In conversation, women are more likely to be interrupted, less likely to introduce successful topics.
12. Women's communicative style tends to be collaborative rather than competitive.
13. More of women's communication is expressed nonverbally (by gesture and intonation) than men's.
14. Women are more careful to be 'correct' when they speak, using better grammar and fewer colloquialisms than men.

Source: Lakoff (1990: 204)

On the surface this argument is not about sexuality as such, but it is possible to make a link between the kind of femininity symbolized by WL and the positioning of women within heterosexual relations. Charlotte Bunch (quoted above) notes disapprovingly that in men's 'limited' view, 'a real woman is one who gets fucked by men' – from which it would follow that only heterosexual women have femininity, this being the key attribute of 'real' women. Whether or not one agrees with Bunch about the prevalence of the assumption she criticizes among men, her formulation does capture something about the way femininity is constructed ideologically in male-dominated societies. 'Feminine' qualities such as weakness and dependency are frequently eroticized, and we will see later in this chapter that WL itself can be deployed for erotic effect. In choosing to contrast WL with 'neutral' rather than 'men's' language, Lakoff herself is making use of the feminist insight that women are sexualized to a degree that men are not. The contexts in which she says women avoid WL are contexts in which competence and success depend on *not* being perceived in purely sexual terms.

At the beginning of the 1990s, the linguist Deborah Tannen published a bestselling book, *You Just Don't Understand* (1990), on the subject of male–female misunderstandings. Once again, sexuality is not the overt focus of Tannen's book, but it is evident that the communication problems of heterosexual couples are central to it. It is also evident that the book can be read (though Tannen herself would contest this reading) as supporting Fishman's argument that heterosexual relationships position women and men asymmetrically: women have to do more interactional work for less interpersonal reward. As one reviewer, Senta Troemel-Ploetz, noted (1991), many or most of the misunderstandings cited by Tannen as examples of quasi-cultural differences between women and men mysteriously end up with the man's needs rather than the woman's being met. Theoretically, it can be argued that Tannen's model of male/female difference is essentially a 'complementarity' model – the linguistic and interpersonal preferences she attributes to men and women are not just randomly different, but arise from a division of labour whereby the two sexes in principle have non-overlapping roles. This recalls the point made above, that women and men are required to complement one another – to be 'opposite' rather than merely different – largely because of the institutionalization of heterosexuality. Heterosexuality (prototypically in the form of marriage) is the key social institution for which and through which gender complementarity is produced. Unlike the radical feminists we have cited, Tannen does not take a critical position in relation to the social institution of heterosexuality, but the existence of that institution is presupposed in her account of gender difference, which arguably makes little sense without it.[3]

The foregoing discussion has drawn attention to the (hetero)sexual dimension of some influential research on language and gender. While heterosexuality may not always be mentioned explicitly in this body of work, it is often strongly implicated in the discussion of gender and power (more precisely, perhaps, of femininity and powerlessness). An important assumption here, reflecting feminist (especially radical feminist) analyses of the relationship between compulsory heterosexuality and women's subordination, is that heterosexual speech is more or less equivalent to *gender-appropriate* speech. The linguistic features that index femininity linguistically also index heterosexual identity, because of the crucial role played by compulsory heterosexuality in the construction of gender identity and gender relations.

Explicit references to sexuality in the language and gender literature are not usually references to heterosexuality, however; instead they are references to 'marked' or minority sexual identities, especially gay and lesbian ones. In these references, too, we can discern the influence of the feminist tendency to treat sexuality primarily as an aspect of the gender system. Just as heterosexual speech is identified with gender-appropriate speech, so it is assumed that non-heterosexuals will be distinguished from heterosexuals by a tendency to gender-*inappropriate* speech. In other words, it is assumed that gay men will tend to talk like women, and lesbians will tend to talk like men. In some cases, this suggestion appears to be little more than a recycling of the popular, untheorized view of homosexuality as gender deviance or 'crossing' (see our discussion in chapter 1). Lakoff, for example, suggests that some features of WL are also used by 'effeminate' men, a category in which she places upper-class Britons and college professors as well as gay men. In other cases, though, particularly where lesbians rather than gay men are the subject of discussion from a radical feminist perspective, what underpins the suggestion is equally likely to be a particular model of the relationship of language to gender and sexuality, as outlined above. If femininity is signalled linguistically by a weak, powerless or deferential style of speaking, and if one motivation for this form of femininity is the dependence on male approval induced by compulsory heterosexuality, then lesbians – women who 'defy the established political system' by refusing heterosexuality and disdaining male approval – may well be expected to eschew 'feminine' speech styles, if only because they have nothing much to gain by adopting them.

THE QUEER CHALLENGE: SEPARATING GENDER AND SEXUALITY

The idea of lesbians as gender deviants or 'outlaws' has been embraced enthusiastically by some activists a generation younger than the early radical feminists. One writer who has linked the lesbian-as-outlaw idea specifically to issues of language and gender is the transgender activist Kate Bornstein. While in transition from her original status as a man to her new self-chosen identity as a (lesbian) woman, Bornstein, like many male-to-female (MTF) trans people, sought expert guidance on changing her speech. She was not, however, very impressed with the instruction she received:

I was taught to speak in a very high-pitched, very breathy, sing-song voice and to tag questions onto the end of each sentence. And I was supposed to smile all the time when I was talking. And I said 'Oh, I don't want to talk like that!' The teachers assumed that you were going to be a heterosexual woman. No one was going to teach you to be a lesbian because being a lesbian was as big an outlaw as transsexual. (quoted in Bell 1993: 112)

Materials about language and speech for MTF transexuals are strikingly indebted to Robin Lakoff's early account of 'women's language', and subsequent popular elaborations of it.[4] This is perhaps odd, given that most language and gender researchers today regard WL more as an idealized symbolic construct than an empirically accurate account of the speech of the 'average' woman in the social milieu Lakoff was writing from (i.e. white, professional, English-speaking American society). Advising MTF transexuals to adopt WL features as a basis for their new female linguistic personae defines an 'appropriate' performance of gender in terms of a gender stereotype. From any feminist point of view this is open to criticism (and we should probably point out that it runs absolutely counter to the spirit of Lakoff's original analysis: she described WL in order to criticize it as an artefact of an oppressive gender system, and was presumably hoping that in doing so she would hasten its demise). Kate Bornstein's particular objection, however, focuses less on the stereotypical nature of WL and more on the sexual connotations of the stereotype: to her it is obvious that this stereotype is heterosexual, and consequently does not provide an appropriate model for someone like herself who identifies as a lesbian. It also seems from the comments quoted above that part of what Bornstein rejects as 'heterosexual' is the subordinate status she takes conventionally feminine speech to symbolize.

The position taken by Kate Bornstein on WL shows some continuity with the radical feminist analysis, but it also shows the influence of an alternative way of looking at the relationship between gender and sexuality, which developed during the late 1980s and 1990s, as new forms of theory and activism emerged around sexual identity and practice. These new developments were influenced by feminism, but at the same time they rejected the assumption that feminism in and of itself could provide an appropriate model for the analysis or the politics of sexuality. Feminism is a political movement concerned with advancing the interests of women, and the key social relation it theorizes is gender. While it is certainly necessary for a theory of gender to discuss sexuality, the argument can be made that an account of sexuality which subsumes it entirely under the heading of gender is both theoretically insufficient and politically unsatisfactory. Sexuality

ADVICE ON SPEECH FOR MTF TRANSEXUALS

From *Miss Vera's Finishing School for Boys who Want to be Girls* (Vera 1997):

The student learns to let her voice rise and fall as she speaks...A man might say, in a near monotone, 'That's a nice dress', but a woman, allowing her vocal pitch to soar, would say 'You look gorgeous!' (131)

[A]nother thing our girls must remember is that as men they speak from a place that is deeper in the throat. As their femmeselves, each must try to start her words at the roof of her mouth. A good way to do that is to start each sentence with an 'h' sound. This gives our girl more breath and brings her voice into the roof of her mouth...Another good tip is to end sentences on an up note, almost as a question. (132)

Girl talk includes learning to listen as well as to speak...In conversation, women tend to have greater willingness to listen, while men are more intent on being heard. (133)

From *From Masculine to Feminine and All Points In Between* (Stevens 1990):

I find that my own language is much less obscene as a woman than it was when I lived as a full-time man. It seems that I find myself thinking about what I am saying more, and concluding that using obscenities as a woman would be alien to the refined front I am trying to present. Even the occasional 'damn' or 'hell' comes difficult to my lips as a woman. Come to think of it, I'm probably a better person for it, too. (76)

When women talk, they move their mouths more than men; here again, smiling comes into play. If you don't believe it, try talking while smiling and talking without smiling. It's much easier to talk with a smile. Your mouth moves more, you're more animated and people tend to have a warmer feeling as they listen to you. (76–7)

[T]he more facial expression, the more smiles, the more you look and listen, the better feminine conversationalist you will be. Good advice for all of us, isn't it? (77)

and gender may be interdependent, but they are not reducible to one another.

One of the earliest and most influential statements of this position comes from the feminist anthropologist Gayle Rubin. In her article 'Thinking sex', Rubin argued that sexuality is more complex than is generally recognized by feminist analyses like those of Charlotte Bunch or Adrienne Rich, which see sexual oppression as derived from gender oppression. In opposition to this view, Rubin argued that lesbians are oppressed not simply because they are unruly women, i.e. not just because of gender, but also because of sexuality. Lesbians are not just any kind of unruly women, Rubin noted: in the eyes of society, they are sexual perverts. And like other sexual perverts – gay men, transvestites, sadomasochists – they suffer for that reason. Rubin agreed with previous feminist analysis that gender and sexuality are indeed related and interact in significant ways. But she disagreed that sexuality might be explained solely through an analysis of gender, and she argued that sexuality and gender constitute distinct arenas of social organization and practice. 'Sex', asserted Rubin,

is a vector of oppression. The system of sexual oppression cuts across other modes of social inequality, such as racial, class, ethnic or gendered inequality, and it sorts individuals and groups according to its own intrinsic dynamics. It is not reducible to, or understandable in terms of class, race, ethnicity, or gender. Wealth, white skin, male gender, and ethnic privileges can mitigate the effects of sexual stratification. A rich, white, male pervert will generally be less affected than a poor, black, female pervert. But even the most privileged are not immune to sexual oppression. (1984: 22)

The sexual stratification and oppression to which Rubin was referring is the social and legal production of a hierarchical system of sexual value in which monogamous married reproducing heterosexuals are at the top of the hierarchy, and promiscuous homosexuals, transvestites and others cluster around the bottom. Rubin accused feminism of maintaining that hierarchy even while inverting it. She criticized the tendency in radical feminist literature to interpret all sexuality in strict relation to heterosexuality and classify those acts that seemed least heterosexual (e.g. non-penetrative sex between two women) as good, and any other kind of sexual act (the use of pornography, sadomasochistic role play, the exchange of money for sex, gay male orgies, heterosexual penetration) as politically retrograde and bad.

Rubin concluded her article with the suggestion that feminism is not the place to look for a radical theory of sexuality. Instead, she argued that the time had come for activists and scholars to move beyond feminism and develop 'an autonomous theory and politics specific to sexuality'.

Feminist conceptual tools were developed to detect and analyze gender-based hierarchies. To the extent that these overlap with erotic stratifications, feminist theory has some explanatory power. But as the issues become less those of gender and more those of sexuality, feminist analysis becomes misleading and often irrelevant...
In the long run, feminism's critique of gender hierarchy must be incorporated

into a radical theory of sex, and the critique of sexual oppression should enrich feminism. But an autonomous theory and politics specific to sexuality must be developed. (Rubin 1984: 34).

Rubin's article was an early inspiration for the perspectives on sexuality and gender that in the early 1990s came to be known as 'queer theory'. The name 'queer theory' is misleading, since there is no one 'theory' to which it refers: developed by philosophers, literary theorists and film theorists, queer theory is a cluster of perspectives, not a single theory. Furthermore, the main target of queer theory's enquiries is not homosexuals, but rather heterosexuality and heteronormativity, defined as those structures, institutions, relations and actions that promote and produce heterosexuality as natural, self-evident, desirable, privileged and necessary. Queer theory interrogates heterosexuality by dismissing its claims to naturalness, and examining, instead, how it is vigorously demanded and actively produced in specific sociocultural contexts and situated interactions.

A major difference between queer theory and radical feminism is that whereas radical feminism continues to see sexual oppression as a reflex of gender oppression (Rich famously concluded 'Compulsory heterosexuality and lesbian existence' with the observation that 'the power men everywhere wield over women ... has become a model for every other form of exploitation and illegitimate control' (1980: 660)), queer theory follows Rubin's advice to see sexuality and gender as separate and only partially overlapping social phenomena. In practice, this difference does not always mean very much. Judith Butler's work, for example, is generally considered to be queer – indeed, her 1990 book *Gender Trouble* is often cited as one of queer theory's inaugural acts. However, her argument that our bodies, sexualities and identities are articulated and produced through what she calls the 'heterosexual matrix' owes much to the writings of radical feminists like Rich and Wittig (as Butler herself acknowledges). One point of lasting disagreement, however, does stand out: whereas radical feminism continues to maintain that certain kinds of sexualities and identities – such as butch-femme lesbians, transsexuals, drag queens, and sex workers who claim to enjoy what they do – conserve and perpetuate some of the most pernicious dimensions of heteropatriarchy, queer theory, in stark contrast, foregrounds those same sexualities and identities as *threats* to heterosexual hegemony, and as potentially agents of subversion and change.

What are the implications of these approaches for our understanding of people's linguistic behaviour? In the study of language-using as a social practice it is axiomatic that language is a resource through which its users construct their identities. An obvious question to ask, therefore, is whether and to what extent sexual identity and gender identity are constructed using the *same* linguistic resources. A less obvious, but equally important, question is: to the extent that the same linguistic resources do enter into the construction of both gendered and sexual identities, how does this actually work? As we have already said, there is a persistent, common-sense assumption that heterosexual identity is implied by a speaker's use of 'gender-appropriate' styles of speaking, whereas 'gender-inappropriate' speech styles imply that the speaker is not heterosexual. We take the view that this assumption oversimplifies what is actually a more complex relationship between gender and sexual identity, and later we will pursue that argument using concrete examples in which the complexity of the relationship is apparent. First, though, we need to say something more general about how language 'works' in the construction of identity, and especially of gendered identities.

INDEXING GENDER

We have already outlined Robin Lakoff's concept of 'women's language', a way of speaking constituted by various features which, according to her argument in *Language and Woman's Place* (1975), identify the person who uses them as a woman. A more technical way of putting this is to say that these features *index* (feminine) gender. To 'index' means to 'point to' something. Hence, when linguists say that particular features of language, such as regional accent or specialized lexicon, 'index' a speaker's identity or social status, what they mean is that those features are associated with specific social positions, and that a speaker, in using them (or appearing to use them), becomes associated with the positions that those linguistic features point to.

The question arises, however, of whether gender is indexed *directly* by language. Lakoff herself suggests that the features she identifies as constituting 'women's language' do not have the single, simple meaning 'this is a woman talking'. She claims that they also communicate things like deference, insecurity and lack of authority.[5] This might imply that gender is indexed *indirectly* rather than directly. The 'primary' meaning of a feature like superpoliteness is 'deference'; but because this trait is associated, in the community Lakoff is discussing, with women rather than men, the use of superpolite features acquires the conventional 'secondary' meaning of 'femininity'. In fact, not long after the publication of *Language and Woman's*

Place it was suggested that what Lakoff described as 'women's language' would be better labelled 'powerless language'. In a study of the styles of speaking used by witnesses in court, the researchers O'Barr and Atkins (1980) found that Lakoff's WL features were used most frequently by low-status witnesses of both sexes, and avoided most consistently by high-status and expert witnesses of both sexes. O'Barr and Atkins suggested that Lakoff had in effect misidentified what was signified by the use or the avoidance of so-called WL features: it was power rather than gender. Arguably, however, there is right on both sides of this argument. Since in male-dominated societies the relationship between the two variables is non-random and socially meaningful (there is a regular, albeit not invariant, association between power and masculinity / powerlessness and femininity), in many contexts the language that signifies one may also signify the other. In a paper entitled 'Indexing gender', the linguistic anthropologist Elinor Ochs (1992) suggested that this duality of meaning is the rule rather than the exception: the relationship between language and gender is almost always indirect, mediated by something else. Ways of speaking are associated in the first instance with particular roles, activities and personality traits (e.g. 'motherhood', 'gossiping', 'modesty'), and to the extent that these roles, activities and traits are culturally coded as gendered (the ones just cited, for instance, are coded as 'feminine'), the ways of speaking associated with them become indices of gender.

Styles that conventionally index gender in the manner described by Ochs may themselves be appropriated to communicate other kinds of meaning in particular contexts. For instance, Cameron (2000) argues that certain 'feminine' styles of speech are now being widely used in the telephone service business to signify a particular, caring and empathetic, attitude to customers. That these ways of speaking retain their gendered connotations can be inferred from the fact that many managers believe women are 'more natural' users of the preferred service style, and there is a preference for employing women in service roles. But in this context gender ('this is a woman talking') is not the only or primary *meaning* of the style, which is also required of male service workers, and routinely used by them. What is indexed is not membership of the gender category 'woman' so much as membership of the occupational category 'server' – though of course it is not coincidental that the speech style associated with serving borrows heavily from that associated with femininity. The point is, no way of speaking has only one potential meaning; the meanings it conveys in one context are not necessarily the same ones it conveys in another, and it may also acquire new meanings over time.

The common-sense assumption that sexual identity is indexed linguistically by the use of either 'gender-appropriate' or 'gender-inappropriate' ways of speaking is complicated by the account we have just given of how indexicality works. The common-sense view presupposes that there is a direct relationship between a speaker's gender and their use of linguistic features x, y and z, whereas the argument of Ochs and others is that this relationship is indirect: linguistic features are associated with gender via their association with something else that can itself be associated with gender. To see more clearly what difference it might make whether we understand the relationship as direct or indirect, consider the hypothetical case of a professional woman who uses a direct, forceful style of speaking and is described by her colleagues as 'talking like a man'. Is this woman using language to signal that she thinks of herself as a man or wants others to take her as a man? Or is she using it to signal a 'professional' identity by indexing qualities like authority and self-confidence, which are also, however, associated with masculinity? We think the second possibility is far more likely. If our hypothetical woman has a problem, it arises from the fact that her way of using language has more than one meaning: what she regards as a way of speaking appropriate to her professional role and status can also be interpreted by others as inappropriate to her gender. (Men doing customer service work have a similar problem – some are uncomfortable with the 'feminizing' effect of the way they have to speak, and some report disparaging remarks on this subject from customers.)

In the hypothetical example we have just given, the same way of speaking signifies both a professional identity and a gendered identity, and in practice these are difficult to separate: the two meanings coexist, and both of them are always potentially relevant. The actual balance between them is not determined in advance by some general principle, but has to be negotiated in specific situations, since meaning is not only in the language itself, but also in the context where language is being used by particular speakers for particular purposes.

At this point we want to try to show how the argument we have just made is relevant to the relationship of gender and sexual identity as these are constructed in actual linguistic practice. The common-sense assumption, as noted above, is that speakers mobilize the gender-indexing capacity of language to index sexual identity. Gender in this account takes precedence over sexuality. Furthermore, the construction of sexuality is assumed to depend mainly on the speaker's production of a speech-style with a particular gendered meaning (for heterosexuals, this will 'match' the speaker's own gender, while for others it may incorporate deliberate deviations from the expected gender norm). In what follows we will try to demonstrate that while the above assumptions may work in some cases, they are contradicted in others; from which we will conclude that a more complex understanding is necessary. The cases we discuss all concern the construction of *heterosexual* identity (gay and lesbian identities are the topic of chapter 4), and among the points they illustrate are the following.

- Although heterosexuality, because of its normative and naturalized status, can be thought of as the 'unmarked' or 'default' sexual identity, it does not necessarily go unmarked in discourse. Language-users in various contexts may be actively engaged in constructing heterosexual identities, both for themselves and for one another.

- The construction of heterosexual identities is not always accomplished by deploying gender-appropriate styles of speech. 'Masculine' or 'feminine' speech styles can be used by men and women to display heterosexual orientation, but equally that orientation can be displayed using styles that are strikingly at odds with the expected gender norm. What is conveyed by using any particular style of speech cannot be interpreted in isolation from questions about the context and content of talk.

- The mapping between gender and (hetero)sexuality is not unidirectional. Just as gendered talk may be (but does not have to be) a means for constructing heterosexual identities, heterosexual talk (i.e. talk which overtly marks the speaker as heterosexual) may be a means for constructing gender identities and/or homosocial relationships among people of the same gender.

EXAMPLE (1): USING GENDERED STYLES TO CONSTRUCT SEXUAL MEANINGS

Our first example is taken from a study of telephone sex workers' language by Kira Hall (1995). Hall studied the linguistic practices of 'fantasy makers' working for telephone sex lines in the San Francisco Bay area of California, concentrating on lines that serve a male heterosexual clientele. Phone sex is of particular interest, sociolinguistically speaking, because what clients pay for is the experience of being aroused by talk alone: there is no visual or tactile contact with the worker, who depends entirely on the resources of language and voice to keep the client on the line for as long as possible (phone sex is generally charged for by the minute, so longer calls mean higher wages). 'Fantasy maker', the preferred occupational term of many of the workers Hall spoke to, is an apt description, since their job is to create a fantasy that appeals to the caller, using language to construct a setting, a narrative, and a central female character who is both the narrator and a major protagonist in the verbal action.

Hall observed that fantasy makers often made use of a speech-style that was strongly reminiscent of Robin Lakoff's 'women's language' with its marked, feminine vocabulary and intonation. Their conversational strategies also recalled some of the interactional patterns Pamela Fishman found women using with male heterosexual partners. One of the women Hall interviewed explained, for instance:

I can describe myself now so that it lasts for about five minutes, by using *lots of adjectives*... and that's both – it's not just wasting time, because they need to build up a mental picture in their minds about what you look like, and also it allows me to use *words that are very feminine*. I always wear *peach, or apricot, or black lace, or charcoal-colored lace not just black*. (Hall 1995: 199–200, emphasis added)

Another interviewee spoke about the 'lilting' quality and 'inviting tone' she tried to put into her voice, while a third noted that she would often use supportive questions like 'do you like that?' to involve shy or silent callers (Hall 1995: 200). Many interviewees linked the erotic qualities of their speech to the 'femininity' of the language they used: in other words, sex was intimately linked with gender. But while they were no less gendered when talking to Kira Hall than when working on the phone lines, they did not use the same linguistic style to perform gender identity in both contexts. 'Women's language' was part of their professional persona, adopted because of its potential to convey a particular sexual meaning in interactions with male clients. Fantasy makers made a clear separation between themselves and their characters, and between the way they constructed gender when they were working and the way they constructed it in other contexts.

In some cases the separation between worker and persona was extreme: while all of them created characters that were female and heterosexual, not all the fantasy makers Hall met identified as heterosexual in non-working life, and one fantasy maker in her sample was not even female. In addition, Hall learned that it is common for telephone sex workers to create a range of characters of different races and ethnicities. In order to cater for different tastes they might offer callers the opportunity to talk to an Asian, Black, Latina or white woman, with all these personae being created by the same individual using the resources of language variation (e.g. accent, intonation, voice quality). Hall was told that the 'best' Black women on the phones are often white in reality, and vice versa. Andy, a Mexican-American male who earns his living on the sex lines ventriloquizing heterosexual women, reeled off the range of women he could produce:

If I want an Oriental, then I have to put a little—you know, then I have to think oriental sort of ((laughs)) and then it comes out a little bit different. Well it's— for example, okay (1.0) ((in alternating high and low pitch)) hull˄o˄::, ˄hi˄i::, ˄how are˄you::? This is Fong ˄Su˄u:. ((in natural voice)) See? [...] and then the Hispanic voice is more like ((clears throat, in high breathy voice)) He:llo::: this is Ésta es Amelia, cómo estás/ (.hhhhh) o:::h lo siento bien (1.0) rica. ((in natural voice)) Then I think I'm like watching Spanish dancers or Mexican dancers—you know, with their big dresses? [...] and then Black is a little bit—you know, on and on it goes. [My Black name is] Winona—Winona. [...] and then there's the Southern sound, you know, and then like I say, there's a British sound and a French sound. For the southern woman I'll use, like, Belle, ((laughs)) something Belle. ((laughs)). Oh, I play right up to it sometimes... You definitely have to use ((in slow southern accent, with elongated vowels)) a Sou:::thern a::ccent. (Hall 1995: 203–4)

TRANSCRIPTION CONVENTIONS

[hhh = exhalation, .hhh = inhalation, (1.0) = timed pause in tenths of a second,— = short pause less than 0.2 secs., :: = lengthened segment, ˄ ˄ = enclosed syllables spoken at higher pitch than surrounding discourse, ? = rising intonation, __ = emphatic stress, (()) = non-verbal communication and/or analyst's commentary, [ ] = editorial additions/clarifications, [...] = portion of original transcript omitted.]

This study is a good illustration of the point that heterosexuality may be actively marked, as opposed to just taken for granted, in discourse. It also illustrates that, while gendered speech styles can indeed be an important resource for constructing heterosexuality in the context of telephone sex, there is more to constructing heterosexuality in this context than simply 'talking like a woman'. Since gendered speech comes in many varieties (differentiated among other things by age, race, ethnicity, personality and social or occupational role), you have to ask what *kind* of feminine speech is being used to construct heterosexuality. Some registers and styles of speaking that are recognizably gendered are nevertheless not conventionally associated with sex (an example is the way of talking to infants sometimes labelled 'motherese', which tends to index femininity, but is only erotic for a small minority of men). Other ways of speaking, however, are not only gendered but also conventionally imbued with erotic significance. When fantasy makers adopt features of Lakoff's 'women's language', or use markedly high pitch, sing-song intonation and breathy voice, what they are doing is not imitating the everyday speech of any group of 'real' women, but producing a stylized performance in which certain gendered characteristics are particularly emphasized and exaggerated. This intensification of gender seems to be one conventional strategy for investing speech with a more strongly sexual meaning.

Another important point this study underlines is that the linguistic construction of identity is not simply about 'authentic' self-expression. The woman the client is talking to is a linguistic creation, and may bear very little resemblance to her creator – though her persona is that of, say, a demure Asian schoolgirl, the fantasy maker herself might be a fifty-year-old white woman, a lesbian or, indeed, as Hall found in one case, a bisexual Mexican-American male. Whatever her persona, the sexual excitement and intense interest in the client which her voice conveys is overwhelmingly likely to be simulated. Telephone sex is particularly congenial to this kind of deception because of the absence of any visual or tactile information. One interviewee told Kira Hall that a successful fantasy maker needs 'big tits in her voice'. In face-to-face sex work, no doubt, the actual size of a woman's breasts would be a more important consideration than their vocal representation. But the interviewee's remark is not just a comment on the specific conditions of telephone sex, it is also a comment on the nature of language as a shared communicative resource. A fantasy maker who puts 'big tits in her voice' is making use of shared knowledge about what kind of voice says 'big tits'. In this case, the phantasmatic tits were voiced through 'words that are very feminine', like 'peach', and by talk about feminine bodies and articles of clothing. Anyone who has that knowledge may use it, whether or not the resulting utterance is an 'authentic' representation (i.e. regardless of the actual size of their breasts). The link between a way of speaking and the social meanings it conveys is not created by the individual speaker; individuals can choose whether and how to deploy particular meanings, but the meanings themselves pre-exist that choice. If linguistic resources were not shared in this way, we would not be able reliably to convey anything about ourselves to others through our linguistic choices. But the way language works also creates the potential for faking: by appropriating the established, shared meanings of particular ways of speaking, speakers like the fantasy makers in Hall's study are able to construct identities which are not 'authentic'. (We will return to this point in chapter 4, where we discuss the vexed question of whether there is or could be an authentically gay speech, and in chapter 5, where we consider the relationship between sexual meaning and speaker intention.)

EXAMPLE (2): DOING GENDER BY TALKING ABOUT SEX

Our next example comes from an ethnographic study of hostess clubs in Tokyo, Japan, by Anne Allison (1994). Like telephone sex lines, hostess clubs are particularly fertile ground for sociolinguistic investigation, because what goes on in them is primarily *talk*. Although the clubs are considered part of Japan's 'water business' (*mizu shōbai*), the term which is used to refer to the sex industry, 'hostess' is not a euphemism for 'prostitute', and hostesses are not employed to have sex with the male guests who come to the club. Rather, hostess clubs are places where men go (encouraged and often paid for by the corporations they work for) to socialize with one another in their roles as men. Conversation is not supposed to be about work, nor about home and family. The hierarchies of the workplace are supposed to be broken down as co-workers relax and talk informally. Women's presence, and especially their linguistic contribution, is crucial to this project. The role of the hostess, Allison says, is 'to smooth the conversational path between men' (1994: 47), and she explains how this is done as follows:

If the man tells a joke, the hostess comments that he's a good teller of jokes...If the man sings a song, the hostess proclaims him one of the finest singers she's ever heard...The skill, as I learned, is to accept, reflect and augment the man as he has chosen to reveal himself. Whether he talks about his 30-foot penis or his joy in collecting stamps, the hostess is supposed to hear him out, comment on what he says, and swear that the qualities he has revealed are exactly what a woman like herself finds irresistibly attractive. The hostess is not supposed to challenge the man's presentation of himself, and she is never to co-opt his authority by reversing their roles. (1994: 177)

In this description of what hostesses do, two points are of particular interest. One is the obvious gender asymmetry. The function of women's talk in this context is to 'accept, reflect and augment the man', and men are not expected to reciprocate – in this respect, hostess-club talk bears comparison with the heterosexual couples' talk described by Pamela Fishman (1983, discussed above). A second interesting point is that this gender asymmetry has an explicitly *sexual* element. The men's talk may or may not be explicitly sexual – some men talk about their 30-foot penises, others about their stamp collections – but, either way, the hostess's response will ideally convey to a man that she finds him 'irresistibly attractive' rather than, say, morally admirable or thrillingly powerful. The flattery hostesses engage in is thus directed to the man as a (hetero)sexual being. As Allison points out, though, in the setting of the hostess club this is not actually a prelude to sex, but is seen rather as a strategy for making men feel more masculine and more powerful.

Explicitly sexual talk serves other purposes in the clubs as well. Allison observed many instances of what she dubs 'breast talk', where men make remarks to hostesses like 'you have large breasts'; 'your breasts are nonexistent'; 'are your breasts on vacation?'; and 'your breasts are more like kiwi fruit than melons' (1994: 48–9). On occasion men appraise women's breasts and bodies in more extended sequences of talk like the following (72–3, Allison's translation):

GUEST 1: Akiko has very pretty legs. She's only 19, you know.
GUEST 2: Yeah, she's a *joshidaisei* [university student].
GUEST 1: She really looks slender, but she has no breasts whatsoever.
GUEST 2: Maybe as she gets older, they'll grow.
GUEST 1: Amazing, no breasts whatsoever to speak of. I mean nothing at all.
GUEST 2: Yeah, not even the hint of a breast.
GUEST 1: (As Akiko walked back to the table from singing) You know, her ass is surprisingly large.
GUEST 2: Yeah, she's very big there. Yet she looks so slender and has no breasts at all.

Such appraisals are typically followed by laughter among the men. Hostesses agree with their assessments, and often encourage men to touch their breasts; according to Allison, however, the touching is often perfunctory, a matter of 'short, ritualized pats' (72). In her analysis, 'breast talk' is a form of banter whose main function is to allow men to relate to one another in an informal, nonhierarchical way. Thus what may appear to be primarily 'heterosexual' talk is in fact primarily *homosocial* talk: the point is for the men to bond with each other, in ways the workplace hierarchy would usually preclude, and the hostess fulfils the function of giving them something to talk about that they can all agree on. It is their relationship rather than her body that is the real focus of the men's attention.

To the extent that sex-talk in hostess clubs is about something other than male bonding, Allison concludes (1994: 184) that it is mainly 'a strategy for constructing gender rather than sexuality or heterosexual interest per se. Because sex talk degrades [i.e. is culturally seen to degrade] the woman but not the man, it emphasizes a gender imbalance that gives the man the pleasure of dominating. Putting the woman down is merely another means for structuring this relationship.' She goes on, however: 'After sufficient inflation of his ego, the man may in fact proceed to a sexual encounter with a woman, probably a different and less expensive woman than the one or ones who made him feel so confident.' This comment suggests that gender and sexuality are not so absolutely distinct as the first part of the quotation above seems to imply. The talk that goes on in hostess clubs is relevant to the construction of both gender and heterosexuality, with male dominance as a key component in both cases.

EXAMPLE (3): DOING HETEROSEXUALITY BY TALKING ABOUT GENDER

Our third example concerns the talk of five fraternity brothers on a US college campus (discussed in detail by Cameron 1997[6]). Unlike the previous two examples, this one does not involve 'institutional' (e.g. workplace) talk, it involves ordinary, informal, domestic conversation. Nor does the conversation occur in a context that is specifically marked as sexual. It takes place in the house the men share, while they are engaged in what is for them a regular communal activity, namely watching a basketball game on television. No women are present, and in the section of the conversation we will focus on here, women are not the topic of discussion either. Instead, four of the fraternity brothers embark on a lengthy discussion of various other men they know on the campus, who are singled out for critical scrutiny because they are, allegedly, 'gay'.

The extract below begins at a point where 'gay men' has been established as the current conversational topic, and attention has turned to a specific case in point, 'that really gay guy in our Age of Revolution class'.

TRANSCRIPTION CONVENTIONS

[[indicates onset of simultaneous speech (overlap); (.) indicates pause of less than 0.1 sec.; = indicates latching, i.e. turn transition with no gap and no overlap; ? indicates rising pitch; { } indicates sequence that is indecipherable or non-verbal; _ underline indicates emphatic stress]

Bryan: uh you know that really gay guy in our Age of Revolution class who sits in front of us? He wore shorts again by the way it's like 42 degrees out he wore shorts again {laughter}   1

Ed: that [guy
Bryan: [it's like a speedo he wears a speedo to class (.) he's got incredibly skinny legs   2

Ed: it's worse   = you know like those shorts women volleyball players wear?
Bryan: you know =

3

Ed: It's like those (.) it's l[ike   [French cut spandex
Bryan: [you know what's even more ridicu[lous? when you
        wear those shorts and like a parka on

4

---

5 lines omitted

Bryan: he's either got some condition that he's got to like have his legs exposed at
        all times or else he's got really good legs =
Ed: = he's probably he[′s like
Carl: [he really likes
                                                  his legs =   5

Bryan: = [he   = he doesn't have any leg hair
                                                          though
Ed: = [he's like at home combing his leg hairs =

6

Bryan: [yes and oh those ridiculous Reeboks that are always {*indeciph*} and
Ed: he real[ly likes his legs =
Al: = very long very white and very skinny

7

Bryan: goofy white socks always striped =   [tube socks
Ed: = that's [right   he's the antithesis of man
                                                              8

What is the relationship between gender and sexuality here? The 'really
gay guy' is identified and labelled by his supposed sexual identity – that is,
he is 'gay' – but the discussion actually centres on his lack of masculinity
(as Ed puts it, 'he's the antithesis of man'). Nothing is said about the
'really gay guy's' sexual preferences or practices, but a great deal is said
about his inappropriate dress and his narcissistic interest in his own body.
It appears, then, that for the participants in this conversation, 'being gay'
is about gender more than sex: a gay man is someone who is insufficiently
masculine rather than someone who has, or desires to have, sex with men.

   There is no doubt that Al, Bryan, Carl and Ed identify as heterosexual and
disapprove of homosexuality. Earlier in the conversation from which the
above extract is taken, they make jokes about a gay ball that had been held
on campus, such as: 'who wears the corsage and who wears the boutonniere?

Or do they both wear flowers cuz they're fruits?' Both the display of ignorance about gay ball etiquette and the use of the pronoun 'they' signify
the speaker's lack of solidarity with the group under discussion, gay men,
while the pejorative term 'fruits' used in this context – by someone who
has marked himself as an outsider to the group – suggests contempt.[7] So
one might expect Al, Bryan, Carl and Ed to take pains to mark their own
masculinity (which would also, within their system of meaning, mark their
heterosexuality), not only in what they say but also in how they choose to
express it. On closer inspection, however, this conversation is *stylistically*
more 'feminine' than 'masculine'.

To begin with, this 'gay men' section of the conversation belongs to the
speech genre of gossip, defined as talk, often of a critical nature, about the
personal characteristics and doings of absent others. In English-speaking
cultures, this genre of talk is strongly associated with women rather than
men. At the level of everyday practice, both men and women gossip; but at
the symbolic or ideological level, gossiping is marked as feminine behaviour.

Another symbolically 'feminine' feature of this conversation about gay
men is its sustained concern with the topics of appearance and dress, which
tend to be thought of as things women talk about while men do not. 'Real
men' are not supposed to take an interest in things like 'French cut spandex'
or 'striped tube socks' – or at least, they are not supposed to display such
an interest in public. There is something particularly paradoxical about the
way the participants dwell on the qualities of the really gay guy's legs (lines
5–8), when the very point they want to stress is that they have no interest
in other men's bodies.

Less obviously but perhaps even more interestingly, the organization of
discourse in this section of the fraternity brothers' talk displays many of the
hallmarks of all-female conversation as described by feminist linguists like
Jennifer Coates (1996). It has been claimed that all-female talk tends to be
collaborative, whereas all-male talk tends to be competitive. But although
it is all-male conversation, the extract reproduced above contains several
of the features linguists have used to define the notion of 'collaborative'
talk, and few if any instances of the features that are generally taken to
define 'competitive' talk. Although some participants (particularly Bryan)
contribute more or longer turns than others, no one attempts to dominate
by holding the floor uninterruptedly for long periods. Nor is there any
sign of conflict and disagreement about the subject under discussion. The
participants build on one another's contributions, producing significant
chunks of simultaneous speech (see line 7) and sometimes repeating each
other's actual words (see Ed's recycling at line 7 of Carl's statement at line 5,

'he really likes his legs'). Their turns are frequently 'latched' (i.e. one follows another with no gap or overlap), a precision-timing phenomenon which is often taken to indicate that participants in talk are attending especially closely to one another's contributions. They also make heavy use of 'you know', which has been associated with rapport-building and solidary relations among women in conversation.

The conclusion we draw from these observations is not that the men in this conversation are indexing feminine gender identities, still less that they are using 'gender-inappropriate' speech styles to display themselves as non-heterosexuals. Instead we want to recall one of the general points we made just before we turned to our three illustrative examples, 'What is conveyed by using any particular style of speech cannot be interpreted in isolation from questions about the context and content of talk', along with another general point made earlier in this chapter: that no way of speaking has only one potential meaning – features that index gender do not do so invariably, nor in most cases directly. Just as the professional woman who 'talks like a man' may be constructing authority rather than masculinity, so the straight men who gossip about gay men may be doing something other than marking femininity.

In Cameron's (1997) analysis of this conversation, what the fraternity brothers are doing is a kind of male bonding. As in the hostess-club case that we considered earlier, their talk is primarily *homosocial*. In that case, men related to one another using heterosexual banter about the bodies of women who were actually present; in this case, by contrast, the men relate to one another through disparaging gossip about other men who are not present. Reinforcing social bonds within a group is one of the key social functions commentators have attributed to gossip: sharing secrets or expressing criticisms about people who are not there underlines the 'in-group' status of those who are there, and brings them closer together. Commentators have also suggested that gossip involving criticism of absent others functions to affirm and strengthen a community's shared moral code. In expressing collective disgust about A who ran off with a man half her age, or B who stole money out of the church collection plate, the gossiping group reasserts its symbolic commitment to the social norms A and B have flouted. In the conversation about the 'really gay guy', similarly, the fraternity brothers underline their difference from him and their shared commitment to the norms of masculinity he has allegedly offended against. The co-operative style of their talk is related to its purpose, which is displaying solidarity and affirming their commitment to shared norms for gender and sexuality. The fact that both this style and the genre of the conversation, gossip, have symbolically 'feminine' associations, is of marginal relevance in this particular context. Though they use different linguistic resources to do it, the fraternity brothers are constructing heterosexual identities just as surely as the Japanese men who engage in 'breast talk' at hostess clubs.

Of course, one might ask why the fraternity brothers feel the need to display their heterosexuality in this context – a context which, one might think, is not specifically marked as 'sexual'. One possible answer is that in a society that is strongly heteronormative, and also male-dominated, male homosocial relations are both highly valued and highly problematic. Highly valued, because social bonds between men play a crucial role in the maintenance of power hierarchies (a point not lost on the Japanese corporations which send their male employees to socialize in hostess clubs). Highly problematic, however, because male homosociality tends to raise the spectre of homosexuality, which is forbidden and carries severe sanctions. One solution is illustrated by the institution of the hostess club: the club exists to facilitate male homosocial relations, but employs women to mediate those relations – for instance, by constantly telling the men how irresistibly attractive they are to women, and by allowing their bodies to serve as objects of male sexual banter. Relations between men which are not mediated by the presence of women have to be managed in other ways. All-male institutions may develop particular constructs of nonsexual love for this purpose – the military 'comrade in arms' or the Christian brotherhood of monastic institutions – which are usually accompanied by an overt prohibition on sex between men. Fraternities are all-male institutions, and their members ('brothers') are often very close. Perhaps this explains why the fraternity men in this conversation engage in a form of homosocial bonding which involves an explicit denial of homosexuality. (We will have more to say about the issue of denial in chapter 5.)

EXAMPLE (4): HETEROSEXUALITY AS A DEVELOPMENTAL IMPERATIVE

Our last example draws on research carried out by the US sociolinguist Penelope Eckert with adolescents and pre-adolescents, which suggests that linguistic strategies for displaying heterosexuality have a special significance for speakers at this transitional life-stage. Although they may not yet be interested in sex as such, (pre-)adolescents are aware that displaying an interest in it (more specifically, in the normative heterosexual form of it) is an important signifier of 'maturity'. *Not* displaying heterosexuality carries the risk that your peers will consider you immature and childish, and that this will negatively affect your status within the peer group. In this example, heterosexual talk has the same homosocial function we noted in examples (2) and (3): it is a bonding mechanism for peers of the same gender, and also, as we will see, a mechanism producing differences of status within the group. But in addition, it is what Eckert calls a 'developmental imperative'. As she explains: 'Childhood is, among other things, about learning to be the next step older. Participation in kid communities requires a continuous learning of new age-appropriate behavior, and age-appropriateness changes rapidly. Social status among one's peers requires growing up – it requires demonstrating new 'mature' behaviors. And in preadolescence, those new behaviors involve engagement in the heterosexual market' (Eckert 1994: 3). What Eckert means by the 'heterosexual market' is a set of social arrange-ments whereby girls and boys, though still socializing mainly with peers of the same gender, reorient their relationships around the norms of het-erosexuality and the status hierarchy those norms create. An individual's popularity becomes linked to their attractiveness to the other sex, and their ability and desire to get a boyfriend or girlfriend. Status is gained by pairing up with someone deemed desirable by the group at large, and it may also be gained by acting as a broker in negotiations about other pairings. Although there is little substance to these early heterosexual liaisons, and they may not be valued for their own sake by either party, they are important because they establish a 'system of social value' (Eckert 2002: 107), a 'market' which organizes social relations and hierarchies within the age cohort as a whole.

The overriding importance of homosociality in pre-adolescents' hetero-sexual activity is evident if we consider the role played by talk among Eckert's subjects. Heterosexual relationships furnished the subject matter for conversations among girls: they talked about which guys were 'cute', who liked whom, and who was going to approach whom to negotiate 'go-ing together' status. By contrast, talk did not play an important part in the heterosexual relationships themselves. In this extract from Eckert's data (1994: 6) a girl is explaining how she started going with her first boyfriend when she was eleven or twelve:

Oh I think someone went and delivered him the message that I liked him, you know. That was it. And so I guess the message came back that OK, he liked me too, so I guess we were going together, so he asked me to go with him. So I sent the message back to him, of course I wouldn't talk to him, heavens no, you know, you didn't talk to – [laughter]

The emotional investment here seems to be in the intimate conversation heterosexual relationships enable you to have with your same-sex friends rather than in any kind of intimacy with the ostensible object of your desire.

As well as active participation in the local heterosexual market, 'appropriate' adolescent behaviour requires a display of knowledge about adult heterosexual practice. Eckert records an incident in a sixth-grade science lesson where the topic of discussion is the workings of cruise control. One eleven-year-old boy has just volunteered that cruise control keeps a car moving at the same speed, when another boy adds: 'When you're going at 60 miles per hour like in a James Bond movie and you press auto control and then you go make out with a woman in the back then you put it on cruise control and you stay at the same speed.' The boy's production of this vignette aligns him with adult heterosexual masculinity, and Eckert points out that it challenges others present to display their own understanding of his references – James Bond movies, making out in the back of cars – by producing an affiliative response such as laughter. In fact, most of his classmates did laugh. The student who does not show appreciation risks coming off as immature, as not understanding what more mature kids understand. As Eckert says, this puts girls in a double bind: if they laugh they are acquiescing in the objectification of their gender, but if they don't they are compromising their age-appropriate credentials.

In our previous examples, performances of heterosexuality were used to position the speaker in relation to three major distinctions: masculine/feminine, heterosexual/homosexual and dominant/subordinate. Eckert's work is important because it shows that heterosexual display can have other meanings, which may in fact be more significant for the participants themselves. In the pre-adolescent peer groups she studied, displays of heterosexuality were used by group members as criteria for making distinctions that included maturity/childishness, sophistication/innocence, coolness/uncoolness, popularity/unpopularity. Distinctions based on gender and sexual orientation were seemingly not attended to in the same way.

But that is not to say those distinctions were irrelevant or insignificant: rather they were taken for granted. Eckert is clear that the status of heterosexuality as a 'developmental imperative' makes certain forms of gender developmental imperatives too. Clearly, boys and girls are gendered beings before they enter the heterosexual market; but at the point when a market emerges, their desire for the social rewards that accrue from participation impels them to shift towards the particular forms of femininity and masculinity that conform to the heterosexual principle, 'opposites attract'. Eckert sees this restructuring of gender identities and relations as a source of some distress for many pre-adolescents, particularly girls, for whom obeying the developmental imperative involves colluding in their own subordination. The point is illustrated by the sixth-grade classroom vignette reproduced above: the boy's performance of heterosexuality indexes both masculinity and dominance over women, which is ratified and normalized by the appreciative response of most girls in the class.

Eckert does not comment specifically on the implications of the social order she describes for young people who have recognized, or who will at some point in their adolescent careers come to recognize, that they do not fit the heterosexual template. What she does underline, however, is the extent to which heterosexuality is institutionalized both in the official culture of US schools and in the informal culture of the peer group. Heterosexuality provides the only developmental path that is recognized by either, and, as Eckert notes, that path is laid down for young people well before they become interested in actually having sex. Even if individuals who decline to participate in heterosexual activity are not actively persecuted, the social cost of non-participation is extraordinarily high, precisely because heterosexuality is the basis for a 'social system of value' rather than merely a sexual one. Eckert's account of this system might well serve to illustrate Adrienne Rich's argument, discussed at the beginning of this chapter, that socializing people to be heterosexual involves far more time, effort and coercion than one might expect if heterosexuality were the natural instinct it is so often claimed to be.

CONCLUSION

In the examples discussed above, we have seen that there is a close relationship between gendered speech and the enactment of heterosexual identity – but also that the relationship is more complicated than it might initially seem. In analysing any specific instance, it is necessary to pay attention to the context and purpose of speech: the linguistic performances of the California telephone sex workers and the Tokyo hostesses, or of the Japanese businessmen and the American fraternity brothers, are gendered and heterosexual performances, but they are undertaken for a variety of reasons, and may be realized in a variety of ways.

At the same time, our examples all show the constraining effects of heteronormativity. They show that a performance of heterosexuality must always also be in some sense a performance of gender, because heterosexuality requires gender differentiation. There is no such thing as a generic, genderless heterosexual: rather there are male and female heterosexuals.

Heterosexual talk as performed by a Japanese businessman is a very different thing from heterosexual talk as performed by the hostess who serves him. Sixth-grade girls and sixth-grade boys position themselves differently in relation to heterosexual discourse. Conversely, our examples suggest that many performances of gender will involve the affirmation of heterosexual identity and/or the rejection of homosexuality, because of the heteronormative assumption that heterosexuality is an indispensable element of 'proper' femininity or masculinity.

For those who identify as heterosexual, then, sexuality and gender are two sides of a single coin – which is not to say they are one and the same thing, any more than the two faces of a coin are indistinguishable from one another. What happens, though, when the relationship between gender and sexuality does not mirror conventional heteronormative expectations? How are gender and sexual identity indexed – and how are the two related – in the speech of lesbians and gay men? These are questions we address in the next chapter.

CHAPTER 4

Sexuality as identity: gay and lesbian language

In the previous chapter we examined the relationship between gender and sexuality as it is played out in language-use among heterosexual men and women. We placed our discussion in the context of the arguments advanced by both feminists and queer theorists, according to which compulsory heterosexuality/heteronormativity is a structural principle that organizes sexuality in general. If that argument is accepted, it makes sense for researchers of sexuality to be interested in the behaviour of heterosexuals *as* heterosexuals – that is, not just as generic representatives of their gender categories. Nevertheless, it is relatively unusual to find linguistic researchers explicitly addressing questions about language and heterosexuality. Far more commonly, interest has focused on the linguistic manifestations of *homosexuality*. For almost a century, social scientists, including sociologists and psychologists as well as linguists, have debated whether homosexuals use language in ways that differentiate them from heterosexuals. That ongoing debate is the topic of this chapter, and our discussion of it will pay attention to two issues in particular.

One, continuing the discussion begun in the last chapter, is the issue of gender. Debates on whether homosexuals have a distinctive language are related to gender in two ways. First, the arguments have tended to be (overtly or covertly) about gay men far more than about lesbians. In scholarship as in popular culture, ideas about how gay men sound or speak are much more salient and widespread than are ideas about how lesbians sound or speak. Second, as we will see, the linguistic characteristics that are commonly imagined to index homosexuality are often ones that also index gender. Homosexual men are thought to talk like women, and lesbians, to the extent that they are imagined to talk in any particular way at all, are believed to talk like men. This argument is the other side of the coin we examined in chapter 3, dealing with heterosexuals: just as heterosexual speech is often equated with gender-appropriate speech, so homosexual speech has often been equated with gender-inappropriate or gender-deviant speech.

Heterosexuals and homosexuals, like men and women, are conceived not merely as different from one another but as the opposite of one another.

The second issue, with which we will begin, is history: the way debates about language and homosexuality have evolved over time. More specifically, we will look at the way linguistic research on homosexuality has been shaped by changing ideas about the nature of homosexuality itself. We will look particularly closely at recent/current understandings of homosexuality and its relationship to language which are framed and dominated by the concept of *identity*. An important goal of this chapter is to look critically at the role identity has come to play in studies of language and homosexuality. But it is important to contextualize this discussion by pointing out that contemporary preoccupations with gay/lesbian identity, and gay/lesbian language-use as an enactment or performance of identity, emerged from a historical process that started with rather different assumptions. Tracing the history of research on language and homosexuality back to its beginnings in the late 1920s, we argue that it has gone through four main phases, which are represented schematically in the table below.

The first phase occurred from the late 1920s to the 1940s, when homosexuality was regarded as a pathology, and was also usually a criminal offence (particularly in the case of male homosexuality). It is worth pointing out here that homosexuality was exceptional in the nineteenth-century cornucopia of perversions in undergoing the kind of specifically linguistic elaboration that made it a plausible object of study for linguists and lexicographers. Language as such was never a concern of the early sexologists. All kinds of sexual perversions were 'written immodestly on [the] face and body', as Foucault noted (1981: 43), but their manifestations were physical, not linguistic (e.g. weak chins in frottists, dull demeanours in onanists, 'decidedly feminine pubic hair growth' in transvestite males). The early compilers of perversions collected many of their case studies by talking to patients, but they were concerned with the content of their patients' confessions, not the form in which the perversions were articulated. While the terms by which sufferers of perversions were frequently characterized – terms like 'nervous' or 'moody' – probably were related to the way patients spoke, there is no indication that the early clinicians thought that perverts might speak a particular language: that they intoned their words in specific, observable ways, or used a special linguistic register that could alert others to their sexual condition.

Homosexuality, however, did come to be associated with specific linguistic traits. A lisp in a man, for example, has for a long time been widely imagined to be, if not a dead giveaway, then at least a strong clue that

Four phases of research on gay and lesbian language

Phase	When?	Characteristics
1	1920s–40s	• homosexuality regarded as a pathology • research on the 'language of homosexuality' focuses on vocabulary and gender inversion
2	1950s–60s	• Homophile and Gay Liberation Movements • homosexuality moves from being considered a medical condition, to being conceived of as a social identity • research on language begins to be conducted by gay and lesbian scholars who have a stake in the political advancement of homosexuals • literature foregrounds divisions between what were seen as old-fashioned and misguided homosexuals, who used gay language, and politically progressive gays and lesbians, who avoided it
3	1970s–mid-1990s	• Gay Liberationist rhetoric expresses confidence that the old-style homosexuals are going or gone, and that a new gay and lesbian community has been formed • previous decades' stress on divisions among homosexuals is toned down, and homosexuality becomes framed as an oppressed minority identity, similar to a minority ethnic or racial identity • influenced by arguments about 'Black English Vernacular' or 'women's language', scholars claim that there is a 'Gayspeak'
4	1990s–present	• 'queer' critique of Gay Liberationist politics • some researchers shift their enquiry from looking at how gay and lesbian identity is reflected through language, to investigating the ways in which those identities themselves are materialized through language • focus shifts from seeing identity as the *source* of particular forms of language, to seeing identity as the *effect* of specific semiotic practices

he may not be heterosexual. If that lisping man should mention hair or flowers or poodles, then the game is all but up. And if he should happen to employ a qualifier like 'lovely', 'adorable' or 'fabulous' while chatting about a hairdo, a hyacinth or Fifi, then the prosecution can rest its case. The man is a fag.

During the first phase, research on the 'language of homosexuality', as it was known – as though the condition of homosexuality manifested itself as a kind of package deal that came complete with a language – focused on vocabulary and on the use by openly homosexual males of female names and pronouns to designate themselves and other men. Research attempted to document this exotic 'lingo', viewing it as a kind of secret code that homosexuals used to communicate their deviant sexuality to others who might be receptive to it.

The second phase of research on gay and lesbian language occurred in the 1950s and 1960s with the emergence of activist struggles around homosexual rights. Research on language began to be conducted by gay and lesbian scholars who had a stake in the political advancement of homosexuals. An important dimension of that advancement was the creation of a new kind of homosexual identity, one that distinguished itself from previous, pathologized identities. This new identity was formed in part by highlighting differences among homosexuals in order to valorize some of them, while subjecting others to critique. Language was important in those debates, because the lingo that had been identified as 'the language of homosexuality' was regarded by many activists and writers as politically retrograde and undesirable. Hence, literature foregrounded divisions between what were seen as old-fashioned and misguided homosexuals, who used the language, and politically progressive gays and lesbians, who avoided it.[1]

What happened by the 1970s and '80s was that the Gay Liberationist rhetoric expressed confidence that the old-style homosexuals were going or gone, and that a new gay and lesbian community had been formed. The previous decades' stress on divisions among homosexuals was toned down, and homosexuality was framed as an oppressed minority identity, similar to a minority ethnic or racial identity. Influenced by arguments of sociolinguists of the time who were documenting 'Black English Vernacular' or 'women's language', scholars began to revive claims that there is a kind of 'Homosexual Language', or 'Gayspeak'. What was now asserted, however – contrary to earlier claims – was that this language did not reflect individual pathologies. Instead it reflected the fact that homosexuals, like other minorities, had particular social identities and constituted a definable, relatively homogeneous social group.

During the 1990s, the identity-based model of homosexuality came under fire. A new generation of political activists argued that identity politics had led the Gay Liberation Movement to increasingly divisive debates about what constituted gay and lesbian identity. They felt that Gay Liberationist politics had become too focused on respectability, and it had marginalized individuals and groups, such as working-class femme dykes or Black drag queens, who did not share particular white middle-class values or outlooks. Resurrecting the shibboleth term 'queer' to name their new political movement, activists highlighted diversity within the non-straight world, and they celebrated the identities of drag queens, transexuals, bisexuals, sadomasochists and butch-femme couples that previous gay and lesbian activism and scholarship had downplayed or devalued. At the same time as queer activism was articulating alternative political agendas, academic scholars working within the new paradigm of queer theory were busy dissecting the idea of identity. Foucault had already demonstrated that identities are not merely given or discovered; instead, they are created and sustained by social relations of power. Following Foucault's lead, others now set out to theorize the processes through which power accomplishes this production. In terms of gay and lesbian language, this perspective led some researchers to shift their enquiry from looking at how gay and lesbian identity is reflected through language, to investigating the ways in which those identities themselves are materialized through language. In other words, focus shifted from seeing identity as the *source* of particular forms of language, to seeing identity as the *effect* of specific semiotic practices.

What all these different approaches to the study of gay and lesbian language have in common is the conviction that there is a relationship between language and sexuality such that language indexes, or can index, sexuality. This in itself is a crucial insight, for, as we have noted several times, language and sexuality have hardly been major research topics in linguistics or sociolinguistics. The literature on gay and lesbian language is the only type of linguistic research where the link between language and sexuality has consistently been foregrounded. Note, however, the 'sexuality' that is indexed is conceptualized in a very specific way. 'Sexuality' here is not interpreted broadly. It does not refer to fantasies, fears, repressions or desires. It means 'sexual identity'. From the earliest research on the language of perverts to much of the very latest work on what some scholars are now calling 'queerspeak' (Livia and Hall 1997a), what is investigated is not how speakers communicate their erotic proclivities or reveal their unconscious lusts. Instead, the focus is on how language is employed by speakers to signal their identity as homosexuals. The equation of sexuality with sexual identity has shaped this literature. It has constrained the questions that have been asked, moulded the methodologies that have been employed, and determined the conclusions that have been drawn. The main issue we want to discuss in this chapter is: what is gained by thinking about sexuality in terms of identity, and what are the limitations of such an approach?

THE LAVENDER LEXICON

The anthropologist Kenneth Read once noted that '[m]ost heterosexuals – subscribing to the popular view that "it takes one to know one" – tend to believe that homosexuals have special, almost subliminal ways of communicating their preference to one another – a "secret language" of identification' (1980: 11). This idea of a secret homosexual language appears to have been established in the first decades of the twentieth century. Already in 1927, one psychiatrist asserted that '[t]he clannishness of homosexuals has led to the development of special slang expressions among them' (Rosanoff 1927, cited Katz 1983: 438–40). In similar language, a 1936 article in *Current Psychology and Psychoanalysis* contained the observation that '[t]here is a widespread use of a strange slang among these human misfits. Once I heard one say: "that queen over there is camping for a jam". I was puzzled. Investigation showed that neither royalty, the wide open spaces, nor the household delicacy were involved' (cited in Duberman 1991: 161–2).[2] Other commentators reported darkly that the urban 'homosexual world has its own language, incomprehensible to outsiders' (Burgess 1949: 234), and that a visitor to a gay bar 'would have some difficulty with the jargon' spoken there (Westwood 1952: 126).

The precise characteristics of the supposedly 'secret language' that homosexuals were thought to speak were usually left vague, but it is clear from the remarks just quoted that whenever it was discussed in any detail, one dimension that always elicited attention was its lexicon. The first English-language text listing more than a few words of this lexicon appeared in 1941 as an appendix to a two-volume medical study of homosexuality.[3] This study was composed of case studies of homosexuals, who were examined for everything from testicle size to sphincter tightness. The two volumes reproduce X-rays of lesbian pelvic areas and graphic sketches detailing the precise morphology of homosexual genitalia. The section on language listed 329 items, most of which were shared by other groups, such as 'Negroes', hoboes and prostitutes. However, 139 of the 329 words were marked by the author – a folklorist and student of literary erotica, Gershon Legman – as being exclusive to 'homosexuals and their associates' (1941: 1154).

Legman's list is characteristic of the first stage of research on gay and lesbian language. Just as case studies like those in Krafft-Ebing's *Psychopathia Sexualis* (1901) or Magnus Hirschfeld's *Sexual Anomalies and Perversions* (1936) listed perverted acts, glossaries like Legman's listed perverted words. It is not immediately clear what the point of such a list might be, and Legman provides no justification for his glossary. But the fact that it was included in a medical study of homosexuality indicates that the words, like the weak chins and pubic hair growth we alluded to earlier, were imagined to be signs or expressions of an inner perverse essence.

FROM 'THE LANGUAGE OF HOMOSEXUALITY: AN
AMERICAN GLOSSARY' (LEGMAN 1941)

church-mouse A homosexual who frequents churches and cathedrals in order to *grope* or *cruise* the young men there. Churches are chosen for this purpose not from any irreverence or cynicism, but rather because crowds of standing and preoccupied people, as in cathedrals, subways, elevators and theatres, are ideal for the homosexual's purpose.

checkers, playing Moving from one seat to another in a motion-picture theatre to find a willing youth. The homosexual sits down next to a likely subject, and makes either a verbal or an elaborately accidental physical overture or 'pass', and if rebuffed, gets up and moves to another row, preferably not too close to the previous location, to try again with someone else.

dethroned Ordered by the attendant to leave a public toilet; said of male homosexuals ('queens' therefore 'dethroned') who frequent the toilet rooms of parks, subways, barrooms, theatres, and other public buildings.

fish Originally a generic term for women or for the vulva; the reference being to the somewhat piscine odor of the female genitalia. The word is used among male homosexuals as a predicate nominative to refer to male homosexuality, especially of the effeminate type, as *to be fish* or *to go fish* (e.g. 'When he touched me I just went *fish*, all over.')

incest A sexual liaison between two homosexuals, such an association being held in comparative contempt by most homosexuals.

man When pronounced emphatically by a homosexual, this term refers to a man who is definitely not homosexual.

sister in distress A homosexual male in trouble, usually with the police.

tea-room queen A homosexual who frequents toilet rooms to find persons amenable to his erotic or erotico-financial plans, or to scrawl homosexual dithyrambs or invitations on the walls.

There are of course numerous problems with lists like Legman's. A major difficulty is the tendency to generalize. A list of words, some of which undoubtedly were used by some homosexuals in some contexts, becomes transformed into a singular and panoramic document: 'The Language of Homosexuality'. In addition, lists of lexical items themselves provide us with little information about how the words were used, in what contexts, under what circumstances, by whom or to whom.

But while the information these kinds of lists provide is limited, they do reveal something about the way homosexuality (male homosexuality, at any rate) was conceived and lived at the time and place of their collection. The mere existence on Legman's list of a term like 'bleeding dirt', for example, which meant 'professional criminals or underworld characters who try to provoke homosexuals to some overt homosexual act, and then extort money from them' gives us some insight into the social context of homosexuality in the 1930s. In a similar way, terms like 'incest' (see box above) and 'ki-ki', which designated '[a] homosexual male who is sexually attracted only to other homosexuals... such homosexuals are commonly considered to indulge in mutual fellation, simultaneous or turnabout, or, less commonly, in mutual pedication [i.e. anal intercourse]' tell us something about how homosexual relations were socially organized at that time. We know from historical research like that undertaken by George Chauncey (1994) and Elizabeth Lapovsky Kennedy and Madeline Davis (1993) that our contemporary assumption that homosexuals desire other homosexuals is of recent date, becoming widely established in North America and northern Europe only in the 1950s and '60s. Before that time, homosexuality was understood and articulated through the lens of heteronormativity. The assumption was that desire itself was heterosexual. This assumption made it inconceivable that males might desire other males *as* males, or that females might desire other females *as* females. Instead, clinicians insisted that males who desired other males possessed a female subjectivity, and that women who desired women were psychologically male (hence the term 'invert', which was widely used in medical and popular contexts to designate homosexuals). This diagnosis was both descriptive and formative of the actual subjectivities of homosexual men and lesbians, who frequently appear to have interpreted their desire in heterosexual terms. Thus, the dominant expectation and practice was that homosexuals (who usually did define themselves, as the examples from Legman's lexicon make clear, in gendered terms) sought sex and relationships with their opposites, i.e. heterosexually identified men, for queens, and heterosexually identified women, for dykes. Hence the humour of campy jokes like: 'What do two queens do in bed together? Each other's makeup' or 'What do you call it when two butches have sex? Banging tools'. Words like 'incest' and 'ki-ki' constitute historical evidence of that earlier era.

It was this gendered dimension of the speech of homosexuals that caught the notice of lexicographers like Legman. Besides the words themselves, what struck observers most was the way in which openly homosexual men employed gendered pronouns in novel ways. This is the single characteristic of language that Legman felt specifically compelled to comment on in his text. 'A very common usage in the speech of male homosexuals', he noted, is the substitution of feminine pronouns and titles for properly masculine ones. Male homosexuals use the terms *she*, *her*, *hers*, *Miss*, *Mother*, and *girl* (almost never 'woman') in referring to themselves and each another, where one might expect 'he', 'him', 'his', 'Mr', 'Father', and 'man' (or 'boy'). This usage is sometimes rather confusingly carried over to references to heterosexuals, though an overtone, in such cases of jocularity or mild contempt usually serves to mark the heterosexuality of the person referred to. (1941: 1155)

This same fascination with the way in which semantic gender is used in the speech of homosexual men is also evident in the following excerpt, taken from a 1951 book entitled *The Homosexual in America*, by Donald Cory, an early campaigner for homophile rights.[4] We quote this example in full because the cinematic overtones of the text effectively convey how homosexuals were represented as a kind of outlandish, exotic tribe, even by sympathetic writers like Cory.

Let us take our place for an evening at one of these [gay] bars, watch the faces, eavesdrop on the conversation. We will look up with the others as a new face appears in the doorway, and we will hear a murmur:
    'Look what's coming!'
    'Isn't it gorgeous!'
This last comment is not in whispered tone. The inflection denotes desire, the volume expresses defiance.
    At one end of the bar, having beers, are three young queens; their eyebrows are plucked, their hair quite obviously bleached, and of course very wavy. Seldom seen in these bars, their presence is discouraged not only by the proprietors, but by the gay clientele. They gesticulate with graceful movements that are not so much feminine as caricatures and exaggerations of the feminine. They talk quickly, and their lips move in a manner not quite like the movements of either men or women. They can be more aptly compared to actors, seeking to imitate, yet not at all believing that they are play acting.
    'So I told Margie that she'd have to find herself a new apartment, because I wasn't going to put up with her carryings-on with all my friends that way, and she got insulted and left in a huff.'
    'She said you raised a stink when she brought a friend home one night.'
    'She did? So you believe her?'
    'I didn't say I believe anyone.'
    'Well, you can't believe a word she says.'
The onlooker or eavesdropper is puzzled, but the initiate is accustomed to the curious change in gender found in the conversations of a few of the homosexual circles. Perhaps no other aspect of their lives is so amusing and, even to many inverts, so revolting. Nothing that these people do stamps them as being apart from the others so much as their conversational use of *she* for *he*, *her* for *him*, in the most matter-of-fact manner. And yet, after a few hours with groups of this sort, there is hardly a homosexual unable to say *Joan* for *Joe*, *Roberta* for *Robert* . . .

A few gay men, standing near the gesticulating group, listen to the conversation with amusement and contempt. 'My, how those faggots camp!' one remarks in a loud voice. A bleached blond turns around and the retort is quickly forthcoming, 'Are you jealous, dearie, because nobody wants your trade?' (1951: 123–4, emphasis in original)

Note the way in which Cory makes it clear that not all 'inverts' speak the language that is bantered back and forth among the three young queens. While he does imply that there is a kind of elective affinity between homo-sexuality and the jargon ('after a few hours with groups of this sort, there is hardly a homosexual unable to say *Joan* for *Joe*'), it is obvious that the speech he describes is not so much a 'language of homosexuality', as it is a kind of register used by some kinds of homosexual men, to the 'amusement and contempt' of other homosexual men.

The difference between Legman's portrayal of the language he docu-ments as somehow indicative or expressive of homosexuality *per se*, on the one hand, and Cory's assertions, on the other hand, that the speech he de-scribes is employed only by a small segment of the homosexual population, is significant, because that difference constitutes the framework that has organized all subsequent work on gay and lesbian language.

This framework took shape as the Homophile and Gay Liberation Move-ments began to form in the 1950s and '60s. A fundamental dilemma that emerged early on in the struggle for gay rights was that the vocabulary and the linguistic gender inversions documented by writers like Legman and Cory proved to be embarrassing for activists. The fact that the inversions and much of the vocabulary were predominantly employed by homosex-uals who were either working-class or upper-class (see Altman 1971, 1982) made such language even more unacceptable to the middle-class gay men and lesbians who were struggling to create a new social role, and win main-stream tolerance and acceptance of homosexuality. To establish a space for themselves as politically progressive activists, and to redefine what it meant to be homosexual, these gay men and lesbians configured people like the bleached blond queens who dished and camped in Cory's bar as misguided, politically retrograde misogynists.

The rhetoric could be harsh. For example, one writer in a widely read gay and lesbian anthology vilified queens who used homosexual jargon as:

relics of a bygone era in their fantasy world of poodle dogs and Wedgwood teacups and chandeliers and all the fancy clothes and home furnishings that any queen could ever desire... a phony world of countless impersonators of Judy

Garland, Bette Davis, Mae West...And it is that same tired old fantasy world peopled by bitchy male hairdressers, snobbish antique dealers, and effete ballet masters. (Hanson 1972: 266)

This author concluded that:

We cannot really expect most fairy princesses to rip down their chandeliers, smash their plaster statues of David, kick their poodles out, or flee from fairyland to reality. But we should expose our Princess Floradora Femadonna so that our younger brothers will not fall into the lavender cesspool and be swept down the sewers of fantasyland. We must make our gay brothers realize that the princess trip is a rotten one, a self-deluding flight into a past that never was, an artificiality, and an escape from reality. It is a selfish, self-serving, irrational and materialistic journey which shuns real human relations for past images and things material, and human relations are what being gay is all about. (1972: 269)

What texts like this did was foreground divisions among homosexuals. They were published contemporaneously with other articles and pamphlets that called for the consciousness raising and mobilization of the 'gay community'. But in the formative years of Gay Liberation, the 'gay community' was not being discovered. As we noted in chapter 2 (pp. 25–6), it was an 'imagined community' in the process of being created. And part of that creation involved contrasting the newly evolving 'gay brotherhood' with other forms of homosexuality, such as those embodied by the bottle-blond queens cameoed by Cory. The campy queens would provide a backdrop against which a new 'gay community' could emerge. As Dennis Altman put it: 'For the homosexual, the new affirmation involves breaking away from the gayworld as it has traditionally existed and transforming the pseudo-community of secrecy and sexual objectification into a genuine community of sister- and brotherhood' (1971: 229). For this reason, it became important for many writers to emphasize that homosexuals were not all the same. Because language usage was one easy way of distinguishing old-style homosexuals (who inverted gendered pronouns and used some of the in-group vocabulary) from new-style, consciousness-raised gays (who avoided using 'gay slang'), the linguistic literature of this time is marked by numerous assertions of difference among homosexuals.

An example is the reaction to an article by Ronald Farrell published in the journal *Anthropological Linguistics*. In the article, Farrell analysed a questionnaire completed by 184 respondents in 'a large midwestern city' and provided a list of 233 vocabulary items that he asserted 'reflect...the preoccupations of the homosexual' (Farrell 1972: 98). This idea of 'the homosexual' was harshly attacked by Conrad and More (1976), who argued that, if Kinsey's reckoning that 10% of the American population is gay was correct, there must be enormous variation among homosexuals, and there can be no such thing as 'the homosexual' or a single homosexual subculture. To refute Farrell's assumptions, they administered a question-naire consisting of 15 words from Farrell's list to two groups of students – one gay (recruited through the campus's Gay Student Union), and the other self-defined as straight. The students were asked to define all the words they could. Conrad and More concluded that not only did all the homosexual students *not* know all the vocabulary (knowledge seemed to increase with age), there was also no statistically significant difference between the gay and straight students' understanding of the terms. In other words, there is no basis, in Conrad and More's opinion, to assume that homosexuals constitute a 'language-defined sub-culture' (1976: 25).

This point was later stated in even starker terms by Penelope [Stanley] and Wolfe (1979), who begin a paper on gay and lesbian language with the assertion that:

Any discussion involving the use of such phrases as 'gay community', 'gay slang', or 'gayspeak' is bound to be misleading, because two of its implications are false: first, that there is a homogenous community composed of Lesbians and gay males, that shares a common culture or system of values, goals, perceptions, and experience; and second, that this gay community shares a common language. (1979: 1)

Penelope and Wolfe base this outright rejection of the notions of gay com-munity or gay language partly on an earlier study by Penelope that examined gay slang. In that study ([Penelope] Stanley 1970), Penelope distributed a questionnaire through homosexual networks, in which respondents were asked to define 26 terms and suggest 2 of their own. On the basis of 67 completed questionnaires, Penelope argued that homosexual slang was not known by all homosexuals: there was, in other words, no homogeneous homosexual subculture that shared a common language. Knowledge of homosexual slang varied according to whether the respondent lived in an urban centre or a rural town. She proposed that homosexual slang should be thought of as consisting of a core vocabulary known by both men and women over a large geographical distance, and a fringe vocabulary, known mostly by gay men in large urban centres. Penelope argued that the core vocabulary, consisting of items such as *butch*, *dyke* and *one-night stand*, is known to many heterosexuals, thereby making it 'not so effective as a sign of group solidarity as the slang of other subcultures' (1970: 50). It is the fringe vocabulary which is 'the most interesting from a linguistic point of view' (1970: 53), partly because it is generally unknown to heterosexuals and hence qualifies as a true marker of group membership, and also because many terms in the fringe vocabulary arise from particular syntactic patterns

(Penelope lists six: compounds (*size queen*, *meat rack*), rhyme compounds (*kiki, fag hag*), exclamations (*For days!*), puns (*Give him the clap!*), blends (*bluff* – a Texas lesbian blend of 'butch' and 'fluff' to signify 'an individual who plays either the aggressive or the passive role') and truncations (*bi, homo, hetero*)).

Penelope also made the important point that knowledge and use of homosexual slang varied according to gender. The slang that writers insisted was homosexual slang was *male* homosexual slang; lesbians did not use it. In fact, Penelope argued that its gender inversions excluded and oppressed lesbians. This difference between gay men and lesbians had been noted in the earliest attempts to document language among homosexuals. Legman had explained it with reference to what he saw as '[t]he tradition of gentlemanly restraint among lesbians [that] stifles the flamboyance and conversational cynicism in sexual matters that slang coinage requires'. He also believed that 'Lesbian attachments are sufficiently feminine to be more often emotional than simply sexual' – hence an extensive sexual vocabulary would be superfluous (Legman 1941: 1156). In other words, lesbians were at once both too (gentle)manly and too womanly to want to talk about sex or take 'flamboyant' liberty with pronouns.

But in addition to these reasons for lesbian demureness, Legman also offered the following assertion, which goes to the heart of how researchers have conceptualized the relationship between language and homosexuality. A crucial reason why lesbians have not developed their own language of homosexuality is because 'lesbian' is not a coherent identity. In Legman's view (1941: 1156), lesbianism is 'in large measure factitious; a faddish vice among intelligentsia, a good avenue of entry in the theatre, and, most of all, a safe resource for timid women and *demi-vierges*, an erotic outlet for the psychosexually traumatized daughters of tyrannous fathers, and a despairing retreat for the wives and ex-wives of clumsy, brutal, or ineffectual lovers.' In other words, while male homosexuality could be considered an identity in its own right, lesbianism, in Legman's view, was merely a phase, a pose, a strategy to become a thespian, or an expression of petulant, confused dissatisfaction with men. Because lesbianism was not an identity, there was no lesbian language.

'GAYSPEAK'

What happened next in the history of research on gay and lesbian language involved something of a sleight of hand. By the 1980s, Gay Liberationist rhetoric was more self-assured, and the idea of a 'gay community' had seemingly made the transition from wishful thinking to social reality. In the eyes of many activists, the consciousness of many homosexuals had successfully been raised, the campy queens had successfully been marginalized, and writers like Edmund White could assert that the previous generations' practice of linguistic gender inversion 'is rapidly dying out, and many gay men under twenty-five fail to practice or even understand it' (1980: 240; also Hayes 1981a: 40). At this point, when a new kind of homosexual culture – based on assertion, not concealment – was becoming increasingly visible, the previously much remarked-upon differences among homosexuals became less salient, and what increasingly became foregrounded, instead, was intra-group homogeneity.

The shift is already apparent in the first scholarly volume entirely devoted to gay and lesbian language, *Gayspeak*, published in 1981. Although the introduction to *Gayspeak* observes that 'homosexuals permeate all dimensions of society as males and females, blacks and whites, rich and poor, rural and urban' (Chesebro 1981: xi), none of the book's contributions actually examines racial, class or geographical difference. Instead, with one important exception by James Darsey that we will discuss in a moment, the various chapters in the book consistently overlay difference with the solidifying image of 'the gay community'; one which, moreover, is said to use language in identifiably 'gay' ways. In explicit recognition of Julia Penelope's critique of the notion of a single gay language or gay community, several contributors to *Gayspeak* do acknowledge that gay men and lesbians do not speak in the same way. But even that acknowledgement is framed in consolidating language. So instead of one 'gay community', we now have two: a 'gay community' and a 'lesbian community', each of which uses language in particular ways.

The most theoretically ambitious papers in *Gayspeak* are two by Joseph Hayes (1981a, b), in which he suggested that Gayspeak (his name for 'the language used by gay men' (1981b: 45)) has three specific functions or dimensions:

(1) it is a secret code developed for protection against exposure (characterized linguistically by use of innuendo and by the avoidance or switching of specific gender reference when discussing one's partner or friends);

(2) it is a code that enables the user to express a broad range of roles within the gay subculture (characterized by camp and an extensive vocabulary defining sexual roles and behaviours – this dimension of Gayspeak, notes Hayes, is the one best known to the general public (1981b: 50)); and

(3) it is a resource that can be used by radical-activists as a means of politicizing social life, for example, when they 'make over' pejorative terms like *fag* or *dyke*, and 'turn them back' as symbols of defiance (1981b: 53).

In essence, Hayes's claim was that Gayspeak was characterized by the use of argot, innuendo, categorizations, strategic evasions (such as omitting or changing gendered pronouns) and, in the case of activist language, conscious revaluation of formerly derogatory terms.

These observations seemed insightful, but already in his response to Hayes's paper (appearing in the same volume), James Darsey pointed out that nothing on that list, in itself, was 'in any way uniquely employed by gay persons' (1981: 63). Darsey criticized Hayes for having 'stumbled into larger areas of behaviour [such as using language to equivocate about the nature of one's relationships, or to forge a political movement] with no compelling evidence that they are in any way uniquely employed by gay persons' (1981: 63). For example, a college student sharing a room with a person of the *opposite* sex might equivocate about the gender of her roommate when speaking to her parents. And resignifying formerly derogatory terms to denote political awareness and defiance is neither a strategy that originated with Gay Liberation nor unique to it. Hayes simply assumed that because many gay men used language in the ways he described, the features he identified as typical of Gayspeak were characteristic of how gay men talk – even though, as Darsey notes, many of those features were 'not exclusively a product of the gay subculture, nor universal within that subculture' (1981: 63).

Darsey condenses his main objection to Hayes's generalizations about Gayspeak into one tight sentence: '[A] study that uses gays as a source of data', he remarks, 'does not necessarily say much about gays' (1981: 59). This is a kind of axiom or logical proposition that expressed in different language means the following: *the fact that gays do X does not make X gay.*

This is an idea with consequences that cut to the heart of research on gay and lesbian language. It highlights two fundamental difficulties that claims about gay or lesbian language must face.

First, research wishing to postulate something like Gayspeak has to document that gays and lesbians in fact use language in empirically delineable ways. This in itself is a fairly tall order, since racial, economic, geographical and age-based differences among homosexuals – in addition to the crucial issues of whether individuals define themselves as homosexual, and are 'out' or not in a variety of contexts – make it difficult or impossible to generalize across the spectrum and pinpoint anything as characteristic of how 'gays' or 'lesbians' talk. There may certainly be linguistic features, especially lexical items, shared among many 'West Coast bears', 'Dykes on Bikes', 'Radical Faeries', 'African-American drag queens', or '30-ish white professional self-identified gay men in major US cities'. But to note those features cannot be the same as claiming that they are synonymous with, or characteristic of, 'gays' or 'lesbians'.

This point leads to the second problem that claims about gay and lesbian language have to confront. Even if it were possible to document that something like Gayspeak existed for particular groups, the question is: in what sense is that language 'gay'?

Take gender inversions as an example. The gender inversions observed by researchers like Legman and Cory did (and still do) undoubtedly exist in the speech of some gay men. But they are not 'gay language' any more than the kind of language used by 'fantasy makers' on phone sex lines is 'women's language'. They are gay in the sense that linguistic gender inversion, for particular historical and cultural reasons, has become iconic of male homosexuality. This is one reason why a high-school coach's mean-spirited shout of 'What's the matter with little Miss Jones over there?' to the boy who just dropped the ball can provoke laughter among others, and feelings of shame in the boy. Gender inversions are not used only by gay men, and even if they were no longer used by a single gay man, they would still connote male homosexuality in the foreseeable future, in the same way that subservient, vacuous blackness can still be connoted through particular phonological, lexical and syntactic characteristics that produce Uncle Tom speech – even though the precise co-occurring features that typify such speech are in no way characteristic of the talk of contemporary African-Americans, and even though nobody could possibly claim that Uncle Tom speech *is* African-American English. Or worse, that African-American English is Uncle Tom speech. To do so would confuse symbolic or ideological representations of language with actual linguistic practice.

This is not to say that some features of English may not occur with more statistical frequency in the speech of gay men than in the speech of non-homosexuals. Stephen Murray (1996: 747) has noted his impression that gay American males use diminutives more frequently than non-gays, especially ones formed through the morpheme -*ette*. He has also remarked on the prevalence and productiveness of the x + *queen* construction, where x is a metonym for some interest of the referent ('gym queen', 'leather queen', 'rice queen', etc.). Recall also Penelope's list of syntactic patterns that she claimed characterized the 'fringe' vocabulary of American gay men in urban centres. An even more familiar linguistic stereotype about Western gay men is that they *sound* different from straight men: they have

IS MIKE TYSON GAY?

Is Mike Tyson gay? Are his violent, macho outbursts and homophobic taunts desperate, perverse attempts to compensate for insecurities about his own manhood and sexuality?

... While there is no evidence that Tyson is gay, he certainly acts like a repressed, self-loathing, misogynistic gay man. Despite his macho pretensions, he can be effeminate in his speech and mannerisms. His lisp fits the gay stereotype, and he would not look out of place in a gay bar. If I saw him in the street, I would assume he was gay. His favourite insults are violent, graphic threats to sodomize men, revealing a perverse preoccupation with anal sex.

... His abusive relationships with women, all about conquest and domination, are a further indication of a misogynistic, self-hating homosexual. Always trying to prove his masculinity, he fits the classic pattern of a gay man who cannot accept his sexual orientation and who uses women sexually as a way of convincing himself – and others – that he is straight.

Source: Peter Tatchell, British gay activist, *New Statesman*, 10 June 2002

a distinctive way of speaking that has sometimes been called 'the voice'. Phoneticians attempting to describe this 'voice' have come up with various lists of its characteristics: suggested constituents include wide pitch range, breathiness, lengthening of fricative sounds like /s/ and /z/ and affrication of plosives /t/ and /d/ so that they sound like [ts] and [dz] (Zwicky 1997). Research on this topic (see Gaudio 1994, Jacobs 1996, Linville 1998 for overviews) suggests that 'the voice' is a culturally recognizable phenomenon: when people are presented with a range of male voices and asked to judge which ones 'sound gay', their responses show a high level of agreement. It is also evident, however, that there is not a perfect fit between *sounding* gay and actually *being* (self-identifying as) gay. Some of the speakers who are picked out by judges as 'sounding gay' will indeed prove to be self-identified gay men, but there will also be gay men who are not picked out because they do not exhibit the relevant vocal characteristics; conversely, the relevant characteristics may occur and be picked out in the voices of certain speakers who identify as heterosexual. Not all gay men have 'the voice' and not everyone who has 'the voice' is gay.

The same point might be made about lexicon. There are a number of slang vocabularies that have been documented for groups of homosexual men in various parts of the world. In the Philippines, for example, an argot called 'swardspeak' is spoken by many male homosexuals (called *swards* or *batuts*), and is widely known by everyone who works in the entertainment and fashion industries (Hart and Hart 1990). Brazilian travestis have an extensive slang vocabulary (documented in ASTRAL 1996; also Kulick 1998: 247) that passed into more widespread use in the mid-1990s, when the scriptwriter of a popular television *novela* created a saucy female character who peppered her speech with it (Browning 1996).

A British example of this phenomenon is the lexicon called Polari. Polari (from Latin *parlare*, 'to speak', and sometimes written as 'Parlarey' or 'Parlarie') consisted of perhaps 100 words, which derive from a variety of sources, including a lingua franca used by travelling entertainers in the eighteenth and nineteenth centuries. While it is not clear how much of the Polari lexicon has ever been in widespread circulation among homosexual men (one recent study suggests that it wasn't much; Cox and Fay 1994: 109), we do know that, by the 1940s and '50s, at least some of the vocabulary was common in cities such as Liverpool, Bristol and London, and it was widely associated with male homosexuality. A popular radio programme of the 1960s, *Round the Horne*, featured two queeny characters, Jules and Sand, who indexed themselves as homosexuals by larding their speech with Polari. Interestingly, the exposure of the lexicon on the BBC seems to have contributed to its demise – once it became widely known, it lost some of its resonance as a specifically gay code, and many younger gay men never learned it. In addition, like other forms of homosexual slang, Polari's links to effeminate pre-Stonewall homosexualities made it a target for Gay Liberationist activists, who regarded it as politically retrograde and discouraged its use. While there have been recent moves to document and revive Polari, all that seems left of it today are a handful of words (Cox and Fay 1994; Lucas 1997).

Our point about slang like Polari, wide pitch ranges, or morphemes like *-ette* is not that these linguistic features don't or can't exist as a kind of 'Gayspeak' that homosexual men can use as an in-group marker, a secret code, a language of humour, or whatever. They clearly do (the apparent absence of a similar 'lesbianspeak' is a point we address below). Our point is that rather than see those features as descriptive of the linguistic practice of particular groups, it is more sensible and more productive to regard them, instead, as symbolically or ideologically laden linguistic resources that are available for anyone – regardless of their erotic orientation – to draw on and recirculate to produce particular effects that may or may not be intentional.

> ### POLARI
>
> As feely homies, when we launched ourselves on the gay scene, Polari was all the rage. We would zhoosh our riahs, powder our eeks, climb into our bona new drag, don our batts and troll off to some bona bijou bar. In the bar, we would stand around parlyaring with our sisters, varda the bona cartes on the butch homie ajax who, if we fluttered our ogleriahs, might just troll over to offer a light.
>
> *[As young men, when we launched ourselves on the gay scene, Polari was all the rage. We would fix our hair, powder our faces, climb into our nice new clothes, don our shoes and cruise to some nice small bar. In the bar, we would stand around chatting with our gay acquaintances, look at the nice genitals on the male man nearby who, if we fluttered our eyelashes, might just wander over to offer a light.]*
>
> (Burton 1979, cited in and translated by Cox and Fay 1994: 109)

Research in the wake of *Gayspeak* did not see the language used by gay men and lesbians in this way. Instead, studies of gay and lesbian language conducted between the 1980s and the mid-1990s were propelled by the politically motivated desire to envisage gays and lesbians as relatively homogeneous 'communities' along quasi-ethnic lines, with their own culture and language (the commonalities and antagonisms between these two 'communities' being topics of continual debate among lesbian feminists and gay men). And just as sociolinguistic work of the period on 'Black English Vernacular' or 'women's language' saw those 'languages' as reflecting the social position and identities of the people who spoke them, the widely shared assumption among scholars studying Gayspeak was that the languages spoken by gay men and lesbians must have their locus in, and be reflective of, gay and lesbian identities. One prominent researcher during this period went so far as to suggest that there may be such a thing as gay-specific grammatical competence: 'gay men's knowledge of English', he proposed, 'may be substantially different from the knowledge of English used by heterosexual persons' (Leap 1996b: 400). This was assumed even though studies as old as Legman's had emphasized the overlap between gay slang and the argot of other groups, and studies like the ones we have discussed by Conrad and More (1976), [Penelope] Stanley (1970) and Cory (1951) had shown that not all homosexuals were familiar with gay slang or used gender inversions in their speech.

Two main consequences arose from the contention that Gayspeak reflected the identities of members of a (consciousness-raised) 'gay community'. The first was that, since gay language was assumed to be instantiated in the speech of people who were homosexual, the only language that was examined was that of people researchers either knew or strongly suspected were gay. (In the same way that many linguists researching child language acquisition studied their own children, studies of gay and lesbian language often reported on the linguistic behaviour of the researcher's friends.) Once again, we can note a parallel with 'women's language': if you believe that 'women's language' somehow inheres in or arises from a speaker's identity as a woman, why look at anyone else? If there is such a thing as 'women's language', then it will be found in the speech of women. But this approach can easily give rise to a circular argument, in which anything a woman says can be taken to be characteristic of women's language. As we noted above, framing the issue in this way confuses symbolic representations of language (the question of how certain ways of speaking are culturally coded as 'feminine') with actual linguistic practice (the question of whether and how these ways of speaking are used in real contexts by real speakers). This obscures the fact that the characteristics thought to make up 'women's language' are in principle available for use by anyone – men, transexual women, male 'fantasy makers', actors. Anyone can try to talk like a 'woman', even if not everyone (including some women) will always succeed. By the same token, people who do not wish to be taken as 'women' – transexual men, adolescent boys, males with high-pitched voices, many women in a variety of social contexts – may find that they unconsciously produce particular co-occurring features that sometimes lead them to be heard as a woman, whether or not they intend that effect.

Because research on gay or lesbian language was based on circular assumptions, it came to be circular: anything a gay or lesbian person said was taken to be characteristic of gay and lesbian language. This kind of framework generates a problem: what do we do with particular women, or particular gays and lesbians, who do not speak as they 'ought' to? In research on 'women's language', this problem was rarely discussed, perhaps because, when it was considered, it led researchers to reject the entire paradigm of seeing 'women's language' as necessarily linked to women (Cameron 1997; Goodwin 1988, 1990). Likewise, in research on gay and lesbian language, the issue was not overtly taken into account, although several scholars did insist vaguely that there was such a thing as 'authentic' gay speech, and that some kinds of gay and lesbian speech were more 'authentic' than others. One collection of essays even had the subtitle *Authenticity, Imagination*

and Appropriation in Gay and Lesbian Languages (Leap 1995b; also
Leap 1995a, 1996a, 1996b; Moonwomon 1995; Moonwomon-Baird 1997:
203).

The second consequence that arose from seeing Gayspeak as tied to a
consciousness-raised 'gay community' was that certain kinds of language
were not studied. Earlier research from the 1950s to the 1970s not only
foregrounded divisions among homosexuals, it also examined conflictual
language. For example, Stephen Murray (1979, 1980) analysed ritual insults
in which combative queens camped to the death with icy snubs about dis-
tended anal openings and microscopic genital endowment. Bruce Rodgers's
lush lexicon *The Queen's Vernacular* (n.d. [1972]) documents enough mink-
draped barbs to keep even the most venomous *vache* armed to the teeth
for days. In studies of gay language in the 1980s and the first half of the
1990s, however, spellbindingly bitchy queens vanish, and argumentative
dykes never appear. Instead, what becomes foregrounded is consensus and
co-operation.

The following text exemplifies the trends we have been discussing. In an
article on lesbian language, Morgan and Wood (1995) discuss a conversation
that occurred between one of the authors and five of her lesbian friends.
Their argument is that lesbians use language to 'co-construct a unified temporary lesbian identity' (1995: 238). In their framework, every topic spoken
about by this group of women, because they are all lesbians, is definitionally either an 'overt' or 'covert' 'lesbian topic'. From this perspective, the
conversational extract below is analysed as follows (1995: 248):

1. Kathy: What else do you pack in lunches?
2. Mandy: (laughs)
3. Linda: Weeell …
4. Kathy: chips
5. Mandy: bananas
6. Linda: fruit
7. Tonya: and a sandwich.

Linda extends her attempt to hold the floor and signals her intent to respond
to Kathy's question in line 1 … Kathy begins the image construction (chips)
by contributing a single word. Mandy follows Kathy's lead with, 'bananas',
also contributing a single word. Linda then adds, 'fruit' to the conversation
image of the sack lunch, also indicating her sense of the rules of this co-
authored sequence, i. e., only contribute one sack lunch word, and do it with
rhythm. Finally, Tonya completes the image using an intonation and construction,
' … and a …' which indicates the last item in a series, both of which signalled the
end of the sack-lunch sequence and the completion of the sack lunch image.

In other words, the speakers in this extract are co-constructing a conversation through conventional turn-taking moves and sequential tying techniques. Confronted only with this transcript, an analyst might be hard pressed to identify its specifically lesbian content. However, because Morgan and Wood know the participants to be lesbians, they interpret this conversation as specifically *lesbian talk*: their conclusion is that Tonya's contribution in line 7 'supports to an even greater extent the way in which these lesbians worked with unrehearsed precision to support the fiction of a cohesive group'. And their ultimate point is that '[c]onarration and conversational collusion function to bind us together in a temporary conversational community, allowing us to strengthen our identity as lesbians and promote the idea of a cohesive community' (248). Because the ones doing this conversational colluding are lesbians, the authors also see this kind of conversation as 'challeng[ing] the hegemonic discourse' of heterosexuality (237; Moonwomon 1995, Painter 1980 and Queen 1998 are other examples of this).

This third stage of research on gay and lesbian language achieved its culmination or epitome in the 1990s with the publication of the first (and, to date, still the only) monograph devoted to gay language: *Word's Out: Gay Men's English* (Leap 1996a). *Word's Out* generalizes about what the author names 'Gay English' from samples that consist almost exclusively of the speech of white professional men living in the author's home town of Washington D.C. It characterizes 'Gay English' as being structured along lines of co-operation (when gay men talk to one another) and secrecy (when they talk to other people); the linguistic features highlighted to document that co-operation and secrecy are commonplace strategies such as euphemisms, and discourse moves like turn taking, which occur in all conversations; and, finally, it is concerned with documenting what the author refers to as 'authenticity', which is to say, with those features of 'Gay English' that are happy – 'optimal, valuable, and life cherishing' – themes, as opposed to previous research's stress on the conflictual and unhappy dimensions of gay men's lives and interactions (1996a: 5–6).

Leap's attempt to delineate a 'gay men's English' was not matched by similar efforts to identify and describe a 'lesbian English'. Studies of lesbian language, such as those we have cited above by Morgan and Wood, Moonwomon and others, are both rarer and more restricted in their scope, and it is perhaps instructive to look more closely at the reasons for this. The rather marginal status of lesbians in this phase of linguistic research certainly did not reflect the persistence of Legman's view, quoted earlier, that lesbian identity itself is 'factitious'. Affirming lesbian identity and increasing the cultural visibility of lesbianism were major preoccupations for activists in the 1980s. So why was there no concerted attempt to show that lesbians too had a language of their own? Are lesbians different from gay men in this respect, and, if so, what explains the difference?

Perhaps the most explicit formulation of that question in the scholarly literature on gay and lesbian language relates to the phenomenon of 'the voice' – a cluster of phonetic features that have come to be associated with gay men's speech, as discussed above. Although, as we have noted, it would be inaccurate to suggest that gay men in general possess 'the voice' (or that straight men never use it), it is clear that vocal characteristics can provide one resource for signalling sexual identity among gay men. Lesbians, on the other hand, do not seem to have a parallel set of vocal characteristics that are popularly considered to distinguish them from straight women. In popular stereotype, lesbians are identified by dress and physical mannerisms rather than by the way they sound. Researchers who have looked for a lesbian equivalent of 'the voice' have concluded that no such thing exists (Moonwomon-Baird 1997; Painter 1980).

One explanation for this difference between gay men and lesbians has been proposed by Arnold Zwicky (1997). Zwicky suggests that gay men who use 'the voice' are marking a desire to differentiate themselves from hegemonic, heterosexual masculinity – this represents a norm which they identify *against*. Lesbians, by contrast, are more likely to identify *with* than against their gender group, and do not have the same desire to sound noticeably different from straight women. Gay men in Zwicky's account privilege sexual identity over gender identity, whereas lesbians do the reverse.

One problem with this argument is that it does not recognize the existence of variation among gay men and among lesbians. In each group one can observe a range of positions with respect to the relationship of sexual and gender identity: gender is expressed differently in the self-presentation of lipstick lesbians and dyke separatists, leather men and drag queens. The idea that lesbians identify most strongly with the larger community of women is plausible if one is thinking about radical feminist 'woman-identified women' (see chapter 3); but not all lesbians fit that particular prototype. Even those who do are often critical of conventional femininity (as indeed are many heterosexual feminists), and distance themselves from it in other aspects of their behaviour, such as styles of dress and bodily demeanour. It is not clear why they should decline to use linguistic resources for the same symbolic purpose.

The broader question Zwicky is grappling with is why gay men, but not lesbians, make use of gender 'crossing' – in other words, adopt linguistic features that are culturally associated with the speech of the 'other' gender. Although the stereotype of the effeminate lisping queen has been discredited, the association of gay men's language with women's language has not disappeared altogether. Many elements of 'the voice' (e.g. wide pitch range, 'swoopy' intonation) have a symbolically feminine meaning. The co-operative, egalitarian discourse style described by Leap in *Word's Out* is strongly reminiscent of women's talk as described by a number of feminist scholars (e.g. Coates 1988, 1996; Holmes 1995). If gender crossing is a resource for signalling non-heterosexual identity, one might expect lesbians to act like mirror images of gay men, adopting symbolically masculine features in their speech. The fact that they apparently do not do this prompts Zwicky to make the suggestion – as we noted above, a problematic one in many cases – that lesbians typically identify more as women than specifically as lesbians.

Another way to address the problem here might be to focus less on issues of identity and more on *structural* constraints. Lesbians and gay men (whatever their individual orientations to particular forms of identity) are not symmetrically positioned in relation to the possibility of gender crossing, because masculinity and femininity are not symmetrical terms. In patriarchal societies masculinity is culturally construed as the 'unmarked' gender position, while femininity is 'marked' – a point recognized by Robin Lakoff (1975) when she contrasted 'women's language' not to 'men's language' but to 'neutral language'.[5] Socially and linguistically, crossing from an unmarked to a marked position is more noticeable than the reverse: just as a woman who wears pants does not make the same kind of statement as a man who dons a dress, so a woman who deliberately eschews a feminine linguistic register in favour of the less marked alternative does not make the same kind of statement as a man who deliberately adopts feminine features in his speech. His gender deviance will be more visible than hers; she will have to go to a greater extreme (e.g. wearing not just pants but a top hat and tuxedo; not just giving direct orders but larding them with obscenities) to get the same effect. Our point is that 'men's language' as a cultural category or stereotype is less focused and elaborate than 'women's language'.[6] Perhaps this is one reason why linguistic gender crossing has not provided the same kind of resource for lesbians as it has for (some) gay men.[7]

The phase of linguistic research we have discussed here made use of ideas about 'identity', 'community' and 'authenticity' which were central to the sexual (both gay and feminist) political debates of the time, but the resulting analytic framework raised as many problems as it solved. As we will see below, some of these problems have persisted; but the Gayspeak approach itself has been progressively eclipsed by a newer paradigm, allied with queer theory.

PERFORMATIVELY QUEER

By the time *Word's Out* appeared in the mid-1990s, the impact of Judith Butler's assertions that gender and sexuality were the effects, not the source, of gendered and sexual practice had begun to be felt among other researchers working on gay and lesbian language, and some were questioning the idea that gay language was a reflection of gay identity (e.g. Barrett 1995). In addition, the concept 'queer', originally formulated in 1990 as a political challenge to 'gay' and 'lesbian', and then extended to name precisely the kind of theories that scholars like Butler were developing, was leading some scholars to reformulate or reject the idea that there was such a thing as a 'gay community' that spoke a particular 'language'. Instead, there were 'queer' ways of using language – ways that disrupted normative conventions and expectations about who could talk about sexuality and how that talk should be structured and disseminated. Just one year after the publication of *Word's Out*, a collection of articles entitled *Queerly Phrased* (Livia and Hall 1997a) appeared. The fourth phase of research on gay and lesbian language was officially inaugurated.

The most significant innovation in *Queerly Phrased* is an insight that builds on earlier articles by Rusty Barrett, who analyses stage performances by African-American drag queens (1995). Barrett (1997) argues that a key dimension of these performances is the way in which the drag queens juxtapose linguistic registers and styles that index socially jarring positions. In other words, in their speech, stereotypical 'white woman style' (which is essentially the speech style characterized by Robin Lakoff as 'women's language') may co-occur with overt sexual references, thereby both highlighting and contravening the expectation that 'ladies don't talk rough'. Or the queens may suddenly switch from 'white woman style' to stereotypical African-American Vernacular English (characterized by forms like the use of the copula 'be' to mark habitual aspect – 'she be nervous' – or the absence of the third person present tense indicative marker /s/ – 'she run'; see Barrett 1998 for details). Celebrity drag queen Ru Paul did this during a television appearance, switching in this manner to answer a question about whether she desired to actually be a woman. No, she replied. She was very happy being 'a big o' black man' (Barrett 1998: 156).

The novelty of Barrett's observations about the speech of the drag queens he discusses is his insistence that their gayness is not signalled through discrete linguistic codes (such as lexicon or gender inversion, as scholars like Legman indicated) or through discursive moves that signal involvement and co-operation, as Leap and others argued. Instead, Barrett's point is that the drag queens' queerness is materialized through the co-occurrence of linguistically incongruous and socially contradictory forms and registers, for example hypercorrect pronunciation while uttering obscenities.

In her contribution to *Queerly Phrased*, Robin Queen (1997) builds on this argument to make a similar point in relation to lesbian language, which she contends is constructed through the juxtaposition of different kinds of registers. Queen analyses fictional texts, and concludes that 'lesbian language' is produced through features that are drawn from and combine (a) stereotyped women's language (Lakoff's 'women's language'), (b) stereotyped non-standard varieties that are often associated with working-class urban males (e.g. cursing, contracted forms like *gotta, gonna*), (c) stereotyped gay male language (e.g. specific lexical items), and (d) what Queen calls stereotyped lesbian language (e.g. use of narrow pitch range, cursing).

Pursuing the same kind of argument in a slightly different direction, Keith Harvey (1998, 2000a, 2000b) has developed a framework for identifying and analysing what he calls 'camp talk' (i.e. talk that indexes the speaker as a homosexual male). Harvey claims that camp talk is language that results from four related rhetorical strategies. He calls these strategies Paradox, Inversion, Ludicrism and Parody. For reasons that will become clear in the following chapter, we disagree with Harvey's emphasis on speaker strategy/intention as the starting point of analysis. We think his framework is insightful, however, and we take the liberty here of re-presenting it in line with our own insistence that the crucial focus of analysis ought to be on the structure and productive effect of an utterance, not speaker intentions. Hence, we would re-state Harvey's claim. So, rather than being the language that results from particular rhetorical strategies, we would argue that camp talk is more productively understood as language that, through the combination of particular surface forms and pragmatic moves, produces four, related, rhetorical effects: Paradox, Inversion, Ludicrism and Parody.

Harvey defines *Paradox* as the juxtaposition of contradictory or clashing meanings.

LINGUISTIC SURFACE FEATURES OF CAMP TALK	EXAMPLES
incongruities of register	'Hello', she lied.
co-occurrence of explicitness/flagrancy and covertness/delicacy	A: You're sweating like a pig. B: I beg your pardon. I don't sweat, dear, I perspire.
co-occurrence of 'high' culture and 'low' experience	talk about mundane or seedy experiences described with reference to high culture, e.g. comparing one's smoker's cough to Violetta's tuberculosis in *La Traviata*

Inversion effects the reversal of an expected order or relation between signs.

inversion of grammatical gender	calling men by female names, referring to a man as 'she'
inversion of expected rhetorical routines	'I hate people who are not serious about meals. It is so shallow of them' (Oscar Wilde, *The Importance of Being Earnest*)
inversion of established value system	'The one charm of marriage is that it makes a life of deception absolutely necessary for both parties' (Oscar Wilde, *The Picture of Dorian Gray*)

Ludicrism (linguistic playfulness), in Harvey's framework, is characterized by utterances that suggest or underscore the indeterminacy or multiplicity of meaning in language.

puns / word play	'My dear, your hair looks as if you've dyed' (Rodgers n.d. [1972]: 207)
double-entendre (definitionally always exclusively sexual)	'When I'm good, I'm very good. But when I'm bad, I'm better' (Mae West)

Finally, *Parody* is realized through stylistic and pragmatic devices that both index and exaggerate speaker orientations to identities and social relations. Harvey claims that camp talk uses two key templates to drive a wedge into the supposed natural and unproblematic relationship between language and identity. These templates are aristocratic mannerisms (invoked in English through the sprinkling of speech with French elements) and femininity (indexed through surface forms stereotypically associated with excessive, catty femininity).

use of French	'This is the *salle à manger* . . . As you can see that slut Lewis never bothers to dust in here, because I haven't actually *mangé* in it for years' (from the novel *The Swimming Pool Library*, cited in Harvey 2000a: 252)
innuendo (not primarily sexual – deprecating in an allusive way)	'Great earring! Last year' (from the film *Jeffrey*)
hyperbole	'When I watch divas, when I read about a gesture of Dorothy Kirsten's or Leontyne Price's, I feel that I've crossed the Alps, that I've witnessed something tremendous and boundary-shattering, but that no one else around me realizes its significance and luminousness' (Koestenbaum 1993: 117)
exclamation	'I am all love, my dear boy – every inch (and there are, oh, so many!), every thought, every sigh – all Love' (from the novel *City of Night*, cited in Harvey 2000a: 255)
vocatives	'Mathilde Marchesi said to her protégée Nellie Melba after her London debut, "*Ma chère* Nellie, how is it that you forgot the two notes in the Quartette?"' (Koestenbaum 1993: 132)

The point of Harvey's discussion of camp talk is as follows. The particular grouping and frequency of these disjunctures of form and register, along with the proliferation of meanings encouraged by puns, double-entendres, innuendo and so on, highlight the non-necessary relationship between meaning and expression, thereby foregrounding the unstable and contingent nature of 'truth'. This is what makes 'camp talk' queer, in the sense of 'disruptive', 'disturbing', 'funny'. Wayne Koestenbaum, discussing a form of camp talk that he calls 'Divaspeak', makes the same point in a slightly different way: 'The diva', he explains, '*turns* a phrase and reverses it – substitutes praise for blame, pride for chagrin, authority for vacillation, salesmanship for silence. I long to imitate this language, if only to inhabit, for a sentence or two, its sublime lack of respect for the truth' (1993: 131, emphasis in original). And Judith Butler expresses all this in more political language, remarking that the effect of camp on 'truth' is to 'deprive . . . hegemonic culture and its critics of the claim to naturalized or essentialized . . . identities' (1990: 138).

CONCLUSION: LEAVING IDENTITY BEHIND

By mapping out the linguistic surface features through which talk comes to be enunciated and heard as camp talk, Harvey has come a long way from Legman's view of 'the language of homosexuality' as consisting of code-words and a perverse propensity to substitute 'feminine pronouns and titles for properly masculine ones' (Legman 1941: 1155). Instead of seeing gay language as a perverse reflection of a perverse identity, or, in 1980s-style scholarship, as an 'authentic' reflection of a consciousness-raised, affirmative identity, Harvey's emphasis is on how particular kinds of juxtapositions in language are used creatively to actively *construct* particular identities and social positions.

From this perspective, it is a short step to seeing language like camp talk as consisting of a set of resources that are available to all speakers of a language, in the same way that something like 'expert talk', which also has specific co-occurring features that make it culturally recognizable as the talk of an expert, is available to anyone who wants to convey, or who is heard as claiming, that they know a great deal about economics, gardening, computers, wine, Barbie dolls or some other specialized topic.

The problem, however, with even the most recent and innovative work on gay and lesbian language, such as that by Harvey, Barrett and Queen, is that it still remains invested in the idea that 'queer language' is somehow necessarily linked to queer (i.e. non-heterosexual) identities. The only language discussed by Barrett and Queen is of speakers or fictional characters who are known from the start to be gay or lesbian. This restricted set of data means that, in practice, it is not easy to see the difference between past frameworks that started from identity categories and looked at how they were reflected in language, and Barrett's and Queen's framework, which they claim starts from semiotic practices to see how those practices produce particular social positions. The fact that Barrett and Queen only look at the language of drag queens and (fictional) lesbians also means that the crucial implication of their work that the position 'queer' might be filled by a subject who is not gay, lesbian or bisexual remains, unfortunately, unpursued.

Harvey, too, remains explicitly attached to the idea that camp talk is gay male language. Despite his own acknowledgement that Paradox, Inversion, Ludicrism and Parody 'may feed into all manner of registers and styles' (2000a: 256), he still insists that camp talk is essentially and primarily a gay male discursive practice (2000a: 256–7).

FROM *THE QUEEN'S THROAT*

Divaspeak is succinct, epigrammatic. How many words need I expend to vanquish you, to work my own will? Is it possible to condense my anger, make a flourish of my failure? Shirley Verrett remembers an early performance – her own – as Carmen: 'It was marvelous – the body was lovely, and I had a lovely voice.' Nellie Melba on Nellie Melba: 'I am Melba. I shall sing where and when I like, and I shall sing in my own way.' Melba's 'I am Melba' is a tautology before which we must fall silent; we can offer no reply to Verrett's 'the body was lovely' – her ability to handle her own body with the tongs of a definite article.

Divaspeak is the ideal language for slap and sting and cut. No one can answer its assaults. Mathilde Marchesi said to her protégée Nellie Melba after her London debut, '*Ma chère* Nellie, how is it that you forgot the two notes in the Quartette?'. The coy French phrase '*ma chère*', can't disguise the fact that Marchesi is a martinet. Use divaspeak and you can pretend to be wounded while remaining invulnerable to arrows. When a fan backstage told Olive Fremstad that after hearing her sing Sieglinde, he now understood Wagner, the diva retorted, 'Isn't that nice, you are more fortunate than I who have given my whole life to the study and still know so little!' Fremstad conceals a bludgeon beneath her saintly sackcloth; she uses the fan's statement as a springboard for her own solo backstage cadenza of pique and retaliation.

Geraldine Farrar dared to tell Arturo Toscanini, 'You forget, *maestro*, that *I* am the star.' One need not be a star to relish Farrar's concise way of gathering a self, like rustling skirts, around her; he or she who will never become a diva, no matter how many social or vocal revolutions occur, may still wish to imitate Farrar, to say, 'You forget, *maestro*, that *I* am the star.'

(Koestenbaum 1993: 131–3)

But if camp talk is the speech of gay men, what about people like Mae West, who effectively claimed the status of camp's Fount in her famous definition of camp as 'the kinda comedy where they imitate me'?[8] And what of the speech of opera divas, which Koestenbaum observes is festooned with enough of the features identified by Harvey as camp talk to put even the most intense drag queen to shame? What of actors, comics, witty heterosexual men? What of unintentional camps like Queen Elizabeth II? What, in the world, of Ivana Trump?

In our presentation of Harvey's framework for analysing camp talk, we deliberately illustrated some of the surface forms he discusses with examples from the speech of individuals who are not gay men. We did this to draw attention to the difficulty that arises when a style of talk is linked axiomatically and exclusively with members of a particular social group. Because in the end, we wonder what is gained by erecting a wall between these different manifestations of camp talk? What theoretical progress is achieved by trying to decide whether or not Mae West's sly lasciviousness or Olive Fremstad's tart retorts are 'authentic' camp? What insights are generated by wrangling, endlessly and inconclusively, over who may have appropriated what from whom, and what difference that makes?

Our own answer to those questions is: nothing, and none. And our conclusion is that those kinds of issues only arise as problems in a theoretical framework that allows identity to be the central mystery, the structuring force behind – and the inevitable answer to – any question that is asked about language.

In her book *Gender Trouble*, Judith Butler argued at great length that what she calls an 'epistemological subject' (1990: 144) has exhausted its usefulness both as an object of philosophical contemplation and as a necessary precondition for political action. The term 'epistemological' in Butler's formulation refers to long-established Western ways of thinking about subjects and their relation to the world. An 'epistemological subject' is a subject that is thought to have a kind of stable existence prior to and outside the cultural field that encompasses it. It is an 'I' that in some sense can choose among different discourses and determine what best corresponds with its (already somehow established) sense of self. It is an 'I' that identity politics assumes needs to be in place in order for political action to be taken. This is the idea of identity that underlies the research that we have discussed in this chapter.

Gender Trouble is an extended call to 'shift from an *epistemological* account of identity to one which locates the problematic within practices of *signification*' (1990: 144, italics in original). In terms of what we are discussing in this book, Butler's call is to move away from the temptation to ground linguistic practices in particular identity categories, and to open up our analysis to exploring (rather than denying or lamenting) the ways that linguistic practices are inherently available to anyone to use for a wide variety of purposes, and to a wide variety of social effects.

All work on gay and lesbian language, even the most recent, has investigated the relationship between language and sexuality in terms of language and *sexual identity*. A point we have stressed throughout this book is that this concept of 'sexual identity' by no means exhausts the range of feelings, sensations, knowledges and relations that compose 'sexuality'. Indeed, an exclusive focus on identity greatly constrains the kinds of questions we can ask about sexuality. Instead of leading us to open up inquiry, it compels us to circumscribe it, and to return again and again to predictable (and finally unresolvable) debates about things like whether or not there is such a thing as a 'gay community', who is 'in' or 'outside' that community, and who or what constitutes 'authentic' instantiations of that community. Identity is doubtless one dimension of sexuality. However, limiting an examination of sexuality to 'sexual identity' leaves unexamined everything that arguably makes sexuality sexuality: namely, fantasy, repression, pleasure, fear and the unconscious.

If we bracket identity, leave it behind and forget about it for a while, how might we approach sexuality through a different kind of linguistic analysis? That is the question to which we turn in the following chapter.

CHAPTER 5

Looking beyond identity: language and desire

At the end of the last chapter we suggested that the study of language and sexuality should encompass not only sexual identity but also other dimensions of sexual experience, among which we mentioned 'fantasy, repression, pleasure, fear and the unconscious'. In this chapter we will discuss these other dimensions under the general heading of 'desire'; and we will try to demonstrate concretely how researchers might approach the topic of *language* and desire. Before we proceed, though, it is useful to say something more about our reasons for wanting to move in this particular direction. What does a focus on desire have to offer that a focus on identity does not?

First, a focus on desire acknowledges that sexuality is centrally about the erotic. This might seem self-evident, but in practice it has not been central to research conceived in an 'identity' paradigm, where the key question is how social actors use language to index their membership of particular groups (e.g. 'gay men', 'lesbians'). Erotic desire is implicitly referenced in this paradigm insofar as the relevant groups are defined by the nature of their desires (most commonly, for someone of the same / the other gender), but it is rarely an explicit presence in the interactions researchers analyse. Bonnie McElhinny points out, for instance, that the literature on gay and lesbian language-use has been dominated by studies of what she calls 'queer peers' (2002: 116–17). Even where the subjects are couples rather than friends or colleagues, the interactions analysts examine tend to be domestic or social rather than sexual. (The 'lunchbox' conversation cited on p. 94 is a good example of talk among 'queer peers'.) Of course there is a rather obvious methodological explanation for this: few people would agree to the recording and analysis of their naturally occurring sexual interactions. In the 'queer peers' case there may also be a political explanation insofar as gay men and lesbians (and those who carry out research with them) want the straight world to understand that there is more to gay/lesbian life than simply sex. But the study of language and sexuality should in principle be able to encompass the linguistic genres (e.g. flirting, personal ads, pornography and erotica, sex talk) in which people perform and represent their erotic desires, the way they construct themselves as desiring subjects and address the real or imagined objects of their desire. Whereas the study of language and identity places the main emphasis on the verbal presentation of self, the study of language and desire acknowledges that sexuality is relational or transitive: desire is always for someone or something. Hence research is impelled to problematize both the subject and the object of desire, and investigate how the relationships between the two are materialized through language.

Another aspect of sexuality that is foregrounded by taking desire rather than identity as a focus is *the extent to which our erotic lives are shaped by forces which are not wholly rational and of which we are not fully conscious.* Sociolinguistic research that treats gay or queer language as an 'act of identity' tends to dwell on the more conscious and calculated aspects of linguistic performance – those in which social actors intentionally lay claim to particular identities, or just as deliberately conceal them. But while we do not doubt the validity of this approach – clearly, people do use language to make claims to sexual identity – it does not exhaust what there is to say about language and sexuality.

In suggesting that there is more to sexuality than deliberate acts of identity, we are, of course, drawing on the conceptual apparatus of what has arguably been the single most influential theoretical discourse on sexuality throughout the last 100 years: psychoanalysis. Psychoanalysis has always emphasized the ways in which human behaviour (especially though not exclusively sexual behaviour) is not just the result of conscious, rational calculation. For psychoanalytic theorists, desire (erotic or otherwise) is fundamentally an irrational phenomenon, whose nature and expression are structured by the unconscious processes of prohibition, repression and fantasy. Regardless of whether or not one agrees with the ways that various schools of psychoanalysis have explained those processes (and feminists and queers have been critical of them for decades), we take it to be axiomatic that sexuality exceeds conscious control. To study sexuality without reference to desire and the unconscious processes which organize it is therefore to miss much that is centrally important about it.

The relationship between language and different kinds of desire is a frequent topic in texts directed at psychoanalytic practitioners, even though therapists 'tend to look *through* language rather than *at* its forms' (Capps and Ochs 1995: 186, emphasis in original; for an example of this kind of text, see Fink 1997). Language and desire has also occasionally been discussed in literary criticism and philosophical texts (e.g. Barthes 1978; Kristeva 1980). However, empirical research that examines how desire is actually conveyed through language in social life is rare. For researchers who want to investigate language as a form of social behaviour, the psychoanalytic perspective on sexuality raises an obvious problem: how can internal and unconscious phenomena like fantasy and repression be located and studied in real texts and conversations?

We do not deny that this is a challenging project; but in the following discussion we hope to show that it is not impossible to explore the non-rational and non-conscious aspects of sexuality using the tools of linguistic analysis. We will highlight some current research in which this project is being pursued, as well as some research which is not about sexuality specifically but which may offer useful models for researchers in that field. First, though, we will look more closely at how desire itself has been theorized, by psychoanalysts and by others whose thinking has been influenced by critical engagement with psychoanalysis.

THEORIES OF DESIRE

The distinguishing feature of desire in much psychoanalysis is that it is always, definitionally, bound up with sexuality. Sexual desire is a constitutive dimension of human existence. For Freud, 'the germs of the sexual impulses are already present in the new-born child' (Freud 1975: 42). Ontogenetic development – that is, the development and maturation of an individual – consists of learning to restrict those impulses in particular ways, managing them (or not) in relation to socially sanctioned objects and relationships. This learning occurs largely beyond conscious reflection, and is the outcome of specific prohibitions and repressions which children internalize and come to embody.

Although Freud was more inclined to speak of 'sexual impulses' or 'libido' than 'desire' (note, though, that *libido* is a Latin word meaning 'wish' or 'desire'), he would undoubtedly have agreed with Lacan's dictum that 'desire is the essence of man' (Lacan 1998: 275). Freud would probably not have agreed, however, with the specific meaning desire has in Lacan's work. Unlike libido, which for Freud was a kind of energy or force that continually sought its own satisfaction, desire, for Lacan, is associated with absence, loss and lack – and, significantly, with language.

A starting point in Lacanian psychoanalysis is the assumption that infants come into the world with no sense of division or separation from anything. Because they sense no separation, and because their physical needs are met by others, infants do not perceive themselves to lack anything; instead, they imagine themselves to be complete and whole. This imagined wholeness is the source of the term 'Imaginary', which is one of the three registers of subjectivity identified by Lacan (the others are the 'Symbolic' and the 'Real'). Lacan argues that this psychic state must be superseded (by the Symbolic, which means language and culture), because to remain in it or to return to it for any length of time would be the equivalent of psychosis.

Exit from the Imaginary occurs as infants develop and come to perceive the difference between themselves and their caregiver(s). Lacan believes that this awareness is registered as traumatic, because, at this point, the infant realizes that caregivers are not just *there*. Nourishment, protection and love are not simply or always just given, or given satisfyingly; instead, they are given (always temporarily) as a result of particular signifying acts, like crying, squirming or vocalizing. Sensing this, infants begin to signify. That is, they begin to formulate their needs as what Lacan calls 'demands'. In other words, whereas, previously, bodily movements and vocalizations had no purpose or goal, they now come to be directed at prompting or controlling (m)others.

Once needs are formulated as demands, they are lost to us, because needs exist in a different order (Lacan's Real, which is his name *not* for 'reality', but for that which remains beyond or outside signification). In a similar way that Kant argued that language both gives us our world of experience, and also keeps us from perceiving the world in an unmediated form, Lacan asserts that signification can substitute for needs, but it cannot fulfil them. This gap between the need and its expression – between a hope and its fulfilment – is where Lacan locates the origins and workings of desire.

The idea that desire arises when an infant registers loss of (imagined) wholeness means that the real object of desire (to regain that original plenitude) will forever remain out of reach. But because we do not know that this is what we want (in an important sense, we *cannot* know this, since this dynamic is what structures the unconscious), we displace this desire onto other things, and we desire those things, hoping – always in vain – that they will satisfy our needs. This means that the demand through which desire is symbolized actually has not one, but two objects: one spoken (the object demanded), and one unspoken (the maintenance of a relationship to the other to whom the demand is addressed). So the thing demanded is a rationalization for maintaining a certain relation to the other: the demand for food is also a demand for recognition, for the other's desire. The catch is that even if this recognition is granted, we can't assume that it will always be granted (Will you still love me tomorrow...?); hence, we repeat the demand, endlessly (for an extremely clear summary of this process, see Grosz 1990: 59–67).

The relationship of all this to sexuality lies in the linkage that psychoanalysis articulates between sexual difference and desire. There is a purposeful conflation in Lacan's writing between sexuality and sex; that is, between erotics and being a man or a woman. (In English, the terms 'masculine' and 'feminine' express a similar conflation, since those terms denote both 'ways of being' and 'sexual positions'.) Lacan's interest is to explain how infants, who are born unaware of sex and sexuality, come to assume particular positions in language and culture, which is where sex and sexuality are produced and sustained. Because becoming a man or a woman occurs largely through the adoption or refusal of particular sexual roles in relation to one's parents (roles that supposedly get worked out in the course of the Oedipal process), sexuality is the primary channel through which we arrive at our identities as sexed beings. In other words, gender is achieved through sexuality. Furthermore, the fact that our demands are always in some sense a demand for the desire of another means that our sense of who we are is continually formed through libidinal relations.

A dramatic contrast to psychoanalytic theories of desire is found in the work of Gilles Deleuze and Félix Guattari. Deleuze and Guattari take great pleasure in criticizing and mocking psychoanalysis. They insist that psychoanalysis has fundamentally misconstrued the nature of desire because it sees desire as always linked to sexuality. This is to misrepresent it: 'Sleeping is a desire', Deleuze observes, 'Walking is a desire. Listening to music, or making music, or writing, are desires. A spring, a winter, are desires. Old age is also a desire. Even death' (Deleuze and Parnet 1987: 95). None of these desires are necessarily linked to sexuality, even though sexuality may well be one dimension (one 'flux') that, together with other fluxes, creates desire. That psychoanalysis distils sexuality out of every desire is symptomatic of its relentless reductionism: 'For [Freud] there will always be a reduction to the One:... it all leads back to daddy' (Deleuze and Guattari 1996: 31, 35). Lacan's insistence that desire is related to absence and lack is a reflex of the same reductionist impulse.

Deleuze and Guattari do not believe that desire has a single origin. In contrast to psychoanalysts like Freud and Lacan, who understand desire in terms of developmental history, Deleuze and Guattari see it in terms of geography. That is to say, they see their tasks as analysts as mapping the ways desire is made possible and charting the ways it moves, acts and forms connections. For students of language, an advantage of this conceptualization of desire, regardless of whether or not one elects to adopt Deleuze and Guattari's entire analytical edifice, is that it foregrounds desire as something that is continually being dis/re/assembled. Thus, attention can focus on whether and how different kinds of relations emit desire, fabricate it and/or block it, exhaust it.

Deleuze and Guattari's rejection of psychoanalysis as the final arbiter of desire is not without problems – Judith Butler, for example, has commented that a reason she has not engaged with their work in her writing is that 'they don't take prohibition seriously and I do' (Butler 1999: 296). But the French philosophers' critical stance towards psychoanalysis does direct attention to desire without requiring that we derive all its formations from a particular source or a specific constellation of psycho-social relations ('. . . it all leads back to daddy'). Their interest in mapping desire as a geologist would map a landscape links them to a much more accessible and sociologically grounded scholar, namely Michel Foucault. And indeed, perhaps the most productive way of thinking about desire would be to see it in more or less the same terms in which Foucault conceptualized power.[1] Foucault is renowned for highlighting power in all his work, and his writings on power have become essential reading for anyone working in the social sciences or humanities. Despite all he wrote on the subject, however, Foucault was explicit about not wanting to erect a coherent theory of power. 'If one tries to erect a theory of power', he argued,

one will always be obliged to view it as emerging at a given place and time and hence to deduce it, to reconstruct its genesis. But if power is in reality an open, more or less co-ordinated (in the event, no doubt, ill-co-ordinated) cluster of relations, then the only problem is to provide oneself with a grid of analysis which makes possible an analytic of relations of power. (Foucault 1980: 199)

In other words, Foucault felt that a general theory of power would get in the way of understanding actually existing relations of power. Note the similarity between this argument and Deleuze and Guattari's insistence that theorizing desire first and then tracing all formations of desire back to that theory (as psychoanalysis does) obscures understanding of what desire is, how it circulates and what it does.

In the remainder of this chapter, we will not be using any one of the various theoretical approaches just discussed as a blueprint for studying desire in language; rather, our discussion will be informed selectively by the contributions of Freud, Lacan, Deleuze and Guattari and Foucault. From Freud, we take the fundamental idea that sexual desire is not a wholly conscious and

A NUTSHELL VERSION OF FOUCAULT'S CONCEPT
OF POWER

1) Power is not an institution, a structure or a possession: no one simply
'has' power. In other words, Foucault rejects the common-sense view
that equates power with dominance. In any given context, power is
exercised over both the dominant and the dominated.

2) This means that power is everywhere. It is not, in itself, either good or
evil, it is the sum of actions that constitute social fields, social relations
and even subjective understandings of oneself. People and groups are
positioned differently in relation to power, and this relationship is
historically contingent, empirically delineable, and continually in flux.
Because power is everywhere, it is not possible ever to escape the effects
of power *per se*, since any social relation will by definition be a
relationship of power. However, it is possible to modify or escape the
particular relations of power that direct one's conduct; hence, political
struggle is meaningful. But it is never final. Foucault stresses that any
new social relations entail structures and limits that are apt to harden
and become rigid. For this reason, the goal of political activism is not
the end of struggle, but to ensure that it may always continue.

3) Power always entails resistance. Resistance is possible because power
relations do not solidify into states of total domination. Power relations
are always fragmented, competing with one another and operating in
different sites along different lines.

4) Although relations of power can be enacted through threat and
prohibition (that is, by saying 'no'), the dominant modality of power,
especially today, is one of expression and creation – in other words, by
saying 'yes'. Power subjugates us (in the double sense of both
dominating us and making us into subjects) by encouraging us to
develop competencies and acquire skills (the ability to speak and act like
a lady, for example). Power subjugates by attaching individuals to
specific identities, and by establishing norms against which individuals
police themselves and others.

5) Finally, power is constitutive of and evident in 'micropractices', such as
child-parent interactions, husband-wife relations, dates, medical
examinations or workplace encounters. In all such instances, the
relations enacted by the participants are channels for and microcosms of
relations of power. Even one's relationship to oneself (in terms of how
one dresses, what one eats, how one acts and thinks about one's own
body, how one speaks, what kinds of erotic pleasures one seeks) can be
analysed as inflections of power, since we come into being as subjects
through forms of knowledge, feeling and practice that are culturally constituted and socially distributed, and, hence, channelled through power.

rational phenomenon, but is partly constituted by unconscious psychic processes (such as repression). From Lacan, we take the insight that desire is inescapably social and linguistic (it emerges only when children begin to acquire language), transitive (it involves both subjects and objects) and relational (desire is always on some level desire for the recognition of an Other). From Deleuze and Guattari, we take two important arguments which are part of their critique of psychoanalysis. One is that desire is not always and necessarily sexual. Although our own primary concern here is with sexual desire, we will consider below what may be learned from linguistic studies dealing with the expression of other kinds of desires. We also follow Deleuze and Guattari in rejecting the Freudian/Lacanian search for the origins of desire in some universal account of human psychosexual development (the Oedipal drama that 'all leads back to daddy'). Like Deleuze and Guattari, we are more interested in 'mapping' desire, locating it and analysing its workings in particular social landscapes. Finally, we take from Foucault the insistence that any relationship (social relationships, sexual relationships, one's relationship to oneself) is a vector of power. Thus, any analysis of desire will simultaneously and unavoidably be an analysis of the relations of power that animate or inhibit that desire.

The question arises, then: if we want to use linguistic data to map the workings of desire rather than searching for its origins, how do we do the mapping? What kind of empirical material can we look at, and what do we look for? In the sections that follow, we return to the two key aspects of sexuality that we highlighted at the beginning of the chapter – its transitivity and its dependence on unconscious/irrational processes – and relate these to recent empirical research on language. We begin by looking at a number of studies which bear on the issue of the transitivity of desire: more specifically, they enable us to analyse the way in which language is used to construct relationships between the subject of desire and its known or imagined object – often transgressing prohibitions and taboos in order to affirm a real or imaginary intimacy between speaker and addressee. We then examine some recent work in discursive psychology, literary theory and anthropology which focuses on repression and prohibition as verbal/interactional accomplishments (i.e. not simply internal processes which are not amenable to linguistic analysis), and which illuminates the role prohibition and repression play in the socialization of children's desires. Finally, we take up the important issue of the relationship between meaning and intention, arguing that routines for the expression of sexual desire cannot be understood within a theory of meaning that makes it wholly dependent on the speaker's intentions or the identity to which s/he lays claim. Rather there is a 'social semiotic' of desire: a set of meaningful resources that both constrain and enable the choices individuals make when they communicate desire.

DESIRING SUBJECTS

An obvious place to look for the construction of desiring subjects is in personal advertisements, where the authors of the ads not only announce themselves as particular kinds of subjects, they also explicitly articulate a relationship between themselves and an imagined object of desire. As Justine Coupland (1996) has observed, personal ads are modelled on the 'small ads' paradigm, which principally serves to sell second-hand consumer goods. The difference of course is that the object being advertised in this instance is the self, and the whole point of the ad is to ensure that the respondent is not just anybody, but a particular, desired kind of person. The personal ad genre is heavily conventionalized, because, in a small number of words, 'the seeker has to give a kind of shop-window description which casts out a net that hopefully catches the desired other as one of the respondents' (Shalom 1997: 190). Analysis of personal ads has consistently found that in casting out this net, heterosexual women tend to offer physical attractiveness and desire men who are 'professional', and heterosexual men offer information about their occupations and desire women who are 'attractive'. So desire in these cases is voiced in and channelled through culturally predictable indices of heterosexual value. Likewise, it should come as little surprise to anyone familiar with queer communities to discover that gay men place most importance, and lesbians least importance, on physical characteristics in their ads (Deaux and Hanna 1984; Gonzales and Meyers 1993; Shalom 1997; Thorne and Coupland 1998).

Personal ads are thus good examples of the way that different kinds of desires get articulated and circulated in society. By documenting the structure and content of the ads, linguists plot a map of desire, showing how particular desires seek to attach to a variety of bodies, objects, statuses and relationships. None of this is sociologically random. On the contrary, personal ads are textbook examples of how people's most intimate desires for connection to others are highly structured along readily observable lines of power.

What about actual erotic intimacy? If the search for desirable others is run through sociologically delineable circuits of power, what happens when those desirable others actually get together? How do they enact desire and create intimacy? In considering that question, it is important to remember that intimacy is, in fact, an interactional achievement. It is a constellation of practices that, like all the other practices that constitute sexuality and desire, are publicly mediated even though they may feel like inner discoveries. Queer theorists like Berlant and Warner (1998) have highlighted the crucial role that the State plays in the constitution of intimacy, by exercising its power to legitimize some types of intimacy (for example, heterosexual couples holding hands and kissing in public) and delegitimize others (for example, homosexual couples holding hands and kissing in public – in most places in the world, this is considered 'indecent behaviour' and is actively discouraged and prosecuted as such). Together with other institutions (for example, religious institutions, the family) and ideological formations (e.g. ideas about what 'real' or 'proper' men and women should and should not do in their intimate lives), intimacies are poignant examples of how desires may feel private, but are unavoidably shaped through public structures and in public interactions.

One consistent finding of researchers who have studied intimate forms of language is that intimacy is often achieved, at least in part, through the transgression of public taboos. An example of this is discussed in Wendy Langford's (1997) examination of Valentine's Day personal messages in the British *Guardian* newspaper. The messages that Langford analyses are ones in which their authors adopt the name and the voice of a cuddly animal for themselves and their partner, for example 'Flopsy Bunny I love you, Fierce Bad Rabbit', or 'Fluffy likes squeezing a pink thing at bed time! Oink says Porker'. A number of taboos are transgressed in these messages, most obviously the prohibition on adults publicly behaving like infants, and by extension also the prohibition on children behaving in an overtly licentious manner. Langford draws on psychoanalytic theory to argue that the development of these alternate animal personalities may be related to the desire to create an attachment to an object which is reliable and unchanging, and which stands outside the emotional traumas of everyday adult life.

Another example of the relationship between intimacy and prohibition is Joanna Channell's (1997) use of Conversation Analysis to track how intimacy is accomplished in the infamous 'Tampax' telephone conversation that allegedly took place between the Prince of Wales and his companion Camilla Parker-Bowles. A central argument in Channell's analysis is that intimacy is accomplished through the transgression of taboos that operate in public and non-intimate discourse; hence the prince's notorious remark about wanting to be in Camilla's knickers so badly that he'll probably end up being reincarnated as a tampon.

TRANSCRIPT FROM CHANNELL, 'I JUST CALLED TO SAY
I LOVE YOU'

M = male speaker, F = female speaker

M Anyway you know that's the sort of thing one has to be aware of. And sort of feel one's way along with – if you know what I mean.

F Mmm. You're awfully good at feeling your way along.

M Oh stop! I want to feel my way along you, all over you and up and down and in and out.

F Oh!

M Particularly in and out.

F Oh, that's just what I need at the moment.

M Is it?

F I know it would revive me. I can't bear a Sunday night without you.

M Oh God.

F It's like that programme 'Start The Week'. I can't start the week without you.

M I fill up your tank!

F Yes you do.

M Then you can cope.

F Then I'm alright.

M What about me? The trouble is I need you several times a week.

F Mmm, so do I. I need you all week. All the time.

M Oh God. I'll just live inside your trousers or something. It would be much easier!

F (laughing): What are you going to turn into, a pair of knickers?

M Or, God forbid, a Tampax. Just my luck! (Laughs)

F You are a complete idiot! (Laughs) Oh, what a wonderful idea.

M My luck to be chucked down a lavatory and go on and on forever swirling round on the top, never going down.

F (laughing): Oh darling!

(Channell 1997: 164)

The sexual innuendo that animates this conversation, culminating in talk about women's knickers, objects that enter a woman's vagina, and women performing intimate ministrations in a lavatory conjures up a chain of images that are mainstays of particular kinds of voyeuristic fantasies and many kinds of pornography. That such images are exploited in pornography is predictable, given that pornography is a discourse that works to incite erotic desire. But in contrast to Valentine's Day messages and private telephone calls, pornography is often thought of as a non-intimate genre – unlike 'Fluffy's' message to 'Porker', or a telephone conversation between two playful lovers, written and visual pornography is not addressed to one specific person with whom the writer, photographer or director is intimately acquainted. However, it is characteristic of many pornographic texts that they seek to *simulate* the intimacy of a non-fictional sexual encounter, and one common technique used to do that is the invocation and transgression of public taboos and prohibitions. Indeed, a crucial characteristic of the pornographic as a genre is that it turns space inside out, by making the most intimate actions public. This dimension of pornographic language is highlighted in John Heywood's (1997) study of narratives published in the gay magazine *Straight To Hell*. Those narratives, which claim to be first-person accounts of real-life sexual experiences, give shape to desire by channelling it through the transgression of multiple boundaries. In the stories, homosexuals have sex with straight men, that sex often takes place in liminal public settings like in the street outside a gay bar, and the sexual acts described flout social norms that separate the acceptable from the unspeakable ('I Slept With My Nose Up His Ass').

REPRESSION AND THE SOCIALIZATION OF DESIRE

Transgressions like those that characterize pornography lead us to the question of why prohibited words, images and actions have the power to entice and excite. With this question, we are back on Freudian terrain, in the realm of repression. In Freudian theorizing, repression is the idea that certain thoughts, feelings and emotions are not only hidden and denied (or, as psychoanalysts say, *disavowed*), but also desired as a source of pleasure *because* they are hidden and denied. In other words, admonitions which are intended to discourage particular desires, in fact, often incite and sustain them. As Freud recognized, the act of prohibition is a crucial instigator of desire. Prohibition is always libidinally invested: it fixes desire on the prohibited object and raises the desire for transgression.

The relationship between disavowal and desire has been extensively discussed by literary and film theorists concerned with the representation of race. Thus for instance Toni Morrison's essay *Playing in the Dark* (1993) explores the role that what she calls 'Africanism' ('the denotative and connotative blackness that African peoples have come to signify' [1993: 6]) has played in the constitution of American literature. Morrison's point is that in this literature, Black people are often either silent, invisible or absent. But though they might be speechless or not present, they nevertheless assert a structuring power on the coherence of American literature and the forms it has taken. Their symbolization as enslaved, unsettling, dark, childlike, savage and raw provided American authors with a backdrop against which they could reflect upon themselves and their place in the world. 'Africanism', writes Morrison, 'is the vehicle by which the American self knows itself as not enslaved, but free; not repulsive, but desirable; not helpless, but licensed and powerful: not history-less, but historical; not damned, but innocent; not a blind accident of evolution, but a progressive fulfillment of destiny' (1993: 52).

Morrison's project is to understand how Africanist characters act as surrogates and enablers, and to see how imaginative encounters with them enable white writers to think about themselves (51). Judith Butler employs a similar analytic strategy in her essay on Nella Larsen's novel *Passing* (Butler 1993b). *Passing* is a story about Clare, a light-skinned Black woman who passes as white, even for her husband, who is a white racist named Bellew. The novel ends when Bellew discovers Clare in the company of African-Americans and deduces her blackness, at which point Clare either falls or is pushed from a window (this is left unclear) and dies. Butler's reading of *Passing* highlights how certain identifications, relational configurations and desires exist in the novel only because the characters refuse to articulate and acknowledge certain other identifications, relational configurations and desires. Like Morrison, one of Butler's concerns is how whiteness is constituted through the disavowal of blackness – Clare's husband Bellew cannot be white without Blacks: he needs Blacks to know himself as white. But this relationship is one of disavowal: Bellew's whiteness is sustained by a continually reiterated *refusal* to acknowledge his relation to blackness – a refusal that is articulated through his racism. In considering this, Butler draws on the important psychoanalytic axiom that *a refusal to acknowledge something* ('I refuse to acknowledge my relation to blackness') *is already a form of acknowledgement*. Hence the refusal to acknowledge particular relationships and desires does not make them disappear. On the contrary, disavowal is a means of maintaining relationships and sustaining desires, even ones that we do not explicitly recognize.

Similar lines of argument have been pursued in some kinds of social science too. For example, the Freudian concept of repression has been reconsidered in linguistic terms in a recent book by Michael Billig (1999). Billig belongs to a group of British psychologists and social scientists who, during the 1990s, elaborated an approach to social and psychological life that they call 'discursive psychology'. As Billig explains, discursive psychology differs from orthodox social psychology and psychoanalysis because it discourages speculation about hidden, inner processes. Instead,

[d]iscursive psychology takes inspiration from the philosophical tradition of Wittgenstein's later philosophy and from the development of ethnomethodology and conversation analysis. These traditions of analysis stress the need to examine in detail the outward accomplishment of social life, showing how social order is produced through discursive interaction. Discursive psychology applies this project to psychological phenomena. It argues that phenomena, which traditional psychological theories have treated as 'inner processes' are, in fact, constituted through social, discursive activity. Accordingly, discursive psychologists argue that psychology should be based on the study of this outward activity rather than upon hypothetical, and essentially unobservable, inner states. (Billig 1997: 139–40)

Billig agrees with Freud that repression is a fundamental dimension of human existence. But he disagrees with the idea that the roots of repression lie in biologically inborn urges, as Freud thought. Instead, he argues that repression is demanded by language: 'in conversing, we also create silences' (1999: 261). Thus, in learning to speak, children also learn what must remain unspoken and unspeakable. This means two things: first, that repression is not beyond or outside language, but is, instead, the constitutive resource of language; and second, that repression is an interactional achievement.

Billig stresses that repression is accomplished in everyday interactions, and he examines the ways in which repudiations and disavowals are achieved through avoidances, topic changes and direct commands. For example, in discussing the socialization of polite behaviour, Billig remarks that 'each time adults tell a child how to speak politely, they are indicating how to speak rudely. "You must say *please*" ... "Don't say *that* word." All such commands tell the child what rudeness is, pointing to the forbidden phrases ... [I]n teaching politeness, [adults] provide ... a model of rudeness' (1999: 94, 95, emphasis in original).

Billig's discussion centres on Freud's own case histories, and he does not apply his arguments to the analysis of interactional material. However, his remarks on the way adults teach children about prohibited behaviour in the very act of prohibiting it suggest a link to research on language socialization that documents how particular fears and desires are conveyed and acquired through recurring linguistic routines. In the existing literature on this topic, the focus is rarely on the socialization of *erotic* desire; in addition, many studies of childhood socialization discuss *fear* rather than desire. Yet it is important to remember that, from another perspective, *fears are desires* – the desire to avoid shame, embarrassment, danger, punishment, etc. This work offers insights which are potentially highly relevant to the study of sexuality.

Patricia Clancy has investigated how Japanese children acquire what she calls communicative style; that is, 'the way language is used and understood in a particular culture' (Clancy 1986: 213; also Clancy 1999). Clancy was interested to see how children are socialized to command the strategies of indirection and intuitive understanding that characterize Japanese communicative style. In working with two-year-old children and their mothers, she discovered that these skills were acquired through early socialization routines in which mothers, among other practices, (a) juxtaposed indirect expressions (e.g. 'It's already good') with direct ones ('No!'), thus conveying the idea that various forms of expression could be functionally equivalent; (b) attributed speech to others who had not actually spoken, thereby indicating to children how they should read non-verbal behaviour; (c) appealed to the imagined reactions of *hito*, 'other people', who are supposedly always watching and evaluating the child's behaviour; and (d) used strongly affect-laden adjectives like 'scary' or 'frightening' to describe a child's (mis)behaviour, making it clear that such behaviour is socially unacceptable and shameful. These kinds of communicative interactions sensitized children to subtle interactional expectations which in adult interactions are not expressed explicitly. They also encouraged children to acquire the specific anxieties and fears (such as the fear of the disapproval of *hito*) that undergird Japanese communicative style.

The socialization of fear is also described by Capps and Ochs (1995), in their study of an agoraphobic woman in Los Angeles. A central attribute of agoraphobia is a sense of having no control over one's feelings and actions (hence one gets gripped by paralysing anxiety attacks). Capps and Ochs hypothesize that this sense of being unable to control one's feelings is, at least in part, socialized, and they examine how this might occur by analysing the interactions that occur between Meg, the agoraphobic woman, and Beth, her eleven-year-old daughter, when Beth talks about how she managed to handle some threatening situation. Whenever this happens, Meg often reframes her daughter's story in ways that undermine Beth's control as protagonist. She does this by portraying people as fundamentally and frighteningly unpredictable, no matter what Beth may think; by casting doubt on the credibility of her daughter's memory of events; by minimizing the threatening dimension of the daughter's narrative, thereby implying that Beth has not truly surmounted danger; and by reframing situations in which Beth asserts herself as situations in which the daughter has done something embarrassing.

Another study co-authored by Ochs (Ochs *et. al.* 1996) specifically discusses desire – not sexual, however, but gustatory. Here, the research team investigated how children come to develop taste. One of their main findings was that children's likes and dislikes of different kinds of food are actively socialized at the dinner table. In a comparison of dinnertime interactions between American and Italian middle-class families, Ochs and her collaborators found that dinners at the American tables were consistently marked by oppositional stances in relation to food, with children complaining that they did not want to eat the food they were served, and parents insisting that they must. One of the reasons why these dinnertime interactions were so oppositional is that they were framed that way by parents. American parents often assumed that children would not like the same kinds of foods that they enjoyed. This could be signalled through the preparation of different dishes, some for children and others for the adults, or by remarks that invited children to align in opposition to adults. For example, when one parent presents a novel food item at the dinner table, the other might remark 'I don't know if the kids'll really like it, but I'll give them...'. In addition, the tendency in American homes was to 'frame dessert as what their children *want* to eat, and vegetables, meat, etc., as what their children *have* to eat' (1996: 22, emphasis in original), thereby creating a situation in which certain foods were portrayed as tasty and desirable, and others as mere nutrition, or even punishment ('Eat that celery or you'll get no dessert').

Italian families, by contrast, highlighted food as pleasure. Parents did not invite their children to adopt oppositional stances (by creating distinctions between themselves and 'the kids' in relation to food), they foregrounded the positive dimensions of the social relations that were materialized through food ('Hey look at this guys! Tonight Mamma delights us. Spaghetti with clams') and they did not portray dessert as a reward to be gained only after one has first performed an onerous duty. The results of these kinds of differences in socializing contexts is that children acquire (rather than simply 'discover') different kinds of relationships to food, different kinds of tastes, and different kinds of desires.

Studies of language socialization like those by Clancy and Ochs and her collaborators do not discuss repression or mention Freud or Lacan. Nevertheless, this kind of work is an important example of how linguists can link with the project of discursive psychology to demonstrate how 'phenomena, which traditional psychological theories have treated as "inner processes" [such as taste, intuition, shame or anxiety] are, in fact, constituted through social, discursive activity' (Billig 1997: 139). Therefore, 'the location of desire outside the processes of dialogue and social order is not necessary' (Billig 1997: 151).

All the work we have considered in this section underlines the importance of analysing not only what is 'there' in a text or the transcript of an
interaction, but also its relationship to what is not said (the disavowed or
repressed) and what cannot be said (the prohibited or taboo). So far, our
examples have been drawn from work that is not about sex. But it is of
course possible to apply the same approach to discourse where sex is the
overt topic. We can illustrate the possibilities of the approach by revisiting
some examples from our own work which we have already mentioned in
earlier chapters.

Our first example takes us back to Deborah Cameron's (1997) study,
which we discussed in chapter 3 above, dealing with an episode of casual
talk produced by five fraternity brothers while watching a basketball game
at home on TV. One key element in their conversation is gossip about
other men who are allegedly gay. On the surface the most obvious thing
about this material is its overtly homophobic content; but as we suggested
in our earlier discussion, at a deeper level the gossip about gay men is
a performative enactment of the speakers' own heterosexuality. This is
necessitated by the presence of a danger that cannot be acknowledged:
the possibility of homosexual desire within the speakers' own homosocial
group. In order to defuse this threat and constitute a solidly heterosexual
in-group, the speakers locate homosexual desire outside the group, in the
bodies of absent others, who are invoked as contrasts. Like the Africanist
characters in fictional texts discussed by Toni Morrison, the 'gay' men who
feature in the fraternity brothers' gossip are vehicles through which others
(in this case, heterosexual men) can know themselves as normal, desirable
and powerful. Yet the way the straight men talk about the bodies of the
despised/disavowed gay men suggests that what they claim to be repelled
by is also (as a psychoanalyst might predict) a source of fascination.

Our second example returns us to the arguments we made in chapter 2
about 'no', the linguistic token of rejection or refusal – arguments which are
developed further by Kulick (in press). Kulick examines how the enunciation (or not) of 'no' in particular social situations works to produce those
situations as sexual, and to materialize individuals as particular kinds of
sexual subjects. He proposes that the subject position 'woman' is produced
in part by the normatively exhorted utterance 'no' when encountering male
desire for sex. The subject 'man', in contrast, is normatively exhorted *never*
to say 'no' when confronted with female desire. As we noted in our earlier
discussion, for a male to say 'no' to female desire for sex would threaten to
signify him as a homosexual. In order to block this signification, extenuating

circumstances need to be asserted, such as extreme physical unattractiveness in the female. All of this configures a kind of cultural grammar in which saying 'no' is part of what produces a female sexual subject, and *not* saying 'no' produces a male sexual subject. 'No' in both its present and absent manifestations facilitates the production of heterosexual subjectivities and heterosexual sexuality.

If we focus here on the issue of repression and disavowal, we see that the heterosexual subjectivities we have just described are dependent on and structured by subject positions that are repressed in discourse. A case where that repression becomes particularly obvious (and, hence, particularly threatening) is in instances when a man is solicited by another man. The problematic subjectivity here is not so much that of the man doing the pursuing – men are culturally defined as subjects who pursue others sexually, and popular stereotypes insist that men who pursue other men are the most fully sexed subjects of all (hence the most repellent heterosexual men in the world feel no embarrassment announcing that homosexuality is 'OK' with them, as long as the homosexuals don't try to seduce *them* . . .). The disturbing subjectivity is that of the man who says 'no'. By saying 'no', this speaker performatively materializes the position reserved in heteronormative praxis for women. By having to utter 'no', the speaker produces a feminine subject; one that importantly does not reject sex so much as facilitate it, by invoking the matrix of persuasion that men are culturally encouraged to use in response to a woman's 'no'. In other words, the 'no' here ensnares the male speaker in the same bind that it raises for female speakers who produce it.

This analysis once again makes clear why it is important to make a distinction between *performativity* and *performance.* According to Kulick's argument, 'no' uttered by a man in response to another man *performatively* materializes the position reserved in heteronormative praxis for women; but the result is to undermine a man's *performance* of masculinity. In this and other situations, if we hope to understand the way that language and sexuality intertwine, the crucial question is not: 'who says it?' Rather, the question to be answered is: 'what does saying it – or not saying it – produce?'

FORGING AND FAKING: BEYOND INTENTION

The case we have just discussed is one where the meaning conveyed by 'no' is not guaranteed by the speaker's intention, and may actually undermine rather than support the speaker's performance of identity. At this point we want to look more closely at the challenge this poses to the kind of sociolinguistic account in which speakers are seen as engaging in 'acts of identity' – particularly if it is assumed that the identities speakers project through their linguistic choices are in some sense intentional: that even if the choices themselves are not consciously reflected upon, they embody the speaker's own sense of who s/he is or wants to be.

Some researchers have explicitly argued that the investigation of language and sexuality crucially depends on being able to access the intentions of the speaker. In a strong statement of this position, Anna Livia (2002: 92) suggests, for instance, that intention is what makes the difference between 'passing' and 'dragging'. A male-to-female transexual and a drag queen might use exactly the same stereotypical linguistic features which conventionally index femininity; but whereas the transexual intends the performance of femininity sincerely and literally ('I am a woman'), the drag queen intends it ironically ('by talking like a woman when I'm actually a man, I communicate a critical stance towards heterosexual masculinity').

One problem with an insistence on somehow knowing speaker intention is that it can easily land us right back in the wrangles over authenticity that we criticized in the previous chapter. Is the point of knowing intention so that we can judge which enactment of gender is the more authentic one? Is a transexual's sincere performance of gender more 'authentic' than a drag queen's ironic one? What about a transexual who wants to perform gender ironically (perhaps someone like Kate Bornstein, whose sceptical view of conventional femininity we quoted on p. 52 above) – is she less 'authentic' than one who insists that she intends to 'pass' sincerely?

A further difficulty with this kind of objection raised by Livia is that, taken to its logical conclusion it seems to be at odds with an understanding of gender as socially constructed. Judith Butler herself invoked drag queens at the end of *Gender Trouble* to make the general point that we all, in effect, 'pass' at doing gender, since gender is not the expression of an inner essence, it is the performative effect of a stylized repetition of acts that approximate particular ideals. Drag queens reveal the constructedness of gender, but it is no less constructed in cases where someone tries to 'pass'. This is not to deny that individuals may feel there is an important difference between 'dragging' and 'passing'. Rather it means that the difference is itself an effect of a particular way of understanding and enacting gender. The difference between 'dragging' and 'passing' is not an irreducible datum which theory should take as its point of departure, but a mode of signification that must itself be explained.

But perhaps the problem is precisely theory. Livia's line of argument leads her to be critical of queer theory as represented in the work of scholars like Judith Butler and Eve Sedgwick. She wants to reassess

how far a theory which comes out of an engagement with literature can be of use to a social science-oriented discipline like linguistics. The dismissal of concepts like intentionality [i.e. that meaning depends ultimately on speaker intentions] comes very much from a model of language as a set of signs which relate more significantly to other signs than to referents [objects, events and states existing in the 'real world'], i.e. a discipline in which the relationship between words takes precedence over their real world consequences. (Livia 2002: 94)

While it is true that the theoretical edifice of any version of queer theory did emerge out of an engagement with literature and philosophy, so did the understandings of intentionality that Livia wants to recoup and reassert as central to an understanding of language and sexuality (we will see this below in our discussion of Austin). That theories originally emerged in the humanities is surely not in itself a problem for social scientists. The issue is whether those theories have the power to illuminate the signifying practices that social scientists examine.

So does a 'dismissal of . . . intentionality' entail an inattention to the 'real world consequences' of language, as Anna Livia argues? We think that the opposite is true. In our discussion so far, we have emphasized the claim made by scholars like Michael Billig that desires are not simply private, internal phenomena but are produced and expressed – or not expressed – in social interaction, using shared and conventionalized linguistic resources. This perspective shifts the focus of inquiry from the identities and the intentions of communicators to the culturally grounded semiotic practices that make them and their communication possible.

That meaning cannot depend solely on the will or intent of the language-user was one of Freud's most fundamental insights, and was expressed in his concept of the unconscious: for Freudians, human behaviour (including, of course, verbal behaviour) is shaped by forces we have no conscious awareness of, let alone willed control over. The person who makes a slip of the tongue, who hates the colour blue but adores yellow, or who feels impelled to wash her hands 100 times a day – this person does not intend or want to do these things, nor understand what makes her do them. The unconscious, as Freud theorized it, is that structure or dynamic which thwarts and subverts any attempt to fully know who we are or what we mean.

As we noted at the beginning of this chapter, we take it as axiomatic that sexuality exceeds conscious control, and believe that no account of language and sexuality can proceed without some awareness of that. However, even if one were to discount psychoanalytic understandings of the unconscious, there are still other arguments for not treating intention as the determining factor producing meaning. Those arguments are not psychoanalytical, they are *structural*. To illustrate what we mean, we must go back to the question of performativity.

The cornerstone of performativity theory is the philosopher J. L. Austin's concept of the performative. As he formulated it, performatives are language as action, utterances that in *saying* something *do* it. They are utterances that in their enunciation change the world – they bring about a new social state. Archetypal performatives are utterances like 'I bet', 'I promise' or 'I now pronounce you husband and wife.'

In the series of lectures in which Austin developed his ideas about performatives (published posthumously in 1962 as the book *How To Do Things With Words* (Austin 1997)), he argued early on that performatives can be divided into two basic kinds – those that work, i.e. those that produce the effects enunciated by the performative (Austin calls these 'felicitous' or 'happy' performatives), and those that do not (these are 'infelicitous' or 'unhappy' performatives). Although later in *How To Do Things With Words*, Austin complicates this distinction by separating what he calls illocution (i.e. the intention behind an utterance) and perlocution (the effect produced by the utterance), and noting that the intention and the effect of a performative often do not coincide, he maintains that one of the characteristics that felicitous performatives must exhibit is that the speaker must mean what she or he says. In other words, if a speaker promises to do something, she or he must mean it. Otherwise, the performative uttered by the speaker is a failed performative. It is, in his words, an 'abuse' (1997: 15–18).

So an important feature of Austin's distinction between successful and failed performatives hinges on the intention of the speaker – whether or not the speaker meant what they said. This foregrounding of speaker intention turned out to be the jugular vein for which the French philosopher Jacques Derrida leapt, in an early, key text in which he discusses Austin, and which helped define his deconstructionist approach to language. In that essay, entitled 'Signature Event Context', Derrida (1995 [1972]) argued that performatives do not work primarily because of the intention of the speaker. He does not argue that intentionality is completely irrelevant to understanding how meaning is produced in language.[2] He insists, however, that an understanding of language that sees it as grounded in and governed by speaker intention is fundamentally and irredeemably flawed.

Instead of working because they embody speaker intention, Derrida argues that performatives work because they embody conventional forms of language that are already in existence before the speaker utters them. Performatives work, and language generally works, because it is quotable.

What does this mean? The best way to explain it is to use Derrida's own example of a signature. He concludes 'Signature Event Context' by signing his name. Why? Because in order for a mark to count as a signature, Derrida observes, it has to be repeatable; it has to enter into a structure of what he calls *iterability*, which means both 'to repeat' and 'to change'. Signatures are perfect examples of iterability, because even though one repeats them every time one signs one's name, no two signatures are ever exactly the same. In addition, in order to signify – that is, in order to produce the effects of authenticity and do *social* work – one's mark *has* to be repeatable. If you sign your name 'XCFRD' one time and 'W4H7V' the next time, and 'LQYGMP' the next time, and so on, it won't mean anything; it will not be recognized as a signature, as a meaningful mark. A more modern example that makes the same point would be a computer password or a bank PIN code. In order to work, the password or the PIN have to be repeated; they may be typed in faster or slower, with more or less pressure on the keys, but they cannot be different each time they are used.

The same is true of the semiotic practices through which desire is encoded. The meaningful expression of desire depends on the existence of codes which are quotable, iterable. For example, the sexual desire of a man for a woman is conveyed through a range of semiotic practices – how he looks at her and for how long; his offering her a cigarette or a drink; his asking her to dance or producing conventional opening lines like 'So baby, come here often?' These actions are not likely to be regarded as random or meaningless by any linguistically and culturally aware person. Why? Precisely because they are iterable signs that continually get recirculated in social life (and in media representations of it). The iterability of particular codes signifying desire is what allows us to recognize desire *as* desire. Because they are iterable, semiotic practices like language are not context-bound, nor are they limited to particular speakers: one might imagine a shoe fetishist creating an erotic ambience and warming up for the evening by pouring a scotch, lighting a few candles, and whispering to his newly purchased pumps 'So baby, come here often?'

Likewise, a woman who produces the line 'So baby, come here often?' to another woman, at a bar, in a gym locker room, on a bus – anywhere – can potentially be heard to be expressing erotic interest in her addressee, not *in spite of* the fact that the line is conventionally represented and used as a typically male come-on, but precisely *because of* that fact. Like any utterance, 'So baby, come here often?' does not have only one interpretation, and a line like that is so stereotypically tied to a particular kind of desperate, lounge-lizard desire that, these days, it is almost impossible to hear it without laughing. But the point is that the interpretation (or not) of a particular utterance as expressive of desire ultimately does not depend on the intention of the speaker. If the recipient of 'So baby, come here often?' laughs, the speaker who intended a come-on may be embarrassed; if the recipient expresses interest or offence, the speaker who intended a joke might be chagrined. In either case, what is the 'true' meaning of the utterance? Whose interpretation is decisive? Intention, as Derrida explains, cannot 'govern' this scene.

In addition to not being governed by the intentions of the speakers who use it, language also exceeds speaker intentionality in its capacity to fail and be forged. Let's return for a minute to the signature. We have already established that in order for a signature to work as a signature, i.e. in order for it to be successful in doing the things a signature should do, it has to be repeated. The thing is, however, that if something is repeatable, this means that it will simultaneously become available for failure: if you sign a cheque while drunk, your signature may not match that on your driver's licence; hence it may not be recognized, in which case it will fail and the cheque will not be cashed. So iterability is the condition both for success *and* for failure.

In addition, if something is repeatable, it also becomes available for misuse and forgery. Anyone reading 'Signature Event Context' can learn to sign 'J. Derrida'. Anyone who discovers someone else's computer password can log onto that person's computer. Anyone who gets hold of someone's PIN code can empty that person's bank account. The crucial point is that these forgeries and frauds are not faults, exceptions, misuses or 'abuses' of language. They are, on the contrary, extremely clear examples of precisely the way language works (i.e. the way language signifies). Thus, your signature (or password or PIN code) works not *in spite of* the fact that it can be repeated. It works because it *must* be repeated. But this repetition is also precisely what makes it available for uses that you cannot foresee and cannot control.

The semiotic codes through which desire is manifested are no exception to this general rule. Desire too is available for appropriation and forgery. We know this from cases where men invoke the desire of the Other to claim – disingenuously or not – that they thought the woman they raped desired them, or that they thought the man they killed was coming on to them. In cases like these, the issue of speaker intentionality is not, from a linguistic or interactional perspective, the main point: it is ultimately impossible to be certain of what the raped woman or the murdered man 'really' meant, or of whether the rapist or murderer sincerely believes the story he is telling. What matters is that certain stories can be told in the belief that they will be found credible and convincing. A rapist or murderer *can* claim that he legitimately read desire in the words and actions of his victim, and he *can* surprisingly – distressingly – often receive the understanding and support of judges and juries for that claim. What is it about the way in which desire is encoded and circulated in society that allows these kinds of forgeries to be meaningful, seem reasonable, and produce real social consequences?

The fantasy makers studied by Kira Hall (1995) who we discussed in chapter 3 are also engaged in a kind of forgery. Not only do they use the codes of sex-talk to forge a desire for the caller which they do not feel, they are also using those codes to construct themselves as kinds of people they are not – as women when they are actually men, as heterosexuals when they identify as lesbian, as Black or Latina when really they are white. Of course it is possible to explain the (in this case highly calculated) linguistic choices of the fantasy makers in terms of their intentions; to say for instance that their primary intention is to keep the caller on the line and so maximize their own earnings. What appeals to intention cannot explain, however, is why their 'forged' contributions succeed in conveying particular forms of desire to the callers who use the service. If phone sex comes off as sex for the customer, it is not because of the intentions or the identities of the fantasy makers. It is, rather, because of their skill in exploiting the iterability of signs which conventionally signify, for instance, 'femininity' (words like 'peach' and 'snuggery'), 'subservience' (speaking quietly and at a high pitch) and 'arousal' (breathiness, moaning).

Indeed, the fact that these semiotic resources produce a sexual scene even though callers do not know (and would undoubtedly be disconcerted to discover) the intentions and identities of the fantasy makers reminds us of Judith Butler's observation, noted above, that, like drag queens, we all 'pass' at doing gender, since gender is not expressive but performative. The same is true, of course, of sexuality. Fantasy makers 'pass' as desiring women not because they *are* desiring women, but because they cite the conventional forms of language that desiring women also cite in order to express desire. Their citation of these forms is no different from the way sexuality is achieved in contexts where people do intentionally express desire. Even there, those intentions will be conveyed through the iteration of the same kinds of resources that the fantasy makers exploit in their work.

And even there, there is always the possibility for those utterances to fail or be forged.

It is, in fact, striking how thoroughly the cultural understanding of women's sexuality seems to be bound up with anxiety about forgery and faking – presumably because the codes for signifying heterosexual femininity are so highly stylized as to block any simple distinction between 'real' and 'fake' versions. If we put together the fantasy makers and other sex workers whose interest in their clients is almost always forged, and the women who, like Sally in *When Harry Met Sally*, perform orgasms they are not actually having, it might well seem that there is no reliable way to tell when a heterosexual woman's desire or pleasure is 'authentic'. The degree of anxiety this generates may be more than just a fear on the part of heterosexual men that they are not as desirable or as sexually accomplished as they would like to think. We suggest that stylized performances like those of Sally or the fantasy makers provoke anxiety because they threaten to bring to conscious awareness the iterative structure of sexuality that needs to stay repressed in order for it to 'pass' as sexuality, which is supposed to be 'natural', authentic and spontaneous. If sexuality is revealed as a code of signification dependent on the structures of iterability, how can we believe in the authenticity of any sexual act or encounter? Anxiety about whether your wife really came or whether a prostitute really enjoyed having sex with you (a common fantasy among male clients, which testifies to the strength of their desire for authenticity, and the ability of sex workers to satisfy it) arises from a complicated interplay between the need to believe that a given performance was authentic, the suspicion that it might not have been, and the need to disavow your knowledge that you can never be sure because fake enjoyment is materialized through the same communicative resources as real enjoyment.

Kira Hall reports that certain acquaintances to whom she mentioned her research with the fantasy makers were disappointed and dismayed to hear that they were not all what they pretended to be (young, attractive, heterosexual and female). Similarly, internet users worry about the possibility that the vivacious 18-year-old girl with whom they are having an erotic or romantic exchange in a chat room might in reality be a lonely 65-year-old man. It is clear that people are not, on the whole, indifferent to the real identities and intentions of the others with whom they interact, and, once again, we would not want to suggest that the intentions/identities of language-users are completely irrelevant to an exploration of language and desire. But it is important to be able to understand 'forged' desire as well as the 'real thing'. One of Derrida's criticisms of Austin was that Austin clearly recognized that performatives were subject to failure, and that infelicities were ever-present structural possibilities. But instead of exploring what those failures and abuses teach us about the language phenomenon under scrutiny, Austin defined them as exceptions and excluded them from consideration. We believe that a perspective on language and sexuality that makes intentionality its focus would be endlessly liable to the same error. Consequently, our conclusion is that the central questions about the relationship of language and desire concern the semiotic practices through which desire is verbalized – whether intentionally and sincerely or otherwise.

CONCLUSION

In response to an earlier proposal (Kulick 2000) which outlined some of the arguments we have made in this chapter, Penelope Eckert (2002) has drawn attention to a number of potential pitfalls awaiting the study of language and desire. 'As linguists', she writes (2002: 100), 'our interest in sexuality is in its social life.' The difficulty she sees with desire is that it tends not to be thought of as having a 'social life': it is typically conceived as something purely private and individual. As a result,

It is desire . . . that brings the mystification into the study of sexuality, and it is in contemplating desire that we are inclined to fall into an asocial and naturalized view of sexuality. The challenge, then, is to adopt an approach that focuses on the social mediation of desire: to construct a view of desire that is simultaneously internal and individual, and external and shared. (Eckert 2002: 100)

This is the challenge we have tried to meet in this chapter, by showing how desire can be an object of linguistic inquiry without becoming mystified in the ways Eckert cautions against. We have emphasized throughout our discussion that desire is, indeed, socially mediated. Although we may experience our sexual desires as uniquely personal and intensely private, their form is shaped by social and verbal interaction – including, as we have illustrated, the silences, the explicit and tacit prohibitions that are part of that interaction. It is in the social world that we learn what is desirable, which desires are appropriate for which kinds of people, and which desires are forbidden. The personal ads discussed above, with their non-random patterns of transitivity (professional man seeks attractive woman, gay man with good body seeks similar) provide an excellent précis of what their writers and readers have learned to regard as 'natural' in the realm of sexual attraction. But for all that they may be deeply felt, it is evident these desires have been inculcated socially. Doubtless, too, their formulaic repetition in countless personal ads makes its own contribution to reproducing and naturalizing them.

When desire is expressed or represented in language (and there are many genres and speech events devoted to that purpose, from personal ads to pornography and from high-flown love sonnets to crude locker-room banter), it is intelligible because it draws on codes of signification that circulate within the wider society – in Eckert's terms, they are 'external and shared'. Individuals cannot choose *not* to have their desires understood in terms of prevailing social norms – that is why some women still say 'no' when they would like to say 'yes' (see chapter 2, note 9), and why some men still refuse to take 'no' as a definitive answer.

Of course Keith Harvey and Celia Shalom (1997: 1) have a point when they suggest, following Lacan, that erotic experience always exceeds the capacity of language to represent it. But arguably the same is true of many other human experiences: pain, for instance, which some clinicians encourage their patients to represent using visual images when they find themselves unable to convey the feeling adequately in words. To treat sex as a special case and to avoid the empirical study of desire is to fall into the trap of mystification. Language – used about anything – is not a perfect representation of experience or reality. But because humans are not able to read each other's minds or experience each other's bodily sensations, we depend on language to communicate (or dissemble) what we think and feel and want. Beyond the most basic level (e.g. the infant's cry which we interpret as pain or hunger), others' thoughts, feelings and desires are only accessible to us in a linguistically mediated form. That is one reason for treating the study of language and desire – an investigation of the forms linguistic mediation takes and the consequences it has – as important not just to the study of language and sexuality, but to the study of sexuality itself.

CHAPTER 6

Language and sexuality: theory, research and politics

In the preface, we stated that one of our main purposes in writing this book was to synthesize a diverse body of research into a coherent field that could be called 'Language and Sexuality'. In the course of this text, we have made a number of arguments about the relationship between gender and sexuality, the nature of sexuality, the status of 'identity', and the relevance of language to all those phenomena. In this concluding chapter, we want to draw together the arguments we have been making into a programmatic statement about where we think the field of language and sexuality stands today, and where it might go in the future. What might be the most interesting directions and important questions for future study?

IDENTITY IN CONTEXT

We can begin with the topic that has inspired most recent discussion among linguistic researchers, and which we have dealt with extensively in the previous chapters: the relationship between language use and the construction and display of sexual identities.

One of the main arguments of this book has been that sexual identity is only one aspect of sexuality: the investigation of language and sexuality needs to move beyond an exclusive focus on identity, if it is going to be able to account for the ways in which sexuality is materialized and conveyed through language. At the same time, however, we have stressed that sexual identities are not completely irrelevant to an understanding of language and sexuality. Identity categories like 'gay', 'lesbian', 'straight' – or *travesti*, *hijra* or *batut* – are clearly salient ones for many people in particular societies. As social positionings that individuals claim, or avoid claiming, or are prevented from claiming, the question is not whether these identities deserve our scrutiny. The question, instead, is what kinds of scrutiny are most illuminating.

We noted in chapter 4 that there has been a tendency for research on language and sexual identity to concentrate on 'minority' identities – those which depart from the mainstream heterosexual norm – and attention has been given in particular to studying the linguistic behaviour of people who identify as gay or lesbian. The linguistic construction of heterosexual identities has not attracted the same interest: where it has been the focus of research it has tended to be discussed as an aspect of gendered linguistic behaviour. Without denying the very close connection between gendered and heterosexual identities (see chapter 3, and the discussion of gender below), in this book we have argued that the study of language and sexuality (or more narrowly, of language and sexual identity) should not be synonymous with the study of those speakers who identify as non-heterosexuals. It should take heterosexual linguistic behaviour as an object of interest in its own right. We are aware, however, that some scholars in the field take a different view, for reasons that are as much political as theoretical. We will therefore return to this issue below in a section devoted specifically to the politics of studying language and sexuality.

Much of the research on minority identities has been done among members of affluent urbanized Western societies – which is not really surprising, since it is in these societies that gay and lesbian lifestyles are most visible and indeed most feasible. The idea that one can base an identity or a lifestyle on same- versus other-sex sexual preference does not have currency or legitimacy in all cultures. However, a number of linguists and anthropologists have turned their attention to the linguistic dimensions of non-mainstream sexual identities that are recognized in cultural traditions other than those of Europe and the USA (e.g. Frank 2002; Gaudio 1997; Hall and O'Donovan 1996; Mark Johnson 1997; Kulick 1998; Manalansan 1995; Wong 2002). Clearly, it is important for the study of language and sexuality to continue to develop its comparative or cross-cultural dimension. This is not only a question of avoiding ethno- and anglo-centrism (though it is partly this as well, of course). It is also a way to enhance theoretical understandings of sexuality as a social construct, by analysing the different ways in which it is constructed in differing social and cultural conditions.

The relationship between linguistic behaviour and the specific social conditions in which speakers use language is an issue that could bear closer examination in Western contexts too. Western researchers working in communities they belong to or know well do not always provide much detailed sociological or ethnographic description of the particular community whose language-use is the object of study. We are told that we are reading about, say, white middle-class gay men living in Washington D.C. (Leap 1996a) or middle-aged lesbians located in Berkeley, California, and Colombus, Ohio (Moonwomon 1995), but we are not always given any fine-grained analysis of what it means, specifically, to be a member of that group of queers and not some other group of queers. Although ideas like 'the gay and lesbian community' or 'the transgendered community' are important political and rhetorical constructs for many gay men, lesbians and transgendered individuals, terms of this kind denote what Benedict Anderson (1983) calls 'imagined communities' (see chapter 2), encompassing a considerable variety of actual communities with their own particular local histories and ways of life. There is, for example, a world of difference between the London lesbian separatists who are the subject of anthropologist Sarah Green's study *Urban Amazons* (Green 1997), and the women recruited in San Francisco by sociologist Arlene Stein for her study of lesbian experience over two generations, *Sex and Sensibility* (Stein 1997). In Green's work, a great deal of attention is given to the specifics of the place, time and political context; Stein grounds her analysis in her subjects' life histories. By contrast, the people who appear in sociolinguistic studies sometimes seem to participate in a sort of generalized gay/lesbian lifestyle located everywhere and nowhere.

It is worth pointing out that community-based studies like Leap's *Word's Out* (1996a), which describes norms of everyday talk among a particular class of gay men in a particular time and place, are still rare. Most studies of gay or queer language-use are studies of single speakers/events (e.g. Podesva *et al*. 2002; C. T. White 1998), highly stylized and deliberate performances of queerness (e.g. Barrett 1995), fictional representations of the speech of queers (e.g. Queen 1997) or textual devices used in queer writing (e.g. Frank 2002). We do not question the legitimacy of analysing these kinds of data – indeed there are purposes for which they are particularly apt. But if we are interested in the linguistic behaviour of a group of people defined by their sexual identity, it is surely important to investigate how that identity is or is not made relevant across a range of situations, from the rituals in which it is most likely to be salient (e.g. placing a personal ad or participating in a drag performance) to the most mundane encounters of everyday life.

Another thing that is important if one is interested in the linguistic behaviour of a group of people is to distinguish between *ideology* – the representations of social types and their ways of speaking and writing which circulate in a given society – and *practice* – what we observe when we investigate the behaviour of real people in real situations. As Wong *et al*. explain: 'the "gay speech" that many have endeavoured to identify is an ideological construct which symbolizes the imagined "gay community"' (2002: 4). As we argued in chapter 4, 'gay speech' should not be taken as a descriptive generalization about the behaviour of real individuals in particular gay communities, for those individuals may not in practice display the speech characteristics that make up the ideological construct. For instance, lisping is part of a stereotypical representation of gay men's speech in English, but in practice, as opposed to ideology, not all gay men lisp and not all speakers who lisp are gay men.

The point of insisting on this distinction is not to eliminate 'unscientific' stereotypes (ideology) from linguistic scholarship so we can concentrate on discovering the true facts about how people really speak (practice). Both ideology and practice are real social phenomena; each of them is interesting, and the study of language and any form of identity is to a considerable extent the study of the relationship between them. The question is how speakers 'take up' the ideological resources available in a given community to construct identities for themselves in practice. The capacity of speech to index membership of particular groups (so that speakers are recognizable to large numbers of others as, for instance, 'northerners', 'hip-hoppers', 'valley girls', 'nerds' or 'queers') clearly depends on shared representations which associate particular ways of speaking with particular social locations and social meanings (northerners are 'bluff', valley girls 'dumb', nerds 'socially inept', etc.). This shared resource can be used by group members to construct recognizable identities as northerners / valley girls / nerds (it also enables people who are not members of those groups to imitate their voices for effect). But real speakers in real situations do not just reproduce familiar linguistic stereotypes. In practice they use ideological resources in complex and creative ways.

A specific case of this kind is discussed in a recent article by Podesva, Roberts and Campbell-Kibler (2002). In a close phonetic analysis of the speech of a gay activist and lawyer speaking on a radio discussion programme about anti-gay discrimination, the researchers argue that this speaker is performing a particular version of gay identity they dub 'non-flamboyant'. He produces some phonetic features that offer clues to his gay identity, but consistently avoids the more stereotypical features of the ideological construct 'gay speech'. Podesva *et al.* suggest that this can be explained in terms of the particularities of the context: while the speaker's gay identity is clearly relevant (he is certainly not trying to conceal it), his professional identity as someone knowledgeable about the law is no less so. He needs, therefore, to find a way of speaking that projects a competent and serious, 'lawyerly' gay identity rather than indexing the stereotypical social meanings many outsiders associate with 'gay speech', such as flamboyance, frivolity and sexual promiscuity. As the authors comment: 'While speaking to potentially hostile audiences, activists often construct themselves *in opposition* to these images' (2002: 187, emphasis added). According to this argument, the ideological representation of gay men's speech is a resource the lawyer uses in his linguistic practice, but not in the sense that he models his performance on it. Rather, consciously or not, he designs his performance *against* it, in the hope of deflecting the 'flamboyant' associations he believes it has for mainstream radio listeners.

Studies of fictional and other highly stylized performances of sexual identity – such as Robin Queen's (1997) analysis of the speech of the lesbian comic-book character Hothead Paisan – are most revealing about the ideological resources available to speakers. Empirical studies of naturally occurring speech – like Podesva *et al.*'s analysis of the lawyer's speech – tell us more about what is done with those resources in everyday social and linguistic practice. Both types of study are important; but arguably there is a particular need for more studies in which the practices of groups of people in particular social contexts, localities and networks are studied in depth and over time. We do not underestimate the practical difficulties this may entail. Working with people whose identities carry a stigma in mainstream society requires the researcher to put a great deal of effort into negotiating access, building rapport and developing trust. The kind of research we are advocating is time- and labour-intensive, and thus dependent on a level of institutional support (both financial and 'moral') that may not be easy to access, particularly in an area of inquiry that is still considered in some quarters to be 'marginal' or of dubious academic respectability. (In our experience this kind of prejudice is not as widespread as it once was, but Queen (2002) reminds us that it remains an issue, especially for less established scholars in the process of developing professional careers.)

PROBLEMS OF IDENTITY

In chapter 4 we discussed Judith Butler's call to shift away from accounts framed in terms of what she calls the 'epistemological subject', and towards accounts in which identity is viewed as the effect (rather than the origin) of practices of signification. As we also observed in that chapter, a number of scholars studying language and identity have begun to respond to that call. Traditionally, sociolinguists talked about people, in their linguistic behaviour, 'marking' identities that by implication were already established and fixed. Today many would rather talk about identities being 'constructed' or 'performed' using linguistic resources. To that extent, sociolinguistics has adopted a more complicated view than it used to have of the relationship between language and what one collection of articles called 'the socially constructed self' (Hall and Bucholtz 1995).

Yet focusing, as we have in this book, on questions about the *sexual* self prompts us to question whether even this more complicated and constructionist approach to identity is sufficient, or whether we need to go further. 'Identity' still tends to suggest a kind of conscious claim-staking by a subject who knows exactly who s/he is, or wants to be (or who s/he isn't and doesn't want to be). Let us clarify that sociolinguists have never suggested speakers are conscious of all the nuances of linguistic behaviour through which identity is signified. Their behaviour cannot in most cases be thought of as intentional and deliberate: it is highly unlikely that people plan such behaviours as convergence (where a speaker alters the statistical frequency of certain linguistic variants in their speech in order to sound more similar to the person they are talking to) or code-switching (where bilingual speakers alternate between the two or more languages in their repertoire). Bilinguals who code-switch cannot always say what motivated them to do so at a given moment: many report that they typically have no awareness from moment to moment of which language they are actually speaking. If convergence and code-switching were conscious choices that people had to stop and make decisions about each time they began to speak, conversation would proceed at a glacial pace. However, sociolinguists do assume that speakers are conscious of the identities which are constructed through behaviours like convergence and code-switching. Even if they are not fully aware of all the means they are using to do it, language users in some sense are intending to present themselves as the particular kinds of people who use language in those particular kinds of ways.

Up to a point, there is nothing wrong with this. People do stake claims to identity by talking in particular ways. They do want, and sometimes deliberately try, to sound like, for instance, 'a local', 'a posh person' or indeed 'a queer'. (Or in the case of the lawyer/activist studied by Podesva *et al.*, 'queer but not too queer'.) But there may also be elements in a person's self which are not underpinned by this kind of more-or-less conscious allegiance to a particular social position. To get at what we mean by this, we want to make a distinction between *identity* and *identification*.

Identification is a psychoanalytic concept concerned with the operations through which a subject is constituted. Identifications are processes through which individuals assimilate an aspect or property of an other, and are, in that process, transformed (for a concise summary, see Laplanche and Pontalis 1973: 205–8). A crucial difference between 'identity' and 'identification' is that identifications are not entirely conscious. On the contrary, identifications are structured just as much by rejections, refusals and disavowals as they are structured by affirmations. In addition, identifications are not imagined to constitute a coherent relational system. In other words, the processes that constitute an individual as a certain kind of subject are not harmonious. Rather, they are conflicting and contradictory, undermining conscious attempts to produce and maintain subjective coherence and consistency. It follows that a person's claim to a particular *identity* could be disrupted or contradicted by *identifications* s/he is unaware or unconscious of.

Like many other phenomena theorized by psychoanalysis, identifications often manifest themselves in people's behaviour not directly, but through inconsistencies, contradictions, incoherences, gaps and silences. These, we have argued, are aspects of language that merit examination under the heading of language and sexuality. At several points in this book, and especially in chapter 5 when we discussed repression, we suggested that what is or can be said is structured in important ways by what is not or cannot be said. We gave examples of how refusals to acknowledge particular relationships, desires or identities does not make them go away. Quite the opposite, refusal is a means of sustaining desire, maintaining relationships and constituting identities, even ones that individuals do not explicitly recognize or embrace. As Judith Butler (1993a: 113) has noted, 'a radical refusal to identify with a given position suggests that on some level an identification has already taken place, an identification that is made and disavowed'. So fraternity brothers' refusal to acknowledge the possibility of homosexual desire in their homosocial group involves an identification with homosexuals that structures their homophobic discourse. White disavowal of any affinity with or desire for blackness is an identification with or for blackness that constitutes an important structuring feature of racist discourse. Cases like these illustrate identifications that are not or cannot be expressed, but that nevertheless are crucial in the constitution of particular subject positions. They also illustrate the way that particular kinds of language are facilitated or blocked by more than speakers' explicitly claimed identities. Hence, to analyse people's use of language only in relation to identities that they consciously claim, or consciously avoid claiming, is to miss much of what animates and sustains the relationship between language and sexuality.

DESIRE, IDENTITY, POWER

Our concern to complicate and move beyond identity as a framework for investigating language and sexuality led us to the notion of desire. As we noted in chapter 5, 'desire' encompasses more than just the preference for partners of the same or the other sex: it also deals with the non-intentional, non-conscious and non-rational dimensions of human sexual life. The unconscious and irrational aspects of sexuality may not be manifested on the surface of people's behaviour in the same way that their behaviour displays the sexual identities they have consciously chosen ('gay', 'lesbian', 'straight', etc.). Following scholars like Michael Billig (1999), however, we have tried to show that they are nevertheless accessible to linguistic investigation. Although they have traditionally been conceptualized as the products of unobservable, internal mental processes, it is possible to reconceive them – and study them – as social and interactional accomplishments.

At the same time, it is important to acknowledge that desire is materialized and conveyed through semiotic resources that are variably distributed among members of the societies in which they are used. As Penelope Eckert (2002) has observed, there will be structured variation in people's use of what we have called the 'social semiotic of desire', because different kinds of people are socialized to desire different things, and/or to express their desires in different ways.

There are some cases where semiotic resources for expressing desire are specific to a particular sexual subculture: examples include the sado-masochist 'safe word' convention (see chapter 2), and the 'handkerchief code' used in certain sexual subcultures to signify preferred sexual roles and activities. Outsiders to the relevant subcultures may be unable to decipher the meaning of a sudden utterance of 'Pickle!' or the display of a brown handkerchief; they may not even perceive these as meaningful communications.

However, variation does not typically take the above form of different subcultures expressing desire through distinctive codes which are not shared with others. More typically, the code itself *is* shared, but there are non-random and meaningful differences in the way it is used by different groups of people (a familiar analogy would be the way a single language, say English, is spoken differently by people from different regions or social classes).

A simple illustration of structured linguistic variation resulting from differentiation in what particular groups of people desire is provided by the case of personal ads (see chapter 5). Personal ads placed by men seeking men, women seeking men, women seeking women and men seeking women make use of the same basic template – the conventions for the genre 'personal ad' are a shared semiotic resource. But analysts have been able to demonstrate that if we look more closely at the linguistic choices advertisers make when 'filling in' the template, there are consistent and meaningful differences among the four possible subtypes. For instance, there is significantly more reference to the respondent's physical characteristics in ads placed by gay men than in ads placed by lesbians. The different choices gay men and lesbians make index differences in what these two groups of advertisers desire. A more complex example is the way sexual invitations and refusals are construed (see chapters 2 and 5). Though women and men may have the same desires (e.g. to invite another to have sex, to say 'yes' to sex or to say 'no' to sex), there is variation in the way they are expected to express those desires (e.g. women are not expected to make propositions or say 'yes' directly to others' propositions). Whatever they do say is liable to be interpreted with reference to these gendered conventions (e.g. a woman who says 'no' to sex may be interpreted as not really meaning to refuse). Clearly, the social differentiation and distribution of desire and its linguistic reflexes (who uses which semiotic resources in what contexts and with what degree of frequency) is an important issue for sociolinguists to explore.

Desire is also an important issue for those scholars whose interest in language and sexuality reflects their commitment to a radical sexual politics; for there is a close connection between desire and power. Consider, for instance, Eckert's observation that

Girls develop a desire to look up at a boyfriend. They see themselves leaning against his shoulder, him having to lean down to kiss her, or to whisper in her ear. They learn to be scared so they can have him protect them; they learn to cry so he can dry their tears. This concentration of desire is perhaps the most powerful force in the maintenance of the gender order. (Eckert 2002: 109)

As we saw in chapter 3, Eckert's recent work has explored the ways in which heteronormativity shapes the forms of gender identity and behaviour that are adopted by young people as they move towards adulthood. In pre-adolescence, the desire that impels girls to take on the trappings of hetero-sexual femininity is not really a desire for sex, or even (except as a means to other ends) a desire to be desired by members of the other sex. It has more to do with a desire to be seen as age-appropriate, which is a pre-requisite to getting and keeping the acceptance and respect of other girls within their peer groups. In time, though, many or most girls will begin to invest emotionally and sexually in a gender order which subordinates them. They will come to eroticize such masculine qualities as size, strength, authority and forcefulness; since heterosexuality is framed as an attraction of opposites, that also means they will want to display the complementary qualities – weakness, subservience and passivity – themselves. This configuration of desire finds expression in a kind of communicative performance (the upward gaze, the angling of the head to receive a man's whispered utterances, the performances of fearfulness or sadness that seek protective or comforting responses) that is not just culturally 'feminine', but is more specifically the performance of a heterosexual woman relating intimately to a man. The repetition of this kind of performance, and of the gratification it affords, reproduces and naturalizes the power relations on which conventional heterosexuality is based.

This is not the only example we could give of the connection between desire and power. We could also mention the link between 'disavowed' desires for prohibited objects and expressions of hatred for a sexual Other – the homophobia displayed by the fraternity brothers we discussed in chapter 3, or the violence associated with so-called 'homosexual panic'. However, Eckert's observation that conventional forms of heterosexual desire reproduce gender inequality is an important one. It bears on the question we raised in chapter 1, about the 'special relationship' between sexuality and gender.

SEXUALITY AND GENDER

In this book we have tried not to treat the study of language and sexuality as just a sub-branch of or a footnote to the study of language and gender. Yet while gender does not subsume sexuality, it is clear that no absolute separation between them is possible. Any investigation of either will involve the other as well. Whenever sexuality is at issue, gender is also at issue – and, importantly, vice versa.

Since desiring subjects and desired objects are never genderless, you cannot 'do sexuality' without at the same time 'doing gender'. 'Homosexual' and 'heterosexual' (and 'bisexual' and 'transexual') appear to be categories that cut across gender divisions; but gender makes all the difference in the world to how the categories are actually inhabited. A heterosexual woman and a heterosexual man are axiomatically expected to be different rather than similar – more exactly, they are supposed to *complement* one another, and this principle of complementarity underpins the norms of acceptable behaviour for each group. This is as true of linguistic norms as of any other social norms. Normatively, for instance, men make sexual propositions and women accept or refuse them; men brag about their sexual exploits (an example is Kiesling 2002 on the 'fuck stories' told by fraternity brothers at their weekly meetings) while women go to great lengths to avoid being labelled 'sluts'.

Lesbians and gay men are not involved in this structural relationship of complementarity, but they too are clearly distinct categories from a sociolinguistic point of view. Even those who believe in the existence of a gay or queer language do not usually suggest that this hypothetical variety is shared by gay men and lesbians. The closest anyone has come to proposing a common basis for queer speech styles regardless of the speaker's gender is the suggestion made by the scholars we discussed at the end of chapter 4: Rusty Barrett (1997), Keith Harvey (2000a) and Robin Queen (1997). These linguists argue that queer speech involves the juxtaposition of incongruous elements. The specific juxtapositions noted by Barrett and Harvey in gay male speech and by Queen in lesbian comic-book dialogue are not, however, the same ones.

But if gender is always implicated in any performance of sexuality, the converse is also true: where gender is at issue, sexuality will also be at issue. This point is less often made than the previous one, and is perhaps more controversial. It is easier to see sexuality as always gendered than to see gender as always and necessarily sexualized. But the work of scholars like Penelope Eckert underscores the crucial role played by heteronormativity, and the desires it engenders, in structuring masculinity and femininity as we know them. Even 'deviant' performances of gender often exhibit a logic that has to do with desire. Recall the Brazilian travestis described in chapter 1, males who take women's names, use feminine pronouns to refer to one another, and painstakingly construct feminized bodies using hormones and industrial silicone (but retain their male genitals). The travestis are not, in their own eyes, enacting a female identity, but a homosexual one: they are motivated by their desire to be desired by masculine men. Or, think of the lesbian 'butch', whose masculine appearance and persona is designed not to communicate that she is or wants to be a man (as we noted in chapter 4, note 7, in some lesbian communities historically there was a distinction between butches and 'passing women', who did actually live as men), but rather to appeal to her preferred object of desire, the 'fem'. Take away the sexual element in gender, and these ways of gendering oneself become difficult to comprehend.

All this suggests that just as researchers of language and sexuality cannot ignore the work that has been done in language and gender studies (or, more generally, the insights of feminist/gender theory), so researchers of language and gender need to pay attention to issues – and theories – of sexuality. Of course, we do not mean to imply that this is not already being done: some of the research we have cited in earlier chapters, such as Penelope Eckert's work on the heterosexual market and Kira Hall's study of telephone sex workers, are good examples of how linguists can theorize the relationship of gender to sexuality and of both to language. But there is still a tendency to put gender and sexuality in separate boxes, and to focus on only one when both are relevant. Leap's *Word's Out*, for instance, announces itself as a study of 'gay men's English', but once it has been made clear that the study is about men, their gender ceases to be an issue in the analysis. The opposite tendency is even more pervasive: countless studies have dealt with gender and gender difference while neglecting to mention sexuality – unless to note in passing that all the subjects were heterosexual, and suggest (often without argument or evidence) that the findings might therefore not apply to lesbians / gay men. Possibly the most remarkable example of this phenomenon is Deborah Tannen's *You Just Don't Understand* (1990), the most successful book about language and gender ever written by a professional linguist. Anyone who has read the book will know that it is fundamentally about communication problems between women and men in heterosexual relationships; but the topic of sexuality is never explicitly raised.

SEXUALITY AND DIFFERENCE

Although we have argued that there is a special relationship between sexuality and gender, it is also important to consider the ways in which sexuality – whether viewed from the perspective of identity or desire – will also be inflected by other kinds of socially salient differences, for instance those of race, ethnicity, generation, class and culture. It is evident, for instance, that differences of race, age or class may be extremely important in some people's erotic lives, and that in certain cultural and historical contexts the desire for particular kinds of difference has been more than just a personal idiosyncrasy: it has been socially institutionalized. A banal example is the way heterosexual desire, in addition to being invested in gender difference, also tends to be structured by age difference (in the unmarked case older men are paired with younger women). In classical Greece, male homosexual desire too was organized around generational difference (as we noted in chapter 4 (see note 1), this 'pederastic' model has also been important for some homosexual subcultures in the modern era). In some times and places, class differences have been widely and overtly eroticized, one of the best known examples being the upper-class male homosexual taste for 'rough trade', i.e. working-class men, which was common in Britain before the decriminalization of homosexuality. In addition to examples like these, the fact that there is significant demand for sex (both hetero- and homo-) with a racial or ethnic Other in contemporary Western societies is suggested by the many advertisements for prostitutes' services that emphasize ethnic characteristics, as well as by the existence of mass market pornographic titles catering to particular racial/ethnic tastes.

The eroticizing of socially salient differences is plainly not neutral with respect to power. It is not only that race, class and generation are themselves axes of power, but also that crossing these significant social boundaries transgresses prohibitions and taboos, and thus can enable the transgressor to feel powerful – even if s/he takes the subordinate rather than the dominant position in a fantasy scenario involving marked power asymmetry. Nick Broomfield's 1996 documentary *Fetishes*, filmed in a New York establishment that specializes in scenarios of dominance and submission, includes a scene with a Jewish client who wants to be humiliated by a sex worker (called 'mistresses' or 'goddesses' here) dressed in Nazi uniform. Prior to the client's session, he is interviewed by one of the establishment's mistresses, who explains that the nature of the session he has requested makes it important for them to know something about his background. After determining whether the client is indeed Jewish, and whether he had any grandparents or close family members who died in the concentration camps ('distant family, distant', he says), the following interaction occurs:

[M = mistress, C = client]

M: OK, very good. If you don't mind – you can talk to me freely...It's very important for these fantasies that goddess Natasha [the mistress who will conduct the client's session] and us to figure out to which intensity, which intensity is good for you. Uh, could you tell me more about which fantasies you like?

C: Well, yes, I have uh/like to be verbally humiliated, I like a lot of humiliation.

M: To which intensity? Is 'Jewboy' enough? Or do you need something more intense like 'you motherfucking Jew', 'you Jew pig'?

C: Uh, it can get, it can get moderate to heavy.

M: Moderate to heavy?

C: Moderate to heavy.

M: OK, so racial slurs?

C: Yes that's fine.

M: Racial slurs and so on? OK, the setting, which kind of setting do you want? Do you want basically 1940s, 1940s Germany kind of setting? Do you want neo-Nazi kind of setting? Concentration camp kind of setting?

c: Uh, 1940s, the neo-Nazi. I don't think the concentration camp *per se* ((M: is too much?)) I think may be too much. I think the whole idea that the Nazis thought they were the superior race and that they wanted to persecute the Jews.

m: OK the goddess being part of a superior Aryan race and you being a lowlife ((inaudible)) Jew.

c: Exactly.

This is a case where an individual gains erotic satisfaction from being positioned in the role of racial subordinate and victim (another scene in the film features an African-American man who pays to enact the part of a plantation slave). In this context (and in absolute contrast with a real concentration camp, or a real slave plantation) it is possible that the client also gains some sense of mastery over the anxiety produced by this positioning, by virtue of being in control of the scenario. It is worth noting that language is central both to the construction of these kinds of scenarios, and to the client's sense of being in control of them: he is made responsible for scripting the encounter before it even begins, and in ensuing dialogue that we do not reproduce here, he is given a 'safe word' by the mistress, so that he can stop the session in case the abuse he has requested becomes too intense.

In scenarios like the ones shown in *Fetishes*, the erotic significance of racialized power differences is made explicit. Elsewhere, there is often a less readily acknowledged sexual component in hatred directed towards a class or racial Other. An obvious example of this would be the practice of lynching in the southern USA during the era of racial segregation. The victims of lynching were African-American men who were persistently imagined by their white tormentors as a sexual threat to the 'purity' of white women. Rape in war is arguably another case in point, symbolizing not only the dominance of men over women but also the dominance of men of one ethnic or national group over the men of the group they are fighting.

The racialization of sexuality and the sexualization of race is not, to our knowledge, a topic many linguistic researchers have as yet taken up, despite the preoccupation of many scholars with issues of identity and difference. (Exceptions include Rusty Barrett's (1995, 1998) work on African-American drag performances, Kira Hall's (1995) observations about the racial/ethnic 'cross-expressing' engaged in by telephone sex workers in order to satisfy the racialized erotic desires of their clients, and Rudolph Gaudio's (2001) discussion of his conversations about race and sexual practice with Nigerian *'yan daudu*, 'men who act like women'.) Most discussions of the issue focus on representations of sexuality – in other words, on ideology rather than practice – and language as such is rarely the main focus of attention. It is evident that representations of sexuality (whether homo- or hetero-), in literature, cinema, verbal and visual pornography, are inflected significantly by racist ideologies. Asian women, for example, are often represented through orientalist discourses which credit them with a hyper-feminine desire to please men sexually and an encyclopaedic knowledge of the mysteries contained in texts like the *Kama Sutra*. Black men, on the other hand, are often represented as hyper-masculine – oversexed and dangerous, particularly to white women. As critics like Frantz Fanon (1986 [1952]) and Marlon Riggs (1989) have argued, the existence of these ideological representations is a factor shaping the performance of non-white sexual identities. Just as the gay lawyer described by Podesva *et al.* must attempt to neutralize his audience's assumptions about gay 'flamboyance', so members of racial and ethnic minorities may have to negotiate ideological presuppositions about their sexual desires, intentions, preferences and prowess.

Such negotiations do sometimes occur in public settings. The relationship of sexuality and race was clearly a major issue, for instance, in such high-profile recent events as the O. J. Simpson murder trial and the Anita Hill / Clarence Thomas hearings, both of which have been discussed by linguists (e.g. Lakoff 2000; Mendoza-Denton 1995). It can also be an issue in more ephemeral encounters. Once, in the London Underground, one of us (the one who is a white woman) was addressed by a young Black man who had run up behind her: he said, 'Don't worry, I'm not going to hurt you, I'm just trying to catch my train.' Exchanges like this may seem trivial, but analysing them sheds light on the phenomenon we might call 'banal racism', by analogy with Michael Billig's term 'banal nationalism' (Billig 1995), referring to the way people often make the category of the nation relevant in discourse which is not explicitly 'nationalist' (for instance, by producing clichés like 'it's a free country' when giving in to somebody's seemingly eccentric desires). In the London Underground case, we can observe that the utterance of 'I'm not going to hurt you' presupposes that it is likely the addressee assumes that the speaker wants to hurt them (it is, for instance, a cliché in film and TV dialogue where the speaker is pointing a gun at the addressee). To make sense of it in this context, both parties have to draw on assumptions about race, gender and sexuality – they are 'made relevant' even though none of them is mentioned explicitly. The speaker has positioned himself in relation to a sexualized racist discourse representing Black men as dangerous to white women, and has interpolated his white woman addressee as someone likely to read his intentions in terms of that discourse.

The general point here is that studying the social differentiation of desire is not just a matter of attending to the most obvious variables, namely gender and sexual orientation. Sexuality is inflected by other social differences. How this plays out in linguistic practice is a question in need of further research.

THEORY AND SEXUALITY

One sign of the emergence of language and sexuality as a 'mature' field of inquiry is the attention now being given by linguistic researchers to the question of how to theorize sexuality, and whether theoretical ideas originating outside linguistics can be helpful in thinking about linguistic phenomena. Not surprisingly, much recent discussion of this issue has focused in particular on the usefulness or otherwise of queer theory. Livia and Hall's *Queerly Phrased* (1997a) opens with an editors' introduction that can be read as a kind of manifesto for queer theory in sociolinguistics. As we observed in chapter 5, however, Anna Livia in her more recent work (Livia 2002) has taken a much more sceptical view. In this she is not alone: in the first half of Campbell-Kibler *et al.*'s volume *Language and Sexuality* (2002) the pros and cons of queer theory are debated at some length, revealing a spectrum of possible positions on the issue among currently active researchers.

Our own view is that queer theory does have something to offer students of language and sexuality, but it is important to try to be clear about what we do and do not mean by that, because there is considerable potential for confusion about the term 'queer theory' itself. In both everyday speech and academic writing, there is a tendency to use 'queer theory' as though it referred to a single, coherent theory about which everyone was in agreement. In fact, though, there is no single 'queer theory', nor, as we observed in chapter 2, is there consensus about the exact meaning and scope of the term 'queer'. Scholars working with the term 'queer' enjoy pointing out that 'queer' denotes that which exceeds definition, that which is undefinable. It is a signifier without a signified. Historian David Halperin defines 'queer' by saying '[t]here is nothing in particular to which it necessarily refers' (1995: 62). Lauren Berlant and Michael Warner (1998: 558) explain the term by asserting that it is 'a space of entrances, exits, unsystematized lines of acquaintance, projected horizons, typifying examples, alternative routes, blockages, incommensurate geographies'.

There is arguably something to be said for a term that seems to have built-in ambiguity, leading anyone who uses it or hears it to question what exactly it means. This semiotic instability ideally promotes critical awareness that the terms we use to describe and orient ourselves in the world are human creations with particular (and changing) histories, values, and relations to power. What is 'queer' for you may not be 'queer' for someone else: realizing this and trying to understand the ways in which different understandings and uses of 'queer' circulate in conversations, political movements or theoretical discussions can lead to a heightened sense of the political work that all seemingly descriptive labels perform. But there is a disadvantage too. Speakers and writers who use the term 'queer' are seldom explicit about their own understandings of the term. Thus when a scholar claims to embrace or reject queer theory, it is often unclear what that scholar is referring to.

So let us be explicit. When we use the term 'queer theory', we mean a kind of theoretical discourse embodying critical perspectives (note the plural) on heteronormativity, which we defined in chapter 3 as those structures, institutions, relations and actions that promote and produce heterosexuality as natural, self-evident, desirable, privileged and necessary. We also noted there that, the name notwithstanding, queer theory is not exclusively concerned with people defined as 'queer' (usually this means homosexual, bisexual and transexual). It is crucial to examine those groups in order to understand (a) the ways in which particular types of identities are produced as problematic and unintelligible, and (b) the ways in which subjects who assume those identities engage in both oppositional and recuperative practices. But many heterosexuals are also queer – men and women who never marry, women with lovers or husbands who are much younger than themselves, women who openly reject motherhood as an option, men who purchase sex from women, women who sell sex to men, to name just a few examples. Queer theory will also focus on heterosexual queers and investigate how they come to be constituted as such. More generally, queer theory is concerned to investigate critically those processes that produce sexed bodies, sexual relations and – importantly – sexual desires. At present, the hegemonic modality through which bodies, relations and desires are made intelligible is heterosexuality: understanding the processes that maintain the hegemony of heterosexuality requires attention to be given not only to the cases in which bodies/relations/desires 'deviate' from the norm, but also to those cases in which they do not.

In practice, the version of queer theory that we find to be most helpful is performativity theory, as elaborated by Judith Butler. A point we have emphasized in this connection, though, is the need to distinguish between *performativity* and *performance*. Sociolinguists are interested in 'performance' in the sense of 'what real people in real social contexts really do with language': this is one of the things that distinguish them from practitioners of 'formal' linguistics, who focus on the abstract properties of language systems rather than the concrete uses to which language is put. Undoubtedly, the study of language and sexuality involves observing and describing particular linguistic performances: in the course of this book we have described, or reproduced others' descriptions of, performances of sexual identity, intimacy, desire, fear and loathing, consent and non-consent. But we have also talked about 'performativity', meaning the underlying conditions that make performance possible, or by virtue of which a given performance does or does not succeed. To say that 'gender / sexual identity / desire is performative' does not mean the same as 'it is performed'. Indeed, if 'performed' is interpreted in its everyday sense to mean a kind of deliberate play-acting, it is obviously unsatisfactory: most of us, most of the time, are not aware of performing anything in this highly self-conscious way. What we are doing, however, is materializing gender / sexual identity / desire by re-peating, consciously or not, the acts that conventionally signify 'femininity' or 'butchness' or 'flirting'. Performativity theory focuses attention on the codes of signification that underlie particular performances, and so chal-lenges the common-sense perception that our verbal and other behaviour is merely a 'natural' expression of our essential selves. For Judith Butler, identity is not the origin but the effect of practices of signification: this is an approach that should appeal, in our view, to researchers for whom language and communication are primary concerns.

Linguists and other social scientists are often suspicious of the kinds of post-structuralist or postmodernist theory in which language is viewed as constitutive of both social and psychic life; queer theory in Butler's formulation is a case in point. To say that language is 'constitutive', however, is not necessarily to indulge in the kind of extreme linguistic determinism that (justifiably) prompts scepticism among most contemporary linguists. We might recall here Michael Billig's (1999) argument that every prohibition implies its opposite: ordering a little boy who plays hopscotch not to act like a fag provides that boy with information both about how non-fags act, *and* about how fags act. Language constitutes reality here not by determining how the boy will turn out – chastising him as a fag will not in and of itself ensure that he does not become one – but by reproducing the categorization scheme ('fag/non-fag') in relation to which he must position himself. As we noted in chapter 2, the production and labelling of categories is a key function of language in relation to sexuality. That, we would argue, is a reason for the field of language and sexuality studies to take seriously those critical theoretical approaches in which language is given a constitutive role.

The interests that led us to write a book about language and sexuality are political as well as intellectual. In this last main section of our concluding chapter we want to comment more explicitly on the political significance of the arguments we have pursued.

As we noted at the beginning of this chapter, the most sustained argument we have made is for an approach to language and sexuality that encompasses questions about desire as well as identity. Some commentators found an earlier formulation of this proposal (Kulick 2000) politically problematic. Robin Queen (2002), for example, expresses concern that moving away from identity categories like 'lesbian' and 'gay' may be depoliticizing, because it 'decentres' the categories around which radical sexual movements are organized. We do not dispute that these categories matter politically: we believe they will continue to matter for the foreseeable future. But desire also matters politically. We have already quoted Penelope Eckert's observation that heterosexual desire is 'perhaps the most powerful force in the maintenance of the gender order' (2002: 109). To the extent that other kinds of power difference can and do become objects of desire and sources of erotic pleasure, the point is applicable to the maintenance of the social order more generally.

Whereas a focus on sexual identity categories will tend to direct attention to one particular hierarchical relationship – between those who approximate the heteronormative ideal and those who do not, or in cruder terms between heterosexuals and non-heterosexuals – a focus on desire has the potential to direct attention to the workings of power across a wider range of social relations and differences (e.g. of gender, generation, race/ethnicity, class). Of course we want to retain a sense of the particular ways in which sexual minority groups are subordinated and oppressed. But we also want to recognize that groups defined on the basis of sexual identity are not internally homogeneous; power relations exist within them as well as between them; and relations between them can be more complex than is suggested by the equation 'straight = powerful, gay/lesbian = powerless'.[1]

We also want, as we explained in the preface to this book, to take a critical stance in relation to certain preoccupations of contemporary identity politics, with its emphasis on celebrating 'authentic' and 'positive' forms of self-expression. Exploring the relationship between desire and various dimensions of power enables us to explore those aspects of sexuality (for instance, those involving hatred and violence, directed to others or to oneself) which are experienced as negative or have negative social consequences.

What makes the study of *language* and desire political? In common with other proponents of 'critical' (politically committed) approaches to language across the social sciences, we take it that the workings of power can be illuminated by close analysis of linguistic data. Relations of dominance and subordination are not just 'there', but have to be 'accomplished', as conversation analysts put it, in the social interactions that make up everyday life. This process has most often been studied in 'asymmetrical', institutional encounters between, for instance, doctors and patients, therapists and clients or teachers and pupils. But power is no less present – and no less significant – in our most intimate exchanges. That point was important for the 'dominance' current in feminist linguistics of the 1970s and 1980s (for example, Pamela Fishman's 1983 work on heterosexual couples' talk, which we discussed in chapter 3). Subsequent work in the 'difference' paradigm (notably that of Deborah Tannen 1990) tended, however, to equate intimacy with equality. The study of language and desire offers, perhaps, a framework in which to return to the relatively neglected but important subject of how power is accomplished in intimate relationships and contexts.

Another question that has been the subject of political debate is *which* or *whose* identities and desires should be primary objects of interest in the study of language and sexuality. It should be acknowledged here that the fora in which that question is now debated were established very largely through the efforts of scholars who identified as gay or lesbian and who wanted to create a space in which to pursue the study of gay and lesbian language practices. This was an important contribution to the 'visibility politics' whose project was to affirm the presence and the value of gay men and lesbians, both inside and outside the academy. But while some researchers feel that the moment of visibility politics has passed, others continue to argue that there are good political reasons to privilege the study of minority over mainstream sexualities. This position often leads them to be critical, in particular, of approaches influenced by queer theory – which, as we have seen, does not define its project as equivalent to 'studying queers'. William Leap, for instance, suggests that 'a general social theory cannot merely incorporate heterosexual and homosexual perspectives into the same analytic paradigm. To do so unavoidably subordinates same-sex experience beneath the authority of the heterosexual norm' (Leap 2002: 46).

In this book we have argued against the position Leap takes here, proposing not only that the study of language and sexuality must deal with both hetero- and homo- variants, but also and more specifically that more attention should be given to the language in which heterosexual identities and desires are made manifest. While we are mindful of the possibility that some straight researchers will take this as a licence to engage in defensive posturing or apolitical navel-gazing (tendencies that have occasionally been seen in research on masculinity and whiteness), we certainly do not think the approach we favour 'unavoidably subordinates same-sex experience beneath…the heterosexual norm'. From our perspective the point of studying heterosexuality is not to make the field more 'inclusive', 'balanced' or 'respectable' by diverting attention from 'deviants' to 'normal' people: it is to subject the prevailing norm to critical scrutiny.

As we noted above, the target of Leap's criticism is not language and sexuality studies as such, but rather queer theory (the 'general social theory' to which he refers in the passage quoted above). Queer theory is essentially (or maybe that should be 'anti-essentially') a critique of heteronormativity, the word 'critique' denoting both a critical stance towards it and a systematic examination of the conditions that enable it to exist. Leap evidently, and perhaps rightly, feels that this focus on heteronormativity shifts attention away from the particularities of gay and lesbian lives. But we see it as important nonetheless, for ultimately it is heteronormativity which shapes the experiences of gay men and lesbians: changing their lives for the better depends on challenging the system that defines them as 'deviant' and their experience as less valuable than the heteronormative variety.

For us, then, the critique of heteronormativity is politically important; and in our view it does require analysts to consider heterosexuality alongside 'same-sex experience'. Like masculinity and femininity, heterosexuality and homosexuality are relational terms defined by contrast with one another: without homosexuals there can be no heterosexuals, and vice versa. '[I]ncorporat[ing them] into the same analytic paradigm' is not a capitulation to heterosexist ideology, it is a theoretical/political recognition that they *are* part of a single heteronormative paradigm.

If that is accepted, it becomes possible to argue that *neglecting* to examine heterosexuality reinforces its normative and dominant status. One of the privileges enjoyed by dominant groups in general is that their identities and modes of behaviour are rarely scrutinized in the same way as the identities and behaviours of subordinated groups. Subordinated groups are 'marked': thus we talk about 'women writers' but not 'men writers', 'Black politicians' but not 'white politicians', 'gay TV personalities' but not 'straight TV personalities'. Dominant groups, on the other hand, are 'unmarked': to be white/male/straight is the default standard for being human. Turning the spotlight critically on whiteness, masculinity or heterosexuality is one way of challenging their status as unmarked, and as such is a political act.

It might be asked – and probably will be – whether linguistic research has anything of practical use to contribute to the sexual political struggles in which activists are engaged. The short answer to that question is that it depends on the research. We certainly would not want to claim that linguistic research on sexuality is by definition relevant to political activism, but nor would we want to deny its potential usefulness. The study of discourse on sexuality, and of what we have called the 'social semiotic of desire', can illuminate a range of politically important issues. How people express their desires to one another – what they do and do not (or can and cannot) say – are crucially important matters in struggles around not only sexual identity or preference but also rape and sexual assault, reproductive rights, and HIV/AIDS.

For example, research carried out by the Women, Risk and AIDS Project (Holland *et al.* 1998) has highlighted the discursive roots of the difficulty many young heterosexual women experience in practising safer sex. This is not because, as is sometimes supposed, young people have somehow remained ignorant of the fact that condom use reduces the risk of HIV infection, nor because they do not perceive themselves to be at risk from HIV. Rather it is because, in the semiotic universe the young women and their partners inhabit, asking a man to wear a condom (or refusing to consent to sex without one) signifies that you do not trust or love him.[2] Women also seem to fear that taking the initiative in this way may indicate a degree of sexual experience and boldness which will get them categorized as sluts. Depressing as this may be, it is necessary for those who work with young people on issues of sexual health to understand that these young women's sexual behaviour is not just impulsive or irrational and self-destructive, but makes sense in terms of the meanings that regulate their exchanges with men. Research like WRAP's suggests that successful educational initiatives cannot concentrate simply on the transmission of facts ('condoms protect against infection'). What needs to change is not only the state of young people's knowledge about sex but also their norms for communicating about it – who can say what, to whom, and with what meaning. Language, therefore, is not just a medium for sex and health education but something that must be discussed explicitly as part of the process. Research that sheds light on existing patterns of interaction and meaning offers activists who want to intervene in those patterns a place to start from.

While activists may indeed dismiss some forms of academic discourse as too abstract or arcane to be of interest or use, it would not be accurate to suggest that anything to do with language is by definition remote from practical politics. Radical sexual movements have always recognized the political importance of language and the need to examine critically the pre-suppositions behind our conventional ways of talking and writing. In pre-vious chapters we have referred to various cases where language has been at issue in debates within radical political communities: examples include debates on whether to adopt category labels such as 'gay' and 'queer', how to define a 'lesbian', and what constitutes sexual consent. Linguistic re-searchers may have a different agenda from political groups, but at the same time their investigations may produce knowledge that can usefully feed into particular political discussions. Conversely, of course, researchers can learn from the experience of activists (and from their own experience as activists, for the same person can be in both categories). As we noted in our preface, the agenda for research on language and sexuality has been shaped as much by political developments outside the academy as by inter-nal academic factors. This, in our view, is as it should be: while we do not think that the study of language and sexuality should be in thrall to any single political orthodoxy, we would not want to see it lose its connection to a broader political project.

This book has been a critical intervention in current discussions about language and sexuality. It will be evident that we have our differences with some of our colleagues in that field, but we hope it is also evident that we value the work that has allowed a field to emerge – a field that did not exist when the two of us began our careers. There can be no doubt that the study of language and sexuality has come a long way in a short time, and that it is still developing rapidly. That sense of movement and of potential – of an open field in which all kinds of questions can still be asked – is one of the things that make the study of language and sexuality exciting and intriguing. In this book we have tried not only to give a sense of what has already been achieved, but also to stimulate present and future researchers to think imaginatively about what might be.

Notes

1. We thank Bambi Schieffelin for bringing this study to our attention; the questionnaire items are reproduced in full in chapter 1 below (p. 3). It turns out that the publication of the article in the *Journal of the American Medical Association* resulted in the dismissal of the editor George Lundberg, who had held his position for seventeen years. The vice-president of the American Medical Association, who fired Lundberg, had no objection to the scientific merits of the article, but he accused Lundberg of hurrying the paper through the normal publication schedule, in an attempt to influence events in Washington (http://abcnews.go.com/sections/living/DailyNews/lundberg980115.html).
The controversy generated by this article is a further example of how talk about sex is political – in this case in the narrow, partisan sense, but also, crucially, in the broad sense of impacting in concrete and contestable ways on the world.

2. This of course is a point that has received a lot of attention from feminists, who have always viewed sex as a site of both 'pleasure and danger' (Vance 1984) for women. Concerns about violent, unpleasurable or degrading sex have been less prominent in the discourse of the Gay Liberation movement and its successors, though some dangers associated with sex (particularly the risk of contracting HIV) have been discussed more extensively since the late 1980s.

1 MAKING CONNECTIONS

1. A note on terminology: we will distinguish *heterosexism*, meaning attitudes and practices based on an ideological belief that heterosexuality is superior to all other forms of sexuality / sexual identity, from *homophobia*, meaning attitudes and practices based on hatred and contempt for homosexuals. The two do frequently go together, but in principle they are distinguishable; something can be heterosexist without being homophobic. (A terminological parallel in the domain of gender relations is the difference between *sexism* and *misogyny* (i.e. woman-hatred.)

2. The phrase 'normative heterosexuality' (another phrase we will sometimes use is '*compulsory* heterosexuality') refers to the particular form of sexual relations

between men and women that is institutionalized as a norm. Normative/ compulsory heterosexuality is not just one alternative among others, but the form of sexuality from which all other possibilities are defined as 'deviations'. This kind of heterosexuality is the basis for the key social institutions of marriage and the nuclear family, and there is enormous pressure on individuals to conform to the expectations it imposes.

2 TALKING SEX AND THINKING SEX: THE LINGUISTIC AND DISCURSIVE CONSTRUCTION OF SEXUALITY

1. The 'vaginal orgasm' was held to have its physical origins in the vagina, and to be produced by direct stimulation of the vagina (prototypically, by the thrusting of the penis during heterosexual intercourse). Post-Second World War sex researchers found, however, that orgasm in women always requires stimulation (whether direct or indirect) of the clitoris. The vagina is a relatively insensitive organ poorly supplied with nerve endings, and while women may indeed have orgasms during intercourse, these are not the result of vaginal stimulation alone. The historian Rachel Maines (1999) points out that for centuries before Freud, 'hysteria' was understood by medical authorities as a condition stemming from lack of sexual release. Manual or mechanical stimulation of the external genitalia was a commonly prescribed treatment for women diagnosed as hysterics; it was carried out by doctors or midwives, and the objective was to produce orgasm (though medical texts often preferred to call it 'the hysterical crisis', avoiding any implication that professionals might be providing sexual services rather than medical treatment). Clearly, the prescribers of this therapy knew that female orgasm does not require vaginal penetration, nor indeed is penetration a reliable method for producing it (many recipients of massage were married and had regular intercourse with their husbands).
2. Philip Larkin, 'Annus Mirabilis', in *High Windows* (1974).
3. The prefixes 'homo-' and 'hetero-' are derived from Greek, and they mean 'same' and 'different'. The category of 'bisexuality' causes problems for this classification scheme, and it is of interest to note that its reality or legitimacy is contested by some people on both sides of the hetero/homo divide. Arguably, this sceptical attitude to bisexuality testifies to the strength of our current conviction that sexual orientation – like sex/gender – is fundamentally a binary opposition, so that a person cannot be 'both at once'. Another interesting case is celibacy: declaring oneself voluntarily celibate and disclaiming any kind of sexual orientation (as some celibate individuals do, though of course not all) does not necessarily exempt one from speculation about whether one is 'really' gay or straight – which suggests that people who are 'neither' are no more intelligible than people who are 'both'.
4. Since this example concerns an ancient language, Latin, there are some obvious caveats about the range and representativeness of the data analysed by Parker, which are taken from a limited corpus of preserved written (especially literary) texts. Clearly this entails a bias towards the usage of an elite (and male) linguistic

community, and towards literary conventions for representing sex whose relation to more everyday ways of speaking is difficult to judge. At any rate it cannot be assumed that the classifications induced from these sources were the only ones current in Roman society as a whole. (We thank Keith Nightenhelser for drawing Parker's work to our attention.)

5. The active/passive distinction remains highly salient in some contemporary societies that do also make the hetero/homo distinction. This can lead to a perception that only the 'passive' partner in a male homosexual encounter is really a homosexual. Kulick (1997, 1998) discusses this issue in relation to Latin American homosexualities in general and travestis in Brazil in particular. See also Greenberg (1988) and Murray (1995, 2000).

6. The two options just mentioned point to a persistent disagreement about whether sexual orientation is an innate characteristic of individuals. Recently, the idea that homosexuals are born and not made has gained more support than it had in the earlier period of gay liberation, in part because it is easier in current political conditions (especially in the US) to press for anti-discrimination measures if the ground for discrimination is something the individual victim has no choice about, like sex or race, rather than something s/he could in principle decide to change. In current discourse we thus have the peculiar situation where prominent gay spokespeople insist that their sexuality is rooted in biology, while homophobic religious fundamentalists declare that on the contrary it is socially constructed (a 'lifestyle choice' which individuals could and should renounce).

7. A group of eighteen-year-old undergraduate students taught by one of us in 2001 reported that 'gay' meaning 'lame' or 'dumb' (as in 'that's so gay') was common currency in the US high schools they attended before coming to college.

8. We can note that the function of signalling political stances is not confined to labels *per se*. It can also extend to the orthographic conventions employed to write those labels. Orthography has been an important source of political claim-staking for many radical feminists, as anyone who still uses, or remembers, spellings like 'wimmin' can attest (the feminist theologian Mary Daly's work is the most luxuriant example of this trend, e.g. Daly 1979; Daly with Caputi 1988). More recently, transgendered activists have advocated a change in the spelling of the word 'transsexual' – removing one of the 's's, thus rendering it 'transexual'. The rationale behind this is the familiar one of 'reclaiming' a word – by excising the 's', activists argue that they are reclaiming the word from the medical establishment that invented it (see Valentine and Kulick 2001). The continuing efforts of some transgendered writers to recast the English language's pronominal system (by advocating the use of third-person pronouns like 's/he' or 'hir') are another example of this phenomenon (see Kulick 1999; Valentine and Wilchins 1997; Wilchins 1995).

9. The belief that women say 'no' when they mean 'yes' is not entirely without empirical support; some women on some occasions do appear to orient to the conventions McConnell-Ginet alludes to. In 1988, the psychologists Charlene

Muehlenhard and Lisa Hollabaugh reported findings from a questionnaire they gave to 610 women undergraduates, who were asked whether they had ever engaged in 'token resistance', i.e. saying 'no' to sex when they fully intended to have sex, and if so what their reasons had been. They found that 39.3% of respondents reported engaging in token resistance at least once. The most important reasons given included fear of appearing promiscuous, moral or religious scruples, and what the authors call 'manipulative' or 'game playing' reasons. These included being angry with a partner, wishing to arouse him further by making him wait, and wanting him 'to beg' (Muehlenhard and Hollabaugh 1988).

10. There were, of course, students who objected to the code or who reported that they simply ignored it. The most visible locus of opposition to it was in a men's group called 'The Boneyard' which announced itself as 'dedicated to the preservation of machismo' (expressed by ostentatious consumption of beer and pornography), and a sister organization for women called 'the Bushwhackers'. These groups, however, were seen, and saw themselves, as representing a disaffected minority on a campus where progressive and 'politically correct' views were mainstream.

11. Cameron (1994) was told by Antioch's Dean of Students that the complaints logged to date under the policy had been made by heterosexual men as well as women, and there had also been complaints from lesbians and gay men.

12. In one notorious recent case, a straight male guest on a US talk-show was told he was going to meet, on TV, a person who had a crush on him: this turned out to be a gay man. Three days later, the straight man went to the gay man's home and shot him dead. Waiting 72 hours hardly suggests that the killer acted in a panic prompted by his victim's 'advance', but the homosexual panic defence was nevertheless instrumental in securing a verdict of second- rather than first-degree murder (for a concise summary of this case, see Kulick in press, and http://www.courttv.com/verdicts/schmitz.html).

13. This tendency, particularly in its overtly sadomasochistic manifestations, has been the target of feminist critique (cf. Linden *et al.* 1982; Reti 1993). But there are also feminists who defend and celebrate the erotics of power (cf. Califia 1983, 1988; Califia and Sweeney 1996; Samois 1981), arguing that power is not necessarily and inevitably connected to institutionalized male dominance, and that, in a nonpatriarchal order, power would remain a source of erotic possibility that could attract some people of both/all genders.

3 WHAT HAS GENDER GOT TO DO WITH SEX? LANGUAGE, HETEROSEXUALITY AND HETERONORMATIVITY

1. Among queer theorists and activists, the term 'heteronormativity' is more commonly used than 'compulsory heterosexuality', which has specific roots in feminism. As we will see (p. 55), queer theoretical analyses of

heteronormativity do not necessarily view its main political function as maintaining male supremacy.

2. A similar line of thought with regard to sex (the only sex that 'counts' in patriarchal societies is sex that culminates in male ejaculation) led one writer to argue that lesbians, as well as many heterosexual women, don't have sex (Frye 1992[1987]).

3. For a more detailed argument to this effect, see Cameron (1992).

4. A sample of these materials is described and critically discussed by Kulick (1999).

5. This claim has been disputed, but here we will let it stand for the sake of argument.

6. The data reproduced in this section were collected by one of the participants in 1990. All participants have been given pseudonyms to protect their privacy.

7. Here we should note that such pejorative terms, when used by insiders (e.g. 'faggot', 'queen', or in a race context 'nigger' and 'boy/girl'), may lose their pejorative force and be understood as in-group markers signalling solidarity, affection, ironic comment on the prejudices of others, etc.

4 SEXUALITY AS IDENTITY: GAY AND LESBIAN LANGUAGE

1. In fact, the Gay Liberationists were continuing a long-running internal debate with a complex history, at least in relation to male homosexuality. Homophile writers such as the French novelist André Gide in the mid-twentieth century defended a 'manly' homosexuality (modelled on the pederasty of classical Greece) and in some instances deplored the 'effeminate' homosexuality of the 'uranist' or 'invert'. One of the arguments that would later recur in Gay Liberation discourse – that effeminate language and behaviour among male homosexuals is a form of misogyny – can also be found in some of the earlier writings on this subject. On the other hand, the ideal of the 'manly' homosexual in Germany between the two world wars took on explicitly fascist and misogynist overtones; in that context, socialists and sex radicals (including for instance the sexologist Magnus Hirschfeld) defended the forms of (unmanly or effeminate) homosexuality that Nazism defined as 'degenerate'.

2. 'The statement meant that the ringleader (queen) of a group of homosexuals was making a play (exhibiting-camping) for a young boy (jam-virgin)' (Duberman 1991: 162).

3. The earliest list that we have been able to find is Rosanoff (1927; reproduced in Katz 1983: 438–40), which lists twelve terms and gives one-line definitions of each of them.

4. Donald Cory is a pseudonym for Edward Sagarin, a sociologist who, a decade after his book first appeared, decided that he was wrong, and that homosexuals were indeed disturbed individuals in need of help. For details see Marotta (1981). The pseudonym Sagarin chose echoes Gide's mid-century defence of pederasty (see note 1, this chapter), which was entitled *Corydon*, an allusion to one of

Vergil's *Eclogues* which describes the love of the shepherd Corydon for the fair (and male) Alexis.

5. The terms 'unmarked' and 'marked' are part of the technical vocabulary of linguistics. They denote a relationship between two paired items where one functions as the 'default' term with respect to the other, and may in certain contexts subsume it. The terms 'man' and 'woman' have this relationship, with 'man' as the unmarked term. A less ideologically loaded example is the pair 'tall' and 'short'. 'Tall' is unmarked with respect to 'short': thus we ask of a person or an object, 'how tall is she/he/it?' rather than 'how short is she/he/it?' 'How tall' is the default expression regardless of our estimate of the height of the person or object in question.

6. A related piece of evidence for the point we are making about the marked-ness and greater elaboration of linguistic femininity comes from the lin-guistic self-(re)fashioning practices of transgendered individuals. Both the individuals concerned and the experts who assist them in acquiring new gender-appropriate voices and styles of speech appear to agree that more work (including both speech therapy and medical/surgical procedures) is needed to construct a convincing feminine speaker (for discussion see Kulick 1999).

7. In their historical study of lesbian culture in Buffalo, New York, Kennedy and Davis (1993) sketch other reasons why gender crossing may have been less available or less useful to lesbians than gay men. For instance, they suggest that the theatrical playfulness of camp would not have been an appropriate strategy for the particular kind of struggle lesbians historically had to wage, where what was at stake was not only their right to express a 'deviant' sexuality, but also their right as women to live independently of men and to inhabit male-dominated public space without male 'protection'. They also note that lesbian culture in the 1940s and '50s was organized around butch-fem roles. Fems would not have engaged in gender crossing, even if butches did. In addition, some women adopted the identity of 'passing women', i.e. women who dressed and acted like men, using male names and false papers: within the community, 'passing woman' was regarded as a different category from 'lesbian'. It may have been the case, then, that linguistic gender crossing indexed the identity of 'passing woman' and was consequently avoided by those who identified as lesbians.

8. Cited in Robertson (1996: 25).

5 LOOKING BEYOND IDENTITY: LANGUAGE AND DESIRE

1. Note, however, that there are differences between 'desire' as elaborated by Deleuze and Guattari, and Foucault's concept of 'power'. These are discussed in detail in Deleuze (2000 [1994]). See also Foucault (2000).

2. Because this point is often missed or ignored in discussions of Derrida (e.g. Livia 2002), here is the exact citation: 'the category of intention will not disappear;

it will have its place, but from this place it will no longer be able to govern the entire scene and system of utterances' (Derrida 1995[1972]: 18).

6 LANGUAGE AND SEXUALITY: THEORY, RESEARCH AND POLITICS

1. For instance, the feminist critic Tania Modleski (1991) has drawn attention to the oversimplification entailed by claims about an overarching 'heterosexual privilege'. Modleski points out that women who became lesbians in the context of the Women's Liberation Movement, while they were aware of (and vocal about) discrimination and prejudice against lesbians, were not inclined to represent heterosexual women as members of a more privileged oppressor class: as lesbians they believed they had gained a degree of autonomy denied to heterosexual women, especially those who were wives. This is a good illustration of why it can be misleading to study one set of power relations in isolation from others: in this case, the positioning of lesbians relative to heterosexual women cannot be fully understood without reference to the way each group is positioned in relation to heterosexual men.

2. The semiotics of condom use in the era of the AIDS epidemic seem to follow this pattern across a range of communities and societies, i.e. not wearing a condom becomes a signifier of love/trust. For instance, the Brazilian transgendered prostitutes studied by Kulick (1998) used condoms with clients but not with their boyfriends.

Bibliography

Allison, Anne 1994, *Nightwork: Sexuality, Pleasure and Corporate Masculinity in a Tokyo Hostess Club*, Chicago: University of Chicago Press.

Altman, Dennis 1971, *Homosexual: Oppression and Liberation*, New York: Outebridge & Dienstfrey.

1982, *The Homosexualization of America*, Boston: Beacon.

Anderson, Benedict 1983, *Imagined Communities; Reflections on the Origins and Spread of Nationalism*, London: Verso.

ASTRAL (Associação de Travestis e Liberados) 1996, *Diálogo de Bonecas*, Rio de Janeiro: ASTRAL.

Austin, J. L. 1997 [1962], *How To Do Things with Words*, 2nd edn, Cambridge, Mass.: Harvard University Press.

Barrett, Rusty 1995, Supermodels of the world unite! Political economy and the language of performance among African-American drag queens, in Leap (1995b) pp. 207–26.

1997, The 'homo-genius' speech community, in Livia and Hall (1997a) pp. 181–201.

1998, Markedness and style switching in performances by African American drag queens, in Carol Myers-Scotton (ed.), *Codes and Consequences: Choosing Linguistic Varieties*, New York: Oxford University Press, pp. 139–61.

Barthes, Roland 1978, *A Lover's Discourse*, New York: Farrar, Straus & Giroux, Inc.

Beauvoir, Simone de 1989 [1949], *The Second Sex*, trans. H. M. Parshley, New York: Vintage Books.

Bell, Shannon 1993, Kate Bornstein: a transgender, transsexual postmodern Tiresias, in Arthur Kroker and Marilouise Kroker (eds.), *The Last Sex: Feminism and Outlaw Bodies*, New York: St Martin's Press, pp. 104–20.

Berlant, Lauren and Warner, Michael 1998, Sex in public. *Critical Inquiry* 24 (2): 547–66.

Billig, Michael 1995, *Banal Nationalism*, London: Sage Publications.

1997, The dialogic unconscious: psychoanalysis, discursive psychology and the nature of repression. *British Journal of Social Psychology* 36: 139–59.

1999, *Freudian Repression: Conversation Creating the Unconscious*, Cambridge: Cambridge University Press.

Broomfield, Nick 1996, *Fetishes*, Lafayette Films and In Pictures.

Browning, Barbara 1996, The closed body. *Women & Performance: A Journal of Feminist Theory* 8 (2): 1–18.

Bucholtz, Mary, Liang, Anita C. and Sutton, Laurel 1999, *Reinventing Identities: The Gendered Self in Discourse*, New York and Oxford: Oxford University Press.

Bunch, Charlotte 2000 [1972], Lesbians in revolt, in Crow pp. 332–6.

Burgess, E. W. 1949, The sociological theory of psychosexual behavior, in Paul H. Hoch and Joseph Zubin (eds.), *Psychosexual Development in Health and Disease*, New York: Grune & Stratton, pp. 227–43.

Burton, P. 1979, The gentle art of confounding naffs. *Gay News* 120.

Butler, Judith 1990, *Gender Trouble: Feminism and the Subversion of Identity*, New York and London: Routledge.

    1993a, *Bodies that Matter: On the Discursive Limits of 'Sex'*, New York and London: Routledge.

    1993b, Queering, passing: Nella Larsen's psychoanalytic challenge, in Butler (1993a) pp. 167–85.

    1999, Never mind the bollocks: an interview by Kate More, in Kate More and Stephen Whittle (eds.), *Reclaiming Genders: Transsexual Grammars at the Fin de Siècle*, London and New York: Cassell, pp. 285–302.

Butters, Ronald R. 1998, Cary Grant and the emergence of *gay* 'homosexual'. *Dictionaries* 19: 188–204.

Califia, Pat 1983, *Macho Sluts*, Boston: Alyson Press.

    (ed.) 1988, *The Lesbian S/M Safety Manual*, Boston: Lace Publications.

Califia, Pat and Sweeney, Robin (eds.) 1996, *The Second Coming: A Leatherdyke Reader*, Los Angeles: Alyson Publications.

Cameron, Deborah 1992, Review of Tannen's *You Just Don't Understand: Men and Women in Conversation. Feminism & Psychology* 2 (3): 465–89.

    1994, Degrees of consent: the Antioch sexual consent policy. *Trouble & Strife* 28: 32–5.

    1997, Performing gender: young men's talk and the construction of heterosexual masculinity, in Johnson and Meinhof (1997) pp. 47–64.

    2000, Styling the worker: gender and the commodification of language in the global service economy. *Journal of Sociolinguistics* 4 (3): 323–47.

Campbell-Kibler, Kathryn, Podesva, Rob, Roberts, Sarah J. and Wong, Andrew (eds.) 2002, *Language and Sexuality: Contesting Meaning in Theory and Practice*, Stanford, Calif.: CSLI Publications.

Capps, Lisa and Ochs, Elinor 1995, *Constructing Panic: The Discourse of Agoraphobia*, Cambridge, Mass.: Harvard University Press.

Channell, Joanna 1997, 'I just called to say I love you': love and desire on the telephone, in Harvey and Shalom (1997) pp. 143–69.

Chauncey, George 1994, *Gay New York: Gender, Urban Culture, and the Making of the Gay Male World, 1890–1940*, New York: Basic Books.

Chesebro, James W. (ed.) 1981, *Gayspeak: Gay Male and Lesbian Communication*, New York: Pilgrim Press.

Clancy, Patricia M. 1986, The acquisition of communicative style in Japanese, in Bambi B. Schieffelin and Elinor Ochs (eds.), *Language Socialization Across Cultures*, Cambridge: Cambridge University Press, pp. 213–50.

1999, The socialization of affect in Japanese mother-child conversation. *Journal of Pragmatics* 31: 1397–421.

Coates, Jennifer 1988, Gossip revisited: language in all-female groups, in Jennifer Coates and Deborah Cameron (eds.), *Women in their Speech Communities: New Perspectives on Language and Sex*, London: Longman, pp. 94–122.

1996, *Women Talk: Conversation between Women Friends*, Oxford: Blackwell.

Conrad, James R. and More, William W. 1976, Lexical codes and subcultures: some questions. *Anthropological Linguistics* 18 (1): 22–8.

Cory, Donald Webster 1951, *The Homosexual in America: A Subjective Approach*, New York: Greenberg.

Coupland, Justine 1996, Dating advertisements: discourses of the commodified self. *Discourse and Society* 7 (2): 187–207.

Cox, Leslie J. and Fay, Richard J. 1994, Gayspeak, the linguistic fringe: Bona polari, camp, queerspeak and beyond, in Stephen Whittle (ed.), *The Margins of the City: Gay Men's Urban Lives*, Hants, England: Arena, pp. 103–27.

Crow, Barbara (ed.) 2000, *Radical Feminism: A Documentary Reader*, New York: New York University Press.

Daly, Mary 1979, *Gyn/Ecology: The Metaethics of Radical Feminism*, London: Women's Press.

Daly, Mary with Caputi, Jane 1988, *Webster's First Intergalactic Wickedary of the English Language*, London: Women's Press.

Darsey, James 1981, 'Gayspeak': a response, in Chesebro (1981) pp. 58–67.

Deaux, Kay and Hanna, Randel 1984, Courtship in the personals column: the influence of gender and sexual orientation. *Sex Roles* 11 (5/6): 363–75.

Deleuze, Gilles 2000 [1994], Desire and pleasure, in Lotringer pp. 248–57.

Deleuze, Gilles and Guattari, Félix 1996, *A Thousand Plateaus: Capitalism and Schizophrenia*, London: The Athlone Press.

Deleuze, Gilles and Parnet, Claire 1987, *Dialogues*, New York: Columbia University Press.

Derrida, Jacques 1995 [1972], Signature event context, in Jacques Derrida, *Limited Inc.*, Evanston, Ill.: Northwestern University Press, pp. 1–23.

Duberman, Martin 1991, *About Time: Exploring the Gay Past*, New York: Meridian.

Easton, Dossie and Hardy, Janet W. 2001, *The New Bottoming Book*, Emeryville, Calif.: Greenery Press.

Eckert, Penelope 1994, *Entering the Heterosexual Marketplace: Identities of Subordination as a Developmental Imperative*, Working Papers on Learning and Identity No. 2, Palo Alto, Calif.: Institute for Research on Learning.

2002, Demystifying sexuality and desire, in Campbell-Kibler *et al.* pp. 99–110.

Ehrlich, Susan 1998, The discursive reconstruction of sexual consent. *Discourse & Society* 9 (2): 149–71.

2001, *Representing Rape*, London: Routledge.

Epstein, Debbie and Johnson, Richard 1998, *Schooling Sexualities*, Buckingham: Open University Press.

Fanon, Frantz 1986 [1952], *Black Skin, White Masks*, London: Pluto Press.

Farrell, Ronald A. 1972, The argot of the homosexual subculture. *Anthropological Linguistics* 14: 97–109.

Fink, Bruce 1997, *A Clinical Introduction to Lacanian Psychoanalysis: Theory and Technique*, Cambridge, Mass.: Harvard University Press.

Fishman, Pamela 1983, Interaction: the work women do, in Barrie Thorne, Cheris Kramarae and Nancy Henley (eds.), *Language, Gender and Society*, Rowley, Mass.: Newbury House, pp. 89–102.

Foucault, Michel 1972, *The Archaeology of Knowledge and the Discourse on Language*, New York: Pantheon.

  1980, *Power/Knowledge: Selected Interviews and Other Writings 1972–1977*, edited by Colin Gordon, New York: Pantheon.

  1981, *The History of Sexuality Vol. I: Introduction*, trans. R. Hurley, London: Pelican Books.

  2000 [1978], Bodies and pleasure, in Lotringer pp. 238–47.

Frank, Heidi 2002, Identity and script variation: Japanese lesbian and housewife letters to the editor, in Campbell-Kibler *et al*. pp. 207–24.

Freud, Sigmund 1957, Mourning and melancholia, in *Standard Edition of the Complete Psychological Works of Sigmund Freud* (24 volumes), edited by James Strachey, London: Hogarth Press, Vol. XIV, 239–58.

  1960, *The Ego and the Id*, New York: W. W. Norton & Company.

  1975, *Three Essays on the Theory of Sexuality*, New York: Basic Books.

Frye, Marilyn 1992 [1987], Lesbian 'sex', in Marilyn Frye, *Willful Virgin: Essays on Feminism 1976–1992*, Freedom, Calif.: Crossing Press, pp. 109–19.

Gaudio, Rudolph 1994, Sounding gay: pitch properties in the speech of gay and straight men. *American Speech* 69: 30–57.

  1997, Not talking straight in Hausa, in Livia and Hall (1997a) pp. 416–29.

  2001, White men do it too: racialized (homo)sexualities in postcolonial Hausaland. *Journal of Linguistic Anthropology* 11 (1): 36–51.

Gonzales, Marti Hope and Myers, Sarah A. 1993, 'Your mother would like me': self-presentation in the personal ads of heterosexual and homosexual men and women. *Personality and Social Psychology Bulletin* 19 (2): 131–42.

Goodwin, Marjorie Harness 1988, Cooperation and competition across girls' play activities, in Sue Fisher and Alexandra Todd (eds.), *Gender and Discourse: The Power of Talk*, Norwood, N.J.: Ablex, pp. 55–94.

  1990, *He-said-she-said: Talk as Social Organization among Black Children*, Bloomington: Indiana University Press.

Green, Sarah 1997, *Urban Amazons: Lesbian Feminism and Beyond in the Gender, Sexuality and Identity Battles of London*, London: Macmillan.

Greenberg, David F. 1988, *The Construction of Homosexuality*, Chicago: University of Chicago Press.

Grosz, Elizabeth 1990, *Jacques Lacan: A Feminist Introduction*, London and New York: Routledge.

Hall, Kira 1995, Lip service on the fantasy lines, in Hall and Bucholtz pp. 183–216.

2001, Performativity, in Alessandro Duranti (ed.), *Key Terms in Language and Culture*, Oxford: Blackwell, pp. 180–3.

Hall, Kira and Bucholtz, Mary (eds.) 1995, *Gender Articulated: Language and the Socially Constructed Self*, London and New York: Routledge.

Hall, Kira and O'Donovan, Veronica 1996, Shifting gender positions among Hindi-speaking hijras, in Victoria L. Bergvall, Janet M. Bing and Alice F. Freed (eds.), *Rethinking Language and Gender Research: Theory and Practice*, London: Longman, pp. 228–66.

Halperin, David 1995, *Saint Foucault: Towards a Gay Hagiography*, New York and Oxford: Oxford University Press.

Hanson, Craig Alfred 1972, The fairy princess exposed, in Karla Jay and Allen Young (eds.), *Out of the Closet: Voices of Gay Liberation*, New York: Quick Fox, pp. 266–9.

Hart, Donn and Hart, Harriett 1990, Visayan Swardspeak: the language of a gay community in the Philippines. *Crossroads: An Interdisciplinary Journal of Southeast Asian Studies* 5 (2): 27–49.

Harvey, Keith 1998, Translating camp talk: gay identities and cultural transfer. *The Translator* 4 (2): 295–320.

2000a, Describing camp talk: language/pragmatics/politics. *Language and Literature* 9 (3): 240–60.

2000b, Gay community, gay identity and the translated text. *TTR Traduction, Terminologie, Rédaction* 13 (1): 137–65.

Harvey, Keith and Shalom, Celia (eds.) 1997, *Language and Desire: Encoding Sex, Romance and Intimacy*, London: Routledge.

Hayes, Joseph J. 1981a, Lesbians, gay men and their 'languages', in Chesebro pp. 28–42.

1981b, Gayspeak, in Chesebro pp. 45–57.

Henkin, William A. and Holiday, Sybil 1996, *Consensual Sadomasochism: How to Talk About it and Do it Safely*, Los Angeles: Daedalus.

Heywood, John 1997, 'The object of desire is the object of contempt': representations of masculinity in *Straight To Hell* magazine, in Johnson and Meinhof pp. 188–207.

Hirschfeld, Magnus 1936, *Sexual Anomalies and Perversions*, London: F. Aldor.

Holland, Janet, Ramazanoglu, Caroline, Sharpe, Sue and Thomson, Rachel 1998, *The Male in the Head: Young People, Heterosexuality and Power*, London: Tufnell Press.

Holmes, Janet 1995, *Women, Men and Politeness*, London: Longman.

Jacobs, Greg 1996, Lesbian and gay male language use: a critical review of the literature. *American Speech* 71 (1): 49–71.

Johnson, Mark 1997, *Beauty and Power: Transgendering and Cultural Transformation in the Southern Philippines*, London: Berg.

Johnson, Sally and Meinhof, Ulrike Hanna (eds.) 1997, *Language and Masculinity*, Oxford: Blackwell.

Katz, Jonathan Ned 1983, *Gay/Lesbian Almanac: A New Documentary*, New York: Harper and Row.

1995, *The Invention of Heterosexuality*, London: Plume Books.

Kempf, Edward J. 1920, *Psychopathology*, St Louis: C. V. Mosby Company.

Kennedy, Elizabeth Lapovsky and Davis, Madeline 1993, *Boots of Leather, Slippers of Gold: The History of a Lesbian Community*, New York: Routledge.

Kiesling, Scott 2002, Playing the straight man: displaying and maintaining male heterosexuality in discourse, in Campbell-Kibler *et al.* pp. 249–66.

Kitzinger, Celia and Frith, Hannah 1999, Just say no? The use of conversation analysis in developing a feminist perspective on sexual refusal. *Discourse & Society* 10: 293–316.

Koedt, Anne 2000 [1968], The myth of the vaginal orgasm, in Crow pp. 371–7.

Koestenbaum, Wayne 1993, *The Queen's Throat: Opera, Homosexuality and the Mystery of Desire*, New York: Poseidon Press.

Krafft-Ebing, Richard von 1901, *Psychopathia Sexualis: With Especial Reference to Antipathetic Sexual Instinct, a Medico-Forensic Study*, 10th edn, Aberdeen: Aberdeen University Press.

Kristeva, Julia 1980, *Desire in Language: A Semiotic Approach to Literature and Art*, Oxford: Blackwell.

Kulick, Don 1997, The gender of Brazilian transgendered prostitutes. *American Anthropologist* 99 (3): 574–85.

1998, *Travesti: Sex, Gender and Culture among Brazilian Transgendered Prostitutes*, Chicago: University of Chicago Press.

1999, Transgender and language: a review of the literature and suggestions for the future. *GLQ* 5 (4): 605–22.

2000, Gay and lesbian language. *Annual Review of Anthropology* 29: 243–85.

in press, No. *Language and Communication*, special issue on Language and Desire edited by Deborah Cameron and Don Kulick.

Lacan, Jacques 1998. *The Four Fundamental Concepts of Psychoanalysis*, New York: Norton.

Lakoff, Robin 1975, *Language and Woman's Place*, New York: Harper & Row.

1990, *Talking Power*, New York: Basic Books.

2000, *The Language War*, Berkeley, Calif.: University of California Press.

Langford, Wendy 1997, 'Bunnikins, I love you snugly in your warren': voices from subterranean cultures of love, in Harvey and Shalom pp. 170–85.

Laplanche, Jean and Pontalis, J.-B. 1973, *The Language of Psychoanalysis*, London: Karnac Books.

Larkin, Philip 1974, *High Windows*, London: Faber & Faber.

Leap, William 1995a, Introduction, in Leap (1995b) pp. vii–xix.

(ed.) 1995b, *Beyond the Lavender Lexicon: Authenticity, Imagination and Appropriation in Gay and Lesbian Languages*, Buffalo, N.Y.: Gordon and Breach.

1996a, *Word's Out: Gay Men's English*, Minneapolis and London: University of Minnesota Press.

1996b, Can there be a gay discourse without a gay language? in Mary Bucholtz, A. C. Liang, Laurel Sutton and Caitlin Hines (eds.), *Cultural Performances:*

Proceedings of the Third Berkeley Women and Language Conference, Berkeley, Calif.: Berkeley Women and Language Group, pp. 399–408.

2002, Not entirely in support of a queer linguistics, in Campbell-Kibler *et al.* pp. 45–64.

Lees, Sue 1986, *Losing Out: Sexuality and Adolescent Girls*, London: Hutchinson.

Legman, Gershon 1941, The language of homosexuality: an American glossary, in George W. Henry (ed.), *Sex Variants: A Study of Homosexual Patterns, Volume II*, New York and London: Paul B. Hoeber, Inc., pp. 1149–79.

Linden, Robin Ruth, Pagano, Darlene R., Russell, Dianne E. H. and Star, Susan Lee (eds.) 1982, *Against Sadomasochism: A Radical Feminist Analysis*, East Palo Alto, Calif.: Frog in the Well Press.

Linville, Sue Ellen 1998, Acoustic correlates of perceived versus actual sexual orientation in men's speech. *Folia Phoniatrica et Logopaedica* 50: 35–48.

Livia, Anna 2002, The future of queer linguistics, in Campbell-Kibler *et al.* pp. 87–98.

Livia, Anna and Hall, Kira (eds.) 1997a, *Queerly Phrased: Language, Gender and Sexuality*, New York: Oxford University Press.

1997b, 'It's a girl!': bringing performativity back to linguistics, in Livia and Hall 1997a pp. 3–18.

Lotringer, Sylvère (ed.) 2000, *More or Less*, New York: Semiotext(e).

Lucas, Ian 1997, The color of his eyes: Polari and the sisters of perpetual indulgence, in Livia and Hall (1997a) pp. 85–94.

McConnell-Ginet, Sally 1989, The (re)production of sexual meaning: a discourse-based theory, in Francine Frank and Paula Treichler (eds.), *Language, Gender and Professional Writing*, New York: Modern Language Association, pp. 35–50.

McElhinny, Bonnie 1993, We all wear the blue. Ph.D. dissertation, Stanford University.

2002, Language, sexuality and political economy, in Campbell-Kibler *et al.* pp. 111–34.

MacKinnon, Catharine 1982, Feminism, Marxism, method and the state: an agenda for theory. *Signs* 7 (3): 515–44.

Maines, Rachel 1999, *The Technology of Orgasm: 'Hysteria', the Vibrator and Women's Sexual Satisfaction*, Baltimore and London: Johns Hopkins University Press.

Manalansan, Martin F. 1995, 'Performing' the Filipino gay experiences in America: linguistic strategies in a transnational context, in Leap (1995b) pp. 249–66.

Manning, Elizabeth 1997, Kissing and cuddling: the reciprocity of romantic and sexual activity, in Harvey and Shalom pp. 43–59.

Marotta, Toby 1981, *The Politics of Homosexuality*, Boston: Houghton Mifflin.

Mendoza-Denton, Norma 1995, Pregnant pauses: silence and authority in the Anita Hill – Clarence Thomas hearings, in Hall and Bucholtz pp. 51–66.

Modleski, Tania 1991, *Feminism Without Women: Culture and Criticism in a 'Post-feminist' Age*, New York: Routledge.

Moonwomon, Birch 1995, Lesbian discourse, lesbian knowledge, in Leap (1995b) pp. 45–64.

Moonwomon-Baird, Birch 1997, Toward a study of lesbian speech, in Livia and Hall (1997a) pp. 202–13.

Morgan, Ruth and Wood, Kathleen 1995, Lesbians in the living room: collusion, co-construction, and co-narration in conversation, in Leap (1995b) pp. 235–48.

Moriel, Liora 1998, Diva in the promised land: a blueprint for Newspeak? *World Englishes* 17 (2): 225–37.

Morrison, Toni 1993, *Playing in the Dark: Whiteness and the Literary Imagination*, New York: Vintage Books.

Muehlenhard, Charlene L. and Hollabaugh, Lisa C. 1988, Do women sometimes say no when they mean yes? The prevalence and correlates of women's token resistance to sex. *Journal of Personality and Social Psychology* 54 (5): 872–9.

Murray, Stephen O. 1979, The art of gay insulting. *Anthropological Linguistics* 21: 211–23.

　　1980, Ritual and personal insults in stigmatized subcultures: gay, black, Jew. *Maledicta* 7: 189–211.

　　1995, *Latin American Male Homosexualities*, Albuquerque: University of New Mexico Press.

　　1996, Review of *Word's Out: Gay Men's English* by William L. Leap. *Anthropological Linguistics* 38 (4): 747–50.

　　2000, *Homosexualities*, Chicago: University of Chicago Press.

O'Barr, William and Atkins, Bowman 1980, 'Women's language' or 'powerless language'? in Sally McConnell-Ginet, Ruth Borker and Nelly Furman (eds.), *Women and Language in Literature and Society*, New York: Praeger, pp. 93–110.

Ochs, Elinor 1992, Indexing gender, in Alessandro Duranti and Charles Goodwin (eds.), *Rethinking Context: Language as an Interactive Phenomenon*, Cambridge: Cambridge University Press, pp. 335–58.

Ochs, Elinor, Pontecorvo, Clotilde and Fasulo, Alessandra 1996, Socializing taste. *Ethnos* 61 (1–2): 5–42.

Painter, Dorothy S. 1980, Lesbian humor as a normalization device, in Cynthia L. Berryman and Virginia A. Eman (eds.), *Communication, Language and Sex*, Rowley, Mass.: Newbury House, pp. 132–48.

Parker, Holt N. 1997, The teratogenic grid, in Judith P. Hallett and Marilyn B. Skinner (eds.), *Roman Sexualities*, Princeton, N.J.: Princeton University Press, pp. 47–65.

[Penelope] Stanley, Julia 1970, Homosexual slang. *American Speech* 45 (1–2): 45–59.

　　1973, Paradigmatic woman: the prostitute, paper presented to the Linguistic Society of America.

Penelope [Stanley], Julia and Wolfe, Susan J. 1979, *Sexist Slang and the Gay Community: Are You One, Too?* Michigan Occasional Paper No. XIV, Ann Arbor: University of Michigan.

Podesva, Robert, Roberts, Sarah J. and Campbell-Kibler, Kathryn 2002, Sharing resources and indexing meanings in the production of gay styles, in Campbell-Kibler *et al*. pp. 175–90.

Queen, Robin 1997, 'I don't speak spritch': locating lesbian language, in Livia and Hall (1997a) pp. 233–56.

1998, 'Stay queer!' 'Never fear!': building queer social networks. *World Englishes* 17: 203–24.

2002, A matter of interpretation: the 'future' of 'queer linguistics', in Campbell-Kibler *et al.* pp. 69–86.

Read, Kenneth 1980, *Other Voices: The Style of a Male Homosexual Tavern*, Novato, Calif.: Chandler and Sharp Publishers, Inc.

Reti, Irene (ed.) 1993, *Unleashing Feminism: Critiquing Lesbian Sadomasochism in the Gay Nineties*, Santa Cruz, Calif.: HerBooks.

Rich, Adrienne 1980, Compulsory heterosexuality and lesbian existence. *Signs* 5: 631–61.

Riggs, Marlon 1989, *Tongues Untied*, San Francisco: Frameline.

Robertson, Pamela 1996, *Guilty Pleasures: Feminist Camp From Mae West to Madonna*, London: I. B. Tauris and Company.

Rodgers, Bruce n.d. [1972], *The Queen's Vernacular: a Gay Lexicon*, London: Blond & Briggs.

Rosanoff, Aaron 1927, *Manual of Psychiatry*, 6th edn, New York: Wiley.

Rubin, Gayle 1984, Thinking sex: notes for a radical theory of the politics of sexuality, in Vance pp. 267–319.

Samois (eds.) 1981, *Coming to Power: Writings and Graphics on Lesbian S/M,* Boston: Alyson Press.

Sanders, Stephanie A. and Reinisch, Julie Machover 1999, Would you say you had 'sex' if. . .? *Journal of the American Medical Association* 281 (3): 275–7.

Sedgwick, Eve Kosofsky 1990, *The Epistemology of the Closet*, Berkeley, Calif.: University of California Press.

Shalom, Celia 1997, That great supermarket of desire: attributes of the desired other in personal advertisements, in Harvey and Shalom pp. 186–203.

Shelley, Martha 2000 [1970], Lesbianism and the Women's Liberation Movement, in Crow pp. 305–9.

Smith-Rosenberg, Carroll 1975, The female world of love and ritual. *Signs* 1: 1–29.

Stein, Arlene 1997, *Sex and Sensibility: Stories of a Lesbian Generation*, Berkeley, Calif.: University of California Press.

Stevens, Jennifer Anne 1990, *From Masculine to Feminine and All Points In Between: A Practical Guide*, Cambridge, Mass.: Different Path.

Tannen, Deborah 1990, *You Just Don't Understand: Men and Women in Conversation*, New York: Ballantine Books.

Tatchell, Peter 2002, What's eating Mike Tyson?, *New Statesman* 10 June: 15–16.

Thorne, Adrian and Coupland, Justine 1998, Articulations of same-sex desire: lesbian and gay male dating advertisements. *Journal of Sociolinguistics* 2 (2): 233–57.

Thorne, Barrie and Henley, Nancy (eds.) 1975, *Language and Sex: Difference and Dominance*, Rowley, Mass.: Newbury House.

Troemel-Ploetz, Senta 1991, Selling the apolitical. *Discourse & Society* 2: 489–502.

Valentine, David and Kulick, Don 2001, Transexuality, transvestism, and transgender, in Neil J. Smelser and Paul B. Baltes (eds.), *International Encyclopedia of* the *Social and Behavioural Sciences, Volume 23*, Oxford and New York: Elsevier, pp. 15888–93.

Valentine, David and Wilchins, Riki Anne 1997, One percent on the burn chart: gender, genitals, and hermaphrodites with attitude. *Social Text* 52/53: 215–22.

Vance, Carole (ed.) 1984, *Pleasure and Danger: Exploring Female Sexuality*, London and Boston: Routledge.

Vera, Veronica 1997, *Miss Vera's Finishing School for Boys who Want to be Girls*, New York: Doubleday.

Weeks, Jeffrey 1985, *Sexuality and its Discontents: Meanings, Myths and Modern Sexualities*, London: Routledge & Kegan Paul.

Westwood, Gordon 1952, *Society and the Homosexual*, London: Victor Gollancz.

White, C. Todd 1998, On the pragmatics of an androgynous style of speaking (from a transsexual's perspective). *World Englishes* 17 (2): 215–23.

White, Edmund 1980, The political vocabulary of homosexuality, in Christopher Ricks and Leonard Michaels (eds.), *The State of the Language*, Berkeley and Los Angeles' Calif.: University of California Press, pp. 235–46.

Wilchins, Riki Anne 1995, What's in a name? The politics of Gender Speak. *Transgender Tapestry* 74: 46–7.

Wittig, Monique 1992, *The Straight Mind and Other Essays*, Boston: Beacon Press.

Wong, Andrew 2002, The semantic derogation of *tongzhi*: a synchronic perspective, in Campbell-Kibler *et al*. pp. 161–74.

Wong, Andrew, Roberts, Sarah J. and Campbell-Kibler, Kathryn 2002, Speaking of sex, in Campbell-Kibler *et al*. pp. 1–21.

Zwicky, Arnold 1997, Two lavender issues for linguistics, in Livia and Hall (1997a), pp. 21–34.

Index